Windows to the Land

Volume One

from Southeast to the Arctic

*Each one is a window through which
the light of Alaska shines.*

Judy Ferguson

Windows to
the Land

VOLUME ONE: ALASKA
NATIVE LAND CLAIMS TRAILBLAZERS

An Alaska Native Story

Voice of Alaska Press
Big Delta, Alaska

© 2012 Voice of Alaska Press
formerly Glas Publishing
P.O. Box 130
Big Delta, Alaska 99737
http://alaska-highway.org/delta/outpost
outpost99737@gmail.com

First Printing: February 2013
Volume One: ISBN 978-0-9716044-8-3

Elmer E. Rasmuson Library Cataloging in Publication Data:
Ferguson, Judy.
Windows to the land, an Alaska Native story / by Judy Ferguson. Delta Junction, Alaska : Voice of Alaska Press, c2013.
2 v. : ill., maps ; cm.
Includes index.
v.1. Alaska Native land claims – v.2. Iditarod.
1. Alaska Natives—Claims. 2. Alaska Natives—History—20th century. 3. Alaska Natives—Land tenure. 4. Iditarod (Race) I. Title.
F904.F47 2013
ISBN 978-0-9716044-8-3 (v.1)
ISBN 978-0-9716044-5-2 (v.2) (Volume Two: available 2014.)
 Cover by Eric Anderson, Deep Water Photographics, and Voice of Alaska Press.
Book design by Voice of Alaska Press and Deep Water Photographics, Box 424, Delta Junction, Alaska 99737.

Front cover photos: Al Ketzler Sr. receiving his honorary doctor of laws degree from the University of Alaska Fairbanks, 2004. Courtesy of Al Ketzler Sr.
    1915 Tanana Chiefs Conference photo. Courtesy of Al Ketzler Sr.
    Horace Mountain, south of Atigun Pass, in Philip Smith Mountains.
    Judy Ferguson photo.
Back cover photos: Elizabeth Peratrovich; courtesy of Nettie and Frank Peratrovich. Emil Notti; Judy Ferguson photo. Marion Dennis Twitchell; Judy Ferguson photo. Clarence Alexander; courtesy of Ecotrust. Landscape is Clarence Alexander's home, Fort Yukon; Judy Ferguson photo.
Bio photo: Judy Ferguson and First Traditional Chief Rev. Dr. David Salmon, 2005, Midnight Sun Intertribal Powwow, Fairbanks, Alaska; Judy Ferguson photo.
First title page photo: Pauline Peters cutting fish, Nulato, Alaska, 1975; Judy Ferguson photo. Second title page photo, courtesy of Deep Water Photographics.

This paper meets the requirements of ANSI/NISO Z39.48-1992 (Permanence of Paper).
Printed in Belgrade, Serbia.

∽ **Dedication** ∽

For three gifted teachers who gave of themselves to teach me: Nettie Peratrovich, DeLois Ketzler Burggraf, and Emil Notti.

Deep thanks to Al Ketzler, Sr., David Salmon, Bill Byler, and Don Wright who shared their lives with patience, respect, and generosity. For Dr. Ray Barnhardt and the late Dr. Angayuqaq Oscar Kawagley for their guidance and support.

For Al "Bear" Ketzler, Jr., whose idea this was, and to all those presented in *Windows to the Land, Volume One*, I dedicate this testimony.

I dedicate this book to Eric Anderson, my teacher and protector in publishing this volume, who always builds others up and patiently teaches his gifts of software and graphic design.

For my husband's patience with my office hibernation, I am ever thankful.

Emmitt Peters' family: parents, Paul and Mary with their grandchildren, Phillip, Nina, and Timmy. Melozi fish camp near Ruby, 1975.

Judy Ferguson photo.

"Our tribe, our culture are the deliberate cultivation of respect. The village, river, grandma, grandpa, sons and daughters: we are the ingredients from which dreams are made. Stand tall, head high with self determination, self respect, and self defense."—Claude Demientieff, Jr., Nenana

Table of Contents

Eskimo—Aleut

1. Alutiiq / Sugpiaq
2. Cupiaq
3. Central Yupik
4. Iñupiaq
5. Siberian Yupik
6. Aleutian Unangax̂ Islands

7. Haida
8. Tsimshian

Athabascan—Eyak—Tlingit

9. Tlingit
10. Eyak
11. Ahtna
12. Deg Xinag
13. Dena' ina
14. Gwich' in
15. Han
16. Holikachuk
17. Koyukon
18. Tanacross
19. Tanana
20. Upper Kuskokwim
21. Upper Tanana

⑭Gwich'in

⑲Tanana

⑮Hän

⑱Tanacross

㉑ Upper Tanana

⑪Ahtna

Northern Tutchone

Southern Tutchone
Tagish

⑧Tsimshian

⑩Eyak

⑨Tlingit

⑦Haida

First People Of Alaska

PREFACE

I visited Alaska in 1965, five years after statehood, the year the Bureau of Indian Affairs closed its federal school on King Island. I was visiting my friend Michael in Nome, the winter the King Island Iñupiaq moved permanently to the mainland. Michael took me to meet the chief, who was skinning a seal. His neighbor was carving ivory, and he invited us over to try our hand using his tools.

Three years later, I moved to Big Delta where I met and married my trapper husband, Reb Ferguson. He had a one-room log cabin. Our transportation was two dog teams and two horses until 1970, when our first son was born and we got a truck.

Down the road, throughout the winter of 1970 to 1971, a Tlingit woman, Maria Joseph Ackerman, opened her trailer home to us. She taught me the art of skin sewing and in the evening, she passed around salami, cheese, and crackers while the television entertained our husbands and the Ackerman children. I loved to listen to her stories of growing up in Haines while she taught me how to make lynx gauntlet mitts, fur hats, mukluks, and a full-length smoked moosehide parka, lined with beaver, wolverine, and bear.

In 1973, our family of three moved up the Tanana River to our new remote cabin with boat and dog sled access only.

When our son Clint was five, my husband and I decided we'd canoe from our home on the Tanana, down the Yukon River, all the way to the ocean.

At a critical window of time during the construction of the Trans-Alaska Pipeline, we launched our canoe. It was the year of the Molly Hootch lawsuit, which resulted in the 1976 Tobeluk v. Lind consent decree, mandating the state to build high schools in Alaska villages. We stepped through an invisible window into a life as old as the river; along its banks, we met elders who were the bridge from before the gold rush to the pipeline era.

Three years later, my husband, son, and I kayaked the Kobuk River before it was protected within the Gates of the Arctic National Park and Preserve, before the 1980 Alaska National Interest Lands Conservation Act. Again we entered an ancient culture before elders passed on, before the government required permits, where we met the inland Iñupiaq.

In the last forty-eight years since I came to Alaska, we have explored many rivers: the MacKenzie, the Eagle, the Porcupine, the middle and upper Tanana, the Yukon, the Nushagak, and the Kuskokwim.

In 1996, I began writing about our subsistence lifestyle. I traveled throughout Alaska to market my early books. As I did, I met elders and I began interviewing. One day sitting in the harbor of my first skin-sewing teacher's hometown,

Haines, I prayed what direction I should next pursue in my writing. Windows to the land, I felt. The people I was meeting throughout Alaska were teaching me about the land, their history, and their culture. Through them, vistas of Alaska I had not known were opening like portholes in the fast ferry in which I was sitting.

It is difficult to grasp in this age of i-Pads, smart phones, and powerful Native corporations that such a time existed: Alaska before telephones and television in the villages, before oil, environmentalism, empowerment, and the information highway. Life was very different.

Windows to the Land is that story told by leaders from every culture about their transition from Russian America along the Aleut and Alutiiq coastline, through the time of the Hudson Bay Company at Fort Yukon, past statehood, and into the grassroots movement of Al Ketzler Sr. and the reorganization of the Tanana Chiefs Conference.

From 2003 through 2012, I met Al Ketzler Sr., DeLois Burggraf, Niilo Koponen, Emil Notti, Don Wright, Frank and Nettie Peratrovich, Larry Brayton, Guy Martin, Tom Begich, and Bill Byler. I met those whose beliefs and fire in the belly led to today's Tanana Chiefs Conference, the formation of Alaska Federation of Natives, and to the Alaska Native Claims Settlement Act (ANCSA). Statehood, ANCSA, and the pipeline led inevitably to the Alaska National Interest Lands Conservation Act (ANILCA). Life in Alaska would never be the same. To understand this, we must hear the voices of those who lived it: their experiences and their concerns.

Windows to the Land, An Alaska Native Story, Volume One: Alaska Native Land Claims Trailblazers depicts those who paid their life's blood for land claims. *Volume II: The Iditarod and Alaska River Trails*, available in late 2013 to early 2014, is the land speaking through its people as they run their rivers and their dogs.

The land and its people have been my teachers, my windows to understanding the Great Land. May the next generation be blessed with the freedom and the space, with this refuge at the top of the world.

Introduction

The purpose of *Windows to the Land* is to introduce the reader to the identity, location, and historical benchmarks for each of Alaska's main indigenous cultures; to show their history first-hand through the lives of the people themselves; and to provide an overview of Alaska's history as seen in the chapter timelines and sidebars. A believer that a picture is worth a thousand words, I have included maps in every chapter and photos on every page. *Volume One: Alaska Native Land Claims Trailblazers* follows the land through each culture. *Volume Two: The Iditarod and Alaska River Trails* is adventure, the Great Land as experienced through each of its indigenous cultures.

Alaska's story may be divided into the following eras: (1) prewestern contact, (2) Russian colonial exploitation, (3) Russian America, (4) the Hudson Bay Company, (5) the 1867 Treaty of Cession in which the United States bought Russia's claim to Alaska, (6) the domination of the American Commercial Company during which Alaska was ruled from revenue cutters, (7) the Organic Act of 1884 when Alaska was made a district governed by an appointed governor and officers, (8) 1896 to 1898 when a flood of whites came with the Klondike gold rush, (9) the Canadian-American boundary dispute, resolved in 1891 when the boundary near Fort Yukon was moved back to the 141 west meridian, (10) Second Organic Act in 1912 when Alaska became a Territory with its own legislature, (11) Alaska statehood in 1959, followed in the modern era by (12) the Alaska Native Claims Settlement Act, (13) the Trans-Alaska Pipeline, and (14) the Alaska National Lands Interest Conservation Act (ANILCA).

At the time of the Alaska purchase in 1867, there were an estimated 35,000 Alaska Natives living in the territory—half of the 74,000 population estimated in 1740. The rest had been killed by disease, starvation, and hardship. At the time, Eskimos, Indians, and Aleuts made up the vast majority of Alaska's population: ninety-five to one hundred percent through its five geographic regions until 1880, when non-Natives began arriving in search of whales, fur, and gold.

Through the age of competing empires—Russian, British, and American—fighting for Alaska's resources, concerns for land claims for Alaska's indigenous people were nonexistent. In the Treaty of Cession, Russia stated that the "uncivilized tribes" were excepted from the enjoyment of privileges, rights, and protections granted the white citizens, Russians, and Creoles who chose to remain in Alaska and become citizens.

After 1880, whites in Juneau began to feel uncomfortable as the minority in a land with no civil government. They began pushing for local control of Alaska's resources, self-rule, representation, and private land ownership. Alaska remained under military rule until 1884, policed by revenue cutters, when Congress finally provided for a measure of civilian government. The first Organic Act of 1884 provided the basic protection of lands for the Alaska Natives but allowed for title controversy by leaving indigenous land title open for "future legislation by Congress." Section 8 stated that:

Indians or other persons in said district shall not be disturbed in the possession of any lands actually in their use or occupation or now claimed by them, but the terms under which such persons may acquire title to such lands is reserved for future legislation by Congress.

In 1914 in United States v. Cadzow, 5 Alaska 125, it was stated that "the aboriginal tribes of Alaska have a right to occupy the public lands of the United States therein, subject to the control of both lands and the tribes by the United States."

The Organic Act of 1884 was the basis for Alaska Native land claims. It promised ultimate settlement.

In 1906, Senator Nelson introduced a bill in Congress extending the provisions of the General Allotment Act to Alaska Natives, but it did not address the tribal entity.

Up to this time, there was no way a Native could get title to land unless he had been recognized as being "civilized." However, failure to appropriate money for the necessary surveys, researching the claims, and documenting the allotments rescinded chances for land title for the 26,000 Natives of the time.

It was left up to Natives to secure an allotment. Without English or a representative to explain the law, only a tiny fraction of the Native population were able to get allotments recorded at the Bureau of Land Management.

In 1926, the Native Townsite Act allowed Natives to get property where they could live as individuals. If they met a number of requirements, it was possible for a community of Native people to secure a townsite, as happened in Stevens Village and Grayling, but the lands were still held by individuals.

The 1930s brought a change of thinking. In 1934, Congress passed a monumental bill, the Indian Reorganization Act. One of its provisions was to repeal the Allotment Acts, which had severely cut down the amount of land held by Indians. Congress gave to the secretary of the interior the power to create new reservations and to enlarge existing ones.

Supplementary legislation two years later extended the provisions of the Indian Reorganization Act to Alaska. It gave the secretary of the interior power to designate as an Indian reservation any area of land which has been reserved for the use and occupancy of the Indians and Eskimos by section 8 of the act of May 17, 1884 [the first Organic Act] . . . or which has been heretofore reserved under any executive order and placed under the jurisdiction of the Department of the Interior or any bureau thereof, together with additional public lands adjacent thereto or any other public lands which were actually occupied by Indians or Eskimos.

With the Indian Reorganization Act thus extended to Alaska, the secretary of the interior could select certain areas as Native reservations. When Secretary of the Interior Ickes proposed setting up a hundred new reservations, there was a public uproar. However, several were instituted.

In 1955, delegates to Alaska's Constitutional Convention proposed in Section 12 of Article 12:

The State and its people further disclaim all right or title in or to any property, including fishing rights, the right or title to which may be held by or for any Indian, Eskimo, or Aleut, or community thereof, as that right or title is defined in the act of admission. The State and its people agree that, unless otherwise provided by Congress, the property . . . shall remain subject to the absolute disposition of the United States.

The Alaska Statehood Act passed by Congress in 1958 again left open the final settlement of Native lands. It was up to the people and to Congress.

Let us follow the river of that story, of the land and of its people.

1860 map, Russian America (Alaska) was to the west of British America (Canada) shows "Recent Discoveries in the Polar Regions."
Mitchell's New General Atlas, Published By S. Augustus Mitchell, Jr, 1860.

Russian America Timeline:

1741: Russians land at Prince of Wales Island. Divine liturgy celebrated offshore. Fur traders establish own families and adopt God-children.

1763: Shelekhov-Golikov Company enslave Aleuts to hunt fur. Systemic violence; families split up. Aleuts become dependent on western goods. Eighty percent die in epidemics.

1784: Shelekhov-Golikov Company kill hundreds of Koniags and enslaved the rest at Kodiak. Colonization begins at Three Saints Bay including a school.

1790s: Long expeditions result in permanent Russian settlements.

1794: Missionaries, including St. Herman of Alaska, arrive Kodiak Island, Orthodoxy to Russian Alaska. Oppose abuse of Natives. Shelekhov hires Baranov as manager who moves to Kodiak. Intermarriage with Koniags.

1795: Baranov buys land from Tlingit near today's Sitka.

1796: Tarkanov winters at Taral on Copper River.

1799: Shelekhov's son-in-law Rezanof gets Czar's fur monopoly.

1802-1804: Other Tlingit destroy Baranov's town. He revenges and builds at New Archangel, capital of Russian America, Sitka. Baranov governor of Russian America.

1818: US and British America (Canada) borders claimed; Britain and US claim trade in Oregon Territory.

1819: Aleksandrovskiy Redoubt, modern Nushagak.

1824: Fr. John Veniaminov at Unalaska. Russo-American Treaty: Russian America's southern border: tip of Alaska Peninsula.

1825: First Native priest, Jacob Netsvetov.

1832: Kolmakovs Odinochka on Kuskokwim River.

1834: Fr. John Veniaminov in Sitka; liturgy translated into Aleut.

1838: Smallpox epidemic; Russian Mission massacre on Yukon River.

1839: Hudson's Bay Co. at Russian America's southern border. Baranov depends on US supply ships; selling fur to Americans.

1812-1841: Natives hunting fur for Russians in Baja California.

1843: First mission school for Yup'ik at Nushagak; Kolmakovskiy Redoubt with church on Kuskokwim River.

1844: Formation of seminary in Sitka.

1850s: Tlingits never conquered; still fighting Russians.

1867: Treaty of Cession, Alaska from Russia to US.

❦

Chapter One

Alutiiq Link to Eyak, Virginia Alice Nicholoff Lacy

Granddaughter of the Native Guides for Anthropologist Frederica de Laguna

As I researched the Alutiiq and Eyak cultures for my children's book, Alaska's First People, *I took my illustrator to Cordova in 2006 where I met with Virginia Lacy, the granddaughter of Makari Chimaviskey, guide for famed anthropologist Dr. Frederica de Laguna in the 1930s.*

Makari Chimaviskey "oldest living Eskimo" and Virginia Lacy's great-grandfather. 1933, Hawkins Island.
Courtesy of Virginia Lacy.

Before the arrival of the Russians, the Pacific (southern) Eskimo called themselves Sugpiaq ("the real people"). The Russians began calling them Aleuts, which eventually applied to three different Native communities. Generally today the Sugpiaq identify themselves as Chugach Eskimo and point to "yesterday's Aleut" as "Alutiiq" today. However, the Native Peoples and Languages of Alaska *map identifies the entire area as "Alutiiq (Sugpiaq)," which includes the islands and coastline of Prince William Sound, Kodiak, and the Alaska Peninsula and Kenai Peninsula.*

In the 1930s, a team of anthropologists, led by Dr. Frederica de Laguna, visited Cordova to study language and culture. The grandmother of Cordova's Virginia Alice Nicholoff Lacy, Matrona Chimaviskey, was the interpreter for de Laguna; Matrona's father, Makari Chimaviskey, was de Laguna's guide and storyteller. Chimaviskey's Alutiiq name was Alingun Nupatlkerlugoq Angakhuna; de Laguna said he was the oldest living Chugach Eskimo in the area.

Virginia is a refined eighty-seven-year-old who lives in a hundred-year-old home built a year after Cordova's founding. She explained the local history and her family's background.

In the 1760s, Russian traders arrived by ship looking for sea otter and other furs at Nuchek on Hinchinbrook Island, the gateway to Prince William Sound. Nuchek is an Alutiiq word that means the "last land before the open water." By

Virginia Lacy's grandmother Matrona Tiedeman, Lacy's great-grandfather Chief Chimaviskey, Frederica de Laguna and party, 1933, Palugvik, Hawkins Island, Prince William Sound.

Courtesy of Virginia Lacy.

1788, a Russian trading post and redoubt had been built. It was a supply point for ships to replenish water and supplies so Nuchek became an important hub.

Nettie Peratrovich, Haida, said from her home in Anchorage, "The Aleuts showed the Russians where the fur seals were. The serf-oriented Russians did to the Natives what had been done to them in their authoritarian feudal system. They made slaves of the Aleuts, impregnated the women to make a slave class, and decimated the men." Virginia continued, "The Russians forced the men to hunt precious sea otter for them and required them to make special bidarkas with three holes so that a Russian could go along to make sure the Natives did not keep any of the furs themselves. They gave guns to the hunters but charged them exorbitant prices for shells for their own use."

By 1800, Russian settlers paid the Chugach chiefs a salary for hunting sea otter, but Natives were also becoming dependent on European goods. Russian customs, language, and Orthodox religion were also becoming part of the Native culture. People of mixed (Russian and Alutiiq) heritage, known as Creoles, served as teachers, managers, explorers, and clergy.

In 1867, the Russians sold their interest in Alaska to the United States.

Virginia's father, August Tiedeman, a German sailor had joined the American Navy and come by ship, the *MacArthur*, to Alaska on a geodetic coastal survey in the 1890s. In Nuchek he jumped ship and not long after, married Virginia's beautiful dark-haired grandmother, Matrona. In 1904, Virginia's mother, Mary Alma, was born, followed by Mary's sister, Freda. The family decided to move to Ellamar, a small city with a promising copper mine along with a company store, large warehouses, school, housing, and dance, and dining halls. However, water in the mine was a constant problem. Much of the work had to be done at low tide. Caissons were built to keep water out of the glory hole. As the mining slowed down, the family moved to Makarka Creek on Hawkins Island, where they lived on a bluff overlooking the stream.

The more protected ports of Valdez and Cordova were growing, and the sea otter industry in Nuchek was dying. By 1909 only thirty people remained in Nuchek. After a devastating smallpox epidemic in which almost everyone died, Virginia's widowed grandfather left with ten to twelve orphans to join his daughter's family at Makarka Point. There he raised the children with Matrona's help, subsisting by digging butter and razor clams, hunting ducks, and fishing.

Virginia said, "As many chiefs did, my grandfather possessed spiritual powers. He could predict weather changes by watching animals' behavior. He claimed to have seen sea otter with human faces. His piercing grey eyes seemed to look right through me."

Matrona's autocratic German husband, August, forbade the use of her Aleut language in the home, so their daughter, Mary, did not learn the language. Virginia did not even know her grandmother knew Aleut until Frederica de Laguna appeared.

By 1925, Nuchek was abandoned and the land title had been transferred to the Chugach National Forest, created in 1907.

Fox farms were becoming popular. North of Hawkins Island near Sheeps Bay, August Tiedeman began a blue fox farm at Alice Cove while also working in the herring saltery.

In the spring of 1933, Frederica de Laguna, her brother and mother, Norman

Nuchek, Alaska, circa 1890.

Courtesy of Virginia Lacy.

Reynolds, and her Danish colleague Kaj Birket-Smith arrived for archeological excavations in Prince William Sound. The Cordova area was still covered with snow and ice, so they spent time interviewing people.

Virginia recalled,

> *When Frederica de Laguna was exploring Palugvik, an ancient site on Hawkins Island about fifteen miles southwest of Cordova, she needed my great-grandfather as a guide. Since he spoke little English, Gammie [Matrona Chimaviskey] translated for her, cooked Native foods, and showed them how to live off the land. They took the anthropologists by boat to Prince William Sound's eastern shores where they visited sites*

and collected artifacts. Gammie introduced them to Eyak speakers who shared their stories while Frederica de Laguna and Kaj Birket-Smith took detailed phonetic notes.

When the de Laguna team returned and shared their notes on the Eyak language with other scholars, it was decided that Eyak was not an Athabascan language but an independent branch that was more distantly related to Tlingit. As a culture, Eyak had heretofore been largely overlooked. Virginia concluded, "My great grandfather died about three years later in 1936 when I was thirteen. I have a photo of him with a replica of a trap he made."

Virginia Lacy wearing a sea otter hat and scarf that she as an Alaska Native is allowed to make. Cordova, 2006.

Judy Ferguson photo.

Today the fur of the animal the Russians once so fiercely hunted, the sea otter, is federally protected. Due to the 1972 Marine Mammal Protection Act, only Alaska Natives are allowed to kill a sea otter and then only for subsistence or for creating handicrafts. Virginia smiled. "In 1992, I shot an otter, (ikumut in Alutiiq), tanned it and made myself a scarf. I wear it today as a reminder of my great-grandfather Makari and my grandmother Matrona, people who helped unlock the connection of the Eyak to our other Alaska Native linguistic families."

Timeline:

1760s: Russians at Nuchek.

1788: Russian fort, Nuchek.

1867: Sale of Alaska.

1907: Chugach National Forest.

1933: De Laguna studying Eyak.

1972: Marine Mammal Protection Act.

∞

Chapter Two

Bruce Robertson, Alutiiq Fisherman

Lesnoi Village, Kodiak and Woody Island

The Alutiiq differ from most Alaska Natives. They and the Aleuts were impacted early by non-natives, resulting in a Creole heritage and early acculturation. They came from a beautiful maritime island culture dependent on fur and fishing. Their culture was badly damaged by the Russian colonial exploitation of the sea otter harvest, the devastating 1964 earthquake, and the oil pollution of the 1989 Exxon Valdez.

Bruce Roberton, ferry from Cordova, 2006.

Judy Ferguson photo.

In 2006 on a ferry from Cordova, I met an Alutiiq fisherman and a former president of Lesnoi Village, Bruce Robertson.

Bruce Robertson, a commercial fisherman born in 1953, is Scottish and "Aleut," referred to today as "Alutiiq." Bruce, the third generation of commercial fishermen, recalled, "Back in the late 1880s, my great-grandfather, William Robertson, got knocked out in a Seattle bar and put on a ship to Kodiak. There he met a full Aleut woman, Anastasia Zillesnoff, and married her." Bruce, like many Alutiiqs of Russian or American Creole derivation, has a culture that spans the islands and coastline of Prince William Sound, Kodiak, and the Alaska and Kenai peninsulas. The culture has the umbrella name *Alutiiq* (formerly "Aleut") which also includes the Sugpiaq or the "Chugach Eskimo."

While watching the vista of Prince William Sound, Bruce explained the Russian and then American entrance into the Kodiak area.

The first to be impacted by the Russians were the people of Sitka, the Aleutian Chain, the Alaska Peninsula, and Kodiak in Prince William Sound. The traders married indigenous women, who gave birth to the Russian Creole generations who became the managers,

5

teachers, and clergy of the Russian-American colony. Bruce's grandfather came from Woody Island near Kodiak, the home of "the Tangirnaq." The island with its lake and trees was a good place to resupply passing ships.

In 1784, Gregorii Shelikhov made the first colony on Kodiak for harvesting sea otter. Two miles across from Kodiak on Woody Island, the Russians started an agricultural colony, followed by an ice industry to supply the iceboxes of the California gold rush in 1852. The Russian-American Commercial Company,

Russian Orthodox church, circa 1940, Woody Island.
Michael Z. Vinokouroff Photograph Collection, ASL-P243-2-017,
Courtesy of Bruce Robertson

(a "corporation formed for the purpose of importing Ice from the Port of New Archangel and other Ports in the Russian Settlements in North America, into the State of California, and trading in the same ..."—Certificate of Trustee), dammed up Woody Island's Lake Tanignak to increase acreage for more ice harvesting. To run the horse-powered saw to cut the ice into blocks, the first horses and iron tracks came to Alaska. The Great Land's first road was built for the horses to haul the ice to the dock, and the first field of oats was to feed them.

Before the 1867 sale of Alaska through the Treaty of Cession, the Alutiiq were forced by the Russians to cut ice through the winter and to hunt sea otter and fur seal in summer.

In 1872 a Russian Orthodox Church was built, replacing Native ceremonies with those of the church. Five years later, Sheldon Jackson, a Presbyterian minister, built the mission at Fort Wrangell. Fifteen years later, he called a meeting of denominations to select their geographical mission areas so the churches would not overlap. The Baptists chose Kodiak, Afognak, and Spruce islands,

Baptist mission and Aleut orphanage built in 1893, Woody Island: Winch Dormitory, the chapel, the mission gardens and the original orphanage headquarters. (Taken before fire of 1925.)

Photo by Margaret Learn Ferris. Courtesy of Bruce Robertson.

Cook Inlet, and Woody Island but they didn't build a mission on Woody until twenty-one years later.

By 1886, Woody Island was the commercial center for the Kodiak area, including the ice harvesting operation, a boat yard, a gristmill, the Alaska Commercial Company (formerly the Russian-American Company) wharf. The only roads in Alaska connected these facilities. For harvesting ice, it was said, Alutiiq employees got "twelve cents a day, a noon meal of fish soup and black rye bread. Last," it said, "but by no means least in the eyes of the Natives, each laborer received thrice a day two-thirds of a gill of vodka." After the Russians took 100,000 sea otter and the same of fur seal every year, by 1911 only about 2,000 sea otter remained, making hunting no longer profitable.

In 1893, Ernest and Ida Roscoe built a Baptist mission and Aleut orphanage on Woody Island, replacing the Russian Orthodox culture. Over the next twenty years, the Spanish Influenza orphaned "a whole ton of kids," Bruce said, and the mission grew to include dormitories, an office, barn, carpenter shop, cannery, silo, and dining room.

Bruce pointed out, "My great-grandfather took out a ninety-two acre homestead, made the first survey on Woody Island, put up a building, fenced the pasture for his cattle, and intended to live there. He and my great-grandmother had two boys and a girl. After fishing season he had a pocket full of money and decided to go down to Seattle to see his institutionalized, handicapped daughter. He never returned. We assumed he got knocked in the head and shanghaied again." Bruce added, "My great-grandmother died of the Spanish Flu so my grandfather, William J. Robertson, and his siblings were put into the Woody Island Baptist orphanage."

In 1911, the United States Navy built a wireless station on the island. Realizing the strategic position of Kodiak in the Pacific, the Civil Aeronautics

Administration built the Kodiak Naval Air Station in 1941. Many Alutiiq moved to Kodiak for work. The Navy kept forty technicians and their families on Woody Island to relay weather and data to the pilots. At the base, the remaining Alutiiq got their fresh water from the base and used the ferry. However, in 1964, the earthquake and tidal wave destroyed the navy's infrastructure and the rest of the Alutiiq moved to Kodiak.

While growing up on Kodiak, Bruce frequently went to Woody Island. "You should've seen it," he declared. "The black sandy beaches. The deep lush growth of the huge timber that cushioned all the noise: so quiet and magical. The white rabbits hopping through the greenery. We only brought matches for lunch. We made a fire, burned it down to embers, dug

William J. and Myra Robertson, grandparents.

Courtesy Bruce Robertson.

clams and mussels, put them in a bed of green grass, and covered them over with hot sand so they steamed. That was our lunch. There was an abundance: rabbits, berries, and freedom."

"Under the Alaska Native Allotment Act of 1906, with its focus on the individual family, we could file for a hundred-sixty-acre Native allotment but in 1971, that ended with the Alaska Native Claims Settlement Act (ANCSA)," Bruce said. With the passage of ANCSA, land to which the tribes could prove indigenous use began to be titled over to the corporations and to the tribes. Those individuals with one quarter Native blood became corporation shareholders.

"Precedent had been set that a person had to have a certain percentage of Alaska Native blood. After the sale of Alaska in 1867," Bruce continued, "if Creole children had too much Russian and not enough Native blood, they could not get Bureau of Indian Affairs [BIA] benefits. But due to the special situation in the Alutiiq culture of having been very early diluted by Russian blood against their own will, resulting in children of mixed blood, Karl Armstrong, the originator of the *Kodiak Mirror* and one of ANCSA's primary negotiators and who later became president of Koniag Corporation and co-founder of the Kodiak Area Native Association (KANA), negotiated in Washington, D.C.

Woody Island as seen from town of Kodiak.

Courtesy of Bruce Robertson

that the Creole blood quantum count as full Native. It had not been the fault of their offspring. Due to Karl's negotiations," Bruce explained, "a lot of people qualified under ANCSA on the village roll."

"Originally I was signed up for Afognak," he said, "since my grandmother, Myra Malutin, came from there. But we also had ties to Woody Island because my grandfather was in the mission there."

When ANCSA was in process, Bruce was still in high school. He was renting a room from Koniag activist Karl Armstrong.

Due to the impending oil pipeline, ANCSA was pushed through very quickly. "Under ANCSA," Bruce explained, "we could select 69,000 federal acres abutting our original village site, on accessible, contiguous available land. If the land wasn't available in our original selected area, we were allowed three times the amount somewhere else. That amount of land wasn't available on Woody Island so we considered part of the Kodiak National Wildlife Refuge. That request exposed a hole in federal protection to pristine areas," he pointed out, "and contributed to the government passing the Alaska National Interest Lands Conservation Act [ANILCA] in 1980. Instead of the wildlife refuge area, they gave us old-growth trees on Afognak Island."

Bruce went on: "Not only were we not prepared for corporation life in the modern business world, but we had to rush to pick our land. [By contrast, the state is still selecting some of its land from the federal government, fifty years after statehood.] Also, the original corporation heads were not necessarily the most skilled but rather were those who didn't already have a steady job and could take the new, risky position. The hurry-up process resulted in putting the cart before the horse. But," he added, "if ANCSA were done today, with all the current land owners, it'd be hung up forever in the courts."

"Many of the corporations put up their land as collateral to get loans unless their area was blessed with oil. So—can you lose your land, your culture?

9

Yes, we could lose it all. During the first Native corporation bankruptcies, 1976–1978, under the IRS Net Operating Loss loophole," he said, "Senator Ted Stevens made it possible for corporations to buy up our debt to lessen what they owed Uncle Sam. They paid pennies on our indebt dollar, applying our loses against their gains, cheating the taxpayer while bailing out the Native corporations."

In 1995, Bruce was asked to be a Leisnoi Corporation board member. Then he served as president of Lesnoi Village until 2002.

Part of the land Lesnoi selected was that of a cattle rancher's federally leased pastureland. The rancher challenged Lesnoi Village's certification and tied their claim up for more than thirty-five years. "We paid five million dollars from corporation earnings and our portion of ANCSA's 7(i) Settlement Agreement monies [the shared profit from those corporations sitting on oil or mineral-rich land] and finally under the Obama administration in 2009, Secretary of Interior Ken Salazar approved our village certification and we won."

But the problems remain. "As individual stockholders," he said, "we are captive landowners. Without a majority vote of the board members, who tend to be an in-house good ol' boys club, we can't trade or sell our stocks. If a stockholder doesn't agree with how a corporation is handling his land, he has no leverage."

Additional issues are if a corporation's land has no economic base, there is no means for growth. "Many of our people were not equipped to make a corporation successful. With all of our land tied up in the corporation model, it is either a great opportunity or a huge risk. And if a people has tundra land with little monetary value, how can they transition to the twenty-first century? What little assets we have in timber pay our bills and our stockholders but that won't last. With no monetary glue and no viable goal, there's nothing to hold the vehicle together; the vision and energy simply dissipate."

Bruce observed that CIRI [Cook Inlet Region, Incorporated] "wound up on top of the heap. I call them urbanized Natives," he said, "because they were already assimilated into the sophisticated modern culture. They knew what to go after and how to negotiate." He explained that federal trading chits can be exchanged for land. When military bases decommissioned, their land and their Federal Communication Commission licenses became a potential trading chit. He said, "CIRI knew what to acquire and how to negotiate, and they wound up smelling like a rose. Up north, because of the Iñupiaq proximity to oil, their corporations got a couple million here and there to keep them satisfied."

Clearly, the 1986 Small Business Administration's disadvantaged program, known as 8(a) "No-Bid Contracts" has been "one of the few things that has helped Native corporations," he said. "Under this, Native corporations can bid well over the top bid. Senator Lisa Murkowski promised to protect that little pot of gold so she won the 2010 election."

Bruce felt it would've been better to retain the model of Alaska Native land allotments with its individual land control or to retain a large land selection in federal trust for hunting and fishing rights, including individual ownership of five to ten acres.

He said, "Today our kids are moving to Anchorage, trying to get jobs. I think the Native population in Anchorage today is over 75,000 to 80,000."

He summed up, "I'm at the time in my life that I don't want to be involved anymore; the benefits are almost meaningless. People have lost interest; it's even hard to get a quorum to vote. In this, the forty-year anniversary of ANCSA, many of the corporations are dying on the vine. The corporation wasn't the model for preserving Native heritage; that is simply without market value." Looking out over the boat railing to Prince William Sound, he mused, "I dream of taking my kids back to Kodiak to live the life I knew, but there is no going back; the world has changed."

Timeline

1784: Shelikhov establishes first Russian fur colony on Kodiak; Woody Island becomes agricultural colony.

1852: California gold rush.

1867: Sale of Alaska through Treaty of Cession.

1872: Russian Orthodox church built on Woody Island.

1886: First roads in Alaska.

1887: Sheldon Jackson calls churches to select their territorical interests in Alaska.

1906: Alaska Native Allotment Act.

1911: Navy builds wireless station, Woody Island.

1964: Good Friday earthquake.

1971: Alaska Native Claims Settlement Act (ANCSA).

1976-1978: IRS Net Operating Loss helps Native corporations.

1980: Alaska National Interests Lands Conservation Act (ANILCA).

1986: "No Bid" contracts and Native corporations.

1989: Exxon *Valdez* oil spill in Prince William Sound.

∾

Chapter Three

The Gwich'in and Hudson's Bay Company, First Traditional Chief David Salmon

King Salmon, the grandfather of former Tanana Chiefs Conference First Traditional Chief David Salmon, was born about 1815 near Arctic Village. His life preceded the coming of the Hudson's Bay Company (HBC or The Bay) to Alaska. In Gwich'in, King Salmon was Khlit Cho; he was said to be eight feet tall, wore his hair tied back, had a long nose, and walked hunched over. His Christian name was John Salmon. He married Jeanne (pronounced Jane). In about 1845, they had a son, William Salmon, on the East Fork of the Chandalar River near Arctic Village.

King Salmon's people depended entirely on the nomadic life style. His peer was the famous chief, Sinate, (Sahneuti Sahnyateh, Sanytyi, Senati, or "father of the runner.") The Gwich'in traded their subsistence products in a complex, multicultural network through which Sinate rose to the top, amassing a fortune in beads.

In 1840, John Bell of the Hudson's Bay Company established the first permanent trading post within the Gwich'in homelands at Fort McPherson. Bell explored the Porcupine River as far as its junction with the Yukon River in 1844.

Two years later, HBC employee Alexander Murray, a Scotsman, established LaPierre House on the Bell River, seventy-five miles east of Old Crow. Continuing downstream, he built Fort Yukon just below the Porcupine River mouth on the Yukon River in 1847.

Few members of Chief Sinate's Kutcha-Kutchin band (Yukon Flats Gwich'in) had ever

Gwich'in as drawn by Alexander Murray in 1848.
Courtesy of the Hudson's Bay Company archive.

Alexander Murray, circa 1846. (1818-1874.)
http://www.mhs.mb.ca/docs/people/murray_ah.shtml.

seen a white man. Impressed by Sinate's abilities and his reputation among his people, Murray appointed Sinate as chief trader, with a symbolic red coat. For several years, Alexander Murray traded at Fort Yukon; his drawings and his journal recorded the first major information on the western Gwich'in. HBC also offered support to their subsistence life. They hired boatmen to pole goods upriver. King Salmon supplemented his trapping by freighting up the Porcupine and Bell rivers and portaging over to the Peel River for the HBC.

However, a few years after his son, William, was born in 1845, King Salmon lost his wife. Later William told his own son, David, how he suffered after he lost his mother. King Salmon never remarried.

Chief of Fort Yukon Sinate, circa 1883.
Schieffelin Brothers prospecting trip, 1882-1883.
ASL-P277-017-016, Wickersham.
Courtesy of Janet Curtiss.

In 1862, the Church Missionary Society persuaded Anglican missionary Reverend Robert McDonald to establish a new mission at Fort Yukon. He eventually translated the Bible into Gwich'in, which had a unifying effect on the tribes. King Salmon accompanied Rev. McDonald on three of his missionary trips, in 1865, 1866, and 1875.

After the purchase of Alaska from the Russians in 1867, the HBC left Fort Yukon and established a new post farther up the Porcupine River. When new surveys of the boundary showed that it was still within United States territory, the post was moved farther upstream to Old Rampart House. During part of their travels each year, King Salmon and his son, William, headquartered near Old Rampart House. Between 1850 and 1880, there was a Vuntut Gwich'in camp at Klo-kut, a fishing and hunting site on the Porcupine River upstream from Old Crow. Klo-Kut was where the people camped, waiting to trade with the Hudson's Bay and to be baptized and married by the missionaries. David remembered it as a very special place.

However, once more the Hudson's Bay Company location turned out to be still within the USA, so in 1891 they moved again to "New" Rampart House (International Boundary Commission, 1918), just east of the border, which is along the 141 west meridian.

For the duration of his life, King Salmon trapped from Old Rampart to Circle on the Yukon River. He died in 1888 near Circle, five years before the city was officially established as a steamboat supply point for the gold mining camps. According to David Salmon, at that time half of Arctic Village's population moved to Circle to provide meat for the miners.

David's father, William Salmon, followed work to the Klondike Gold Rush, market hunting for the miners. When William was thirty-five, he married Alice of Crow Flats, a region renowned for a devastating intertribal war. The wedding was in Klo-kut. In 1900, with the people of Old Crow and Venetie, William and his wife migrated down the Porcupine River, up the Black River, past the future site of Chalkyitsik, and up the Salmon Fork, where they founded Salmon Village. In 1912, Alice gave birth to David Salmon. David was born when both the clan structure and Indian law were foundational to the people. Broken laws carried a sentence of death or of being ostracized, because survival of the group was paramount. The rules applied to the whole social infrastructure of the group: marriage, family, even gossip, and especially to the hunt. Boys were carefully taught by their fathers and girls were trained by their mothers in all the skills needed for survival. As the modern era brought the need to protect the land, in 1915 with construction of the Alaska Railroad under consideration, Judge Wickersham called a conference of the Tanana Chiefs. Forty-seven years later again with protection of the land the focus,

Old Rampart, the Canada-U.S. border station in 1869-70 before the location was corrected.
http://www.stratalink.com/
stratavarious/porcupine2

New Rampart House after boundary established correctly. Note the Gwich'in community by the near edge and back of the clearing.
Dr. Ernest A. Cook Photograph
Collection, UAF-2003-109-213.

the Tanana Chiefs Conference (TCC) reorganized in 1962. After the passage of the Alaska Native Claims Settlement Act, Chief Andrew Isaac of Mansfield Lake/ Tanacross became TCC's original first traditional chief in 1972. When he died in 1991, Peter John of Minto replaced Andrew Isaac as the first traditional chief. After Peter John died in 2003, David Salmon filled the office.

Because David was raised hearing his father's generations-old stories, as the first traditional chief he became a living conduit for the oral tradition of his people, the bridge between ancient and modern.

I first met David Salmon at the Fairbanks Athabascan Fiddling Festival in 1998. A pastor and an Episcopalian priest from Chalkyitsik, his twinkling eyes and open manner touched me. I asked if he would consider my interviewing him sometime when he was in town. He said yes. I was in process of writing another book, but I hoped to call him when the time was right. Six years later, it finally seemed like the moment. I called the Fairbanks

Episcopalian Diocese and then reached David at his home in Chalkyitsik. A friend of his, Janet Thompson Curtiss, answered the phone. In the background, I could hear a home church service going on. David answered the phone with, "Praise the Lord! Hallelujah!"

In response to David becoming TCC's first traditional chief, his family planned a potlatch and a revival in Chalkyitsik on June 18, 2004. Dignitaries from Doyon and TCC and many other guests were invited. Janet Curtiss asked me to cover the event for *Heartland* magazine, and the *Fairbanks Daily News-Miner* agreed.

I met thirty-six-year old Janet at Wright's Air Service in Fairbanks for the flight to Chalkyitsik. As we flew over the White Mountains, she excitedly told me that there would be a special time during the three-day potlatch when David would formally adopt her as his granddaughter.

Half Gwich'in but raised in Anchorage, Janet hadn't often been to the village. Because of that and a difficult childhood, she wanted a stronger connection to her heritage. At the age of ninety-two, David Salmon had waded into the chilly Black River to baptize Janet and several others. A man dedicated to his people's salvation, David was a door to Janet for healing and for relationship, for connecting the past to the present. As we landed in Chalkyitsik, his adult granddaughters Patty Salmon and Isabelle Salmon-Carroll welcomed us. Boys with four-wheelers ferried us and our baggage to David's house. As each guest arrived, he beckoned them over. Armed with red survey tape, always chuckling, he tied an honorary headband around the head of each guest.

Accompanying him to dinner were Doyon Limited President and CEO Orie G. Williams, Tanana Chiefs Conference President Harold "Buddy" Brown, Episcopal Archbishop Mark MacDonald, Interior

David Salmon greeting guests honoring them with survey ribbon headdresses, 2004, Chalkyitsik.
Judy Ferguson photo.

Regional Housing Authority Executive Director Steve Ginnis, evangelist Gary Simple and his family, Alice Carroll of Circle, many guests, and musicians who boated and flew in from distant villages.

We gathered the first night of the potlatch where David announced over the microphone, "This is a night to join me—whether you can dance or not—just for me tonight, dance. When you honor me, you honor God! That's who I work for! Hehhh ho!" A night of amazing jigging, two-stepping, and Gwich'in square dancing followed, young and old forming an expanded family in sheer delight. This wonderful dancing took me by surprise; later I read anthropologist Craig Mishler's research. After 1847, most of the non-Natives in Fort Yukon were immigrants from the Orkney Islands and from northern Scotland, along with a few French Canadians. The Hudson's Bay Company traders and prospectors brought their lively tunes and violins from across the sea. In 1860 at a Christmas Ball, the principal trader and postmaster at Lapierre House on the Bell River documented the festive

Kenny Charlie of Minto playing guitar while Gary Simple jigs.

Judy Ferguson photo.

music. James Flett, an Orkney man and an old voyageur, was married to an Indian wife; he wrote about the gala affair performed to Scottish reels of four and jigs. The introduction of Scottish and Orcadian folk music and dancing to the Gwich'in can be attributed to James Flett and his friends.

16

Ariana Herbert and Everett Nathaniel two-stepping in the Chalkyitsik tribal hall, 2004.

Judy Ferguson photo.

Arrow points to ten-year-old David Salmon and his mother in boat with his father standing on shore, 1922.

Dr. Ernest Cook Photographic Collection. Courtesy of David Salmon.

That proof was easy to see in Chalkyitsik as cousins, aunts, uncles, husbands, wives, and children danced until long past midnight.

The next night over a dinner of roasted moose, beaver, caribou, king salmon, whitefish, ham, chicken, beef, and succulent black duck, David told me his story.

> *Before the Hudson's Bay Company [HBC] arrived, my grandfather, Khlit Cho/King Salmon, Christian name John Salmon, 1815-1888, kept his family on the move, hunting caribou and sheep.*
>
> *My father's life straddled the old way and the coming of the prospectors. He told me many stories of the old life.*
>
> *I was born and raised at Salmon Village on the Salmon Fork, off the Black River. Every fall, wearing no rubber boots, we track-lined our boat upstream with winter supplies from Fort Yukon to Salmon Village, all the way, hunting and fishing. Twelve days, it took. Gee, today that is flown in twenty-two minutes!*
>
> *In those days, tuberculosis was rampant. Dr. and Mrs. Burke of St. Stephen's Episcopal mission at Fort Yukon took care of the sick and orphaned. There was no government assistance.*
>
> *When I was ten years old, my mother died of tuberculosis, just like my father's mother had died when he was little. I wondered, "Who's going to take care of me now?"*
>
> *My father had been home during those long months of my mother's sickness and he had not gone out trapping. After my mother died, he decided my young sister would stay home with my older sister, but I'd go out with him on the trapline. As I left the village, following behind my father and our toboggan pulled by four dogs, I snowshoed out into No*

17

Man's Land. All I had was my little bow and arrow. If you had seen me, gee, you'd have felt sorry.

In the late afternoon every day, we made beds of spruce branches covered by caribou hides; by dark, we were tucked in our cotton-covered, duck-down bags in our tent. Before I went to sleep, my father would pray, "Please don't let my son die out here alone."

Sometimes when we were breaking trail, there was no time to set up a tent so we'd sleep out. I had a caribou parka and rabbit-lined beaver mitts. Sometimes during the day when he was out setting traps, I'd spend the day waiting by the campfire. I could see Salmon Village in my mind and I'd cry because I wanted to go home.

Every day, we'd break almost two feet of snow. When I got tired, I cried. I cried all the time. My young sister was at home. I wondered what was going to happen to me, was I going to die? My father said, "What are you crying for? In old days, parents often died; then their children stayed with other families." He said, "When I lost my mother, I suffered too. You'll cry today and you'll cry tomorrow. But one day, you'll become a man and then, you'll be strong. If I left you behind in the village, maybe you'd get sick and die too. But trapping and hunting are the way we get our food; there's no other way. I am teaching you to survive. There is no other way."

After the trail was in and after a day of checking our marten sets, we would camp in our low-wall canvas tent. As the wolves howled, my father would smoke his long pipe and teach me to skin. He'd say, "Did I ever tell you about...?" (I'd think, "Yes—every night.") Then he'd tell me long-ago stories of the old people in Crow Flats, of "The Little Boy Who Went to the Moon," of his father, and of the Hudson's Bay Company. We had no radio, and the stories went right to my heart. He

Third from left, David Salmon at St. Stephen Mission, Fort Yukon; far right: Dr. Burke.
Courtesy of David Salmon.

told me about Fort Yukon and sometimes Washington, D.C. They were like a far-off dream. I never thought I would go to any of those places.

My father had no calendar or clock. He could tell the time by the stars. As he talked, I'd think about what people were doing back in Fort Yukon, dancing and playing fiddle music. But out here, all I could hear was the wolves singing.

There were a lot of weasels in that country, and talk about marten! There was one in every trap! They were so thick that we couldn't check our traps fast enough before the live ones ate those in the traps! No one had been in that country since the old days.

We ate a lot of moose meat but by the end of our trip, we had no store food left except some tea and a little sugar that my father saved for me.

After two and half months, we came in. We had lots of fur to take to Fort Yukon, and for a time, my suffering was over.

Before the next trapping season, my father decided I was too young for trapping, and that it was too much for my older sister to keep my little sister, Annie, at home. He took us both to St. Stephen's mission in Fort Yukon. At first, I was scared of the horses in Fort Yukon and of the white people. But Mrs. Burke was very kind to us. I couldn't speak any English, but at the store, I learned about Cracker Jacks: inside the box, there was a toy! Every day, the kids at the mission followed Mrs. Burke around like she was a mother duck.

That September, when a little girl was playing, she accidentally caught the curtains on fire. Suddenly the mission was in flames. We made a bucket brigade to the only water, down at the river, but we could not save the mission. We moved into another building while a new school was built.

Fourth from left, church lay reader David Salmon, 1952.

Courtesy of David Salmon.

Fourth and fifth from left, Episcopalian priest David Salmon and his wife Sarah Salmon with their son William, his wife and their children, circa 1964.

Courtesy of David Salmon.

Two years later, my father came for me and my sister. He put us and a year's supplies into a boat driven by a heavy inboard motor. We went far upstream, past Salmon Village, and into the Grayling River. My older sister had gotten married. With her and her husband, we built a base cabin. In the early winter, we mushed deep into the wilderness on the Grayling River where we trapped for the next ten years. We were the only people from the Grayling River to the Canadian border: us, the animals, and the mountains.

In the evenings while we skinned, my father told me stories of the Hudson's Bay Company, how they taught the Natives to jig and to play the fiddle.

In my late teens, I got my last mother: my father remarried another woman named Alice.

At the mission, I had met Sarah Enoch. My father arranged for us to be engaged. At eighteen when I was still legally too young, I married Sarah, who was also eighteen. Sarah helped me to read and write better. (All my life, I tried to learn from other people.)

Sarah and I trapped out of Grayling River, but I mushed in to get our mail at Salmon Village. When I was twenty-nine, I was made chief of the village. In 1941, hoping for a school from the government, the people asked me to move from Salmon Village to the Black River, where we established Chalkyitsik. We cut and rafted logs in, and by winter, we had a school. There was no air freight at that time so during the summer, I barged in supplies from Fort Yukon for the Native stores I set up in Arctic Village and in Chalkyitsik. I did a lot of firsts: I introduced pot-

latch, dog races, and the first Christmas tree in our village. We were a happy little community, but we had no church.

During the late 1950s, while I was working construction in Fort Yukon, I began studying the Bible with Deacon Albert Tritt. In 1958, I too became a deacon. But when Tritt died, there was no one else left. I wanted a church for Chalkyitsik. St. Stephen's mission in Fort Yukon sent me to Bible school in Michigan. With the requirement of four years of college and three years of seminary, it was tough in those days for us Natives to become an ordained

David Salmon at church he built in Chalkyitsik, 2004.

Judy Ferguson photo.

priest. I asked Bishop Gordon in Fairbanks if the church would relax the requirements for the Natives. In 1962, I became the first ordained Native Episcopal priest.

In the old days, Indian law governed everything: the group, marriage, family, gossip, and the hunt. That code protected the arctic nomads during starvation times. Violation of those laws meant exile or a death sentence. Until the 1930s Indian Law kept Native order, protecting individual and family ethics.

Wishing that code might apply to today's urban generation, David sighed, running his fingers through his thick, white hair.

You young people attend school now. How can you understand rules made for Bush survival? But life is in the old chiefs' words. Listen awhile; then, let the young take over.

After dinner, guests drifted over to see the beautiful church David had built. Passing his birch-bark canoe on the way, David explained it was similar to one he had previously made for the Alaska Native Heritage Center in Anchorage. At seventy, a master craftsman, he had also chain-sawed the logs for the church as perfectly as any milled logs.

At the community hall, adults and children gathered on the porch swatting mosquitoes as musicians began tuning their instruments. Saucy fiddle, guitar, and banjo music began filling the hall. Men, women, and children staccatoed their moccasined toes to Scottish jigs introduced 165 years ago. Between dance sets, David's granddaughters, Patti and Isabelle, presented him with a moose-hide bible cover and a feather headdress made by the Native elders in the community. Buddy Brown honored him with a special necklace of dentalia given to him by Will Mayo. Buddy and Doyon's Orie Williams gave David gaily handkerchiefed rifles along with many other gifts.

Chief David Salmon at his Chalkyitsik potlatch, 2004.
Judy Ferguson photo.

After guests had retreated to their quarters about 3:00 a.m., David leaned back in his easy chair and recalled important benchmarks.

During the 1930s, he had campaigned for a reservation for the Yukon Flats. He also pushed for reindeer as a domestic industry. Pointing with his time-worn hands, he said:

> *Half of the people supported me, but the other half did not. They said, "You're trying to make us Indians!" But only a few years later when western law converted reservations to tribal land, they discovered then that they were Indians! They wished they'd chosen a reservation so they had sovereignty over their subsistence lands!*
>
> *Also, it was a poor choice that under ANCSA, villages were obliged to become individual tribes in order to receive certain monies. It would have been better for their unity if all the villages in the Yukon Flats had been identified as one tribe for they are the same people.*

The following day after hot coffee, pancakes, and bacon, David ripped the air with a triumphant, "Heh heh ho!" Holding court from his chair, David hosted the second day of his three-day potlatch under an outside awning where church services were being televised. David was the mentor to evangelist Gary Simple of Sacred Ground Ministries in Venetie. Gary sang while David prayed. They traveled frequently as a team to Yukon River villages.

David, who was an expert musician, did not play his fiddle at his potlatch that evening. Wearing his new short-feathered headdress, he tapped his walk-

Chief Peter John and Chief David Salmon, 1992.
Courtesy of David Salmon.

ing stick, drumming his feet to the bluegrass jig. Reveling, he drank in the people dancing their jigs, swirling like the river, for joy, for pride, for healing… Near him, Janet's face was wet for joy.

Over the years, David ministered from Point Hope to Annette Island and often to the Lower Forty-eight. He served as archdeacon of Interior Alaska and of Yukon Territory.

During the 1960s, David traveled to Tanana for some of the first Tanana Chiefs Conferences. There he met Chief Andrew Isaac and began talking in depth with Chief Peter John. In the early 1980s, the men organized the elders' organization Denakkanaaga. "The old chiefs' words," David always said, "are life to the young." He traveled widely, sharing traditional Indian law and subsistence tool-making with children throughout Alaska.

In 2002, the University of Alaska honored David's knowledge of Native law by giving him an honorary doctorate of laws degree.

David said, "By tradition, Indian law requires fathers to teach the necessary tools of life to their sons. The scriptures are my tools of life. I tell others that when they honor me, they are honoring God, the one I serve. With such tools, our people will survive another thousand years."

In 2004-2005, David and I collaborated on the children's book Alaska's Little Chief, *the story of David's childhood and Alaska's fur-bearers.*

Every year at the Fairbanks Midnight Sun Intertribal Powwow, David would open with prayer and release the eagle. In 2005 at the installation of Fort Yukon's new chief, David gave an overview of Gwich'in history, citing the names of the great chiefs and the history of the

Evangelist Gary Simple at David Salmon's burial, Chalkyitsik, October 2007.

Judy Ferguson photo.

annual gathering of the Gwich'in tribes. May 30, 2007, four months before he died, David blessed the ground at the official ground-breaking ceremony for the Morris Thompson Center at 101 Dunkel Street, at what soon became the cultural and visitors' center.

In October 2007 when David died, he passed in peace and victory. Seated by his side was the succeeding first traditional chief, Don Honea. For burial, David was dressed in full Gwich'in regalia

Rev. Chief Dr. David Salmon, circa 2005.
Janet Curtiss photo.

and laid to rest next to his wife in Chalkyitsik. His disciple, Pastor Gary Simple, stood by the large wooden cross bathed in the October sunshine at David's graveside. Across the state, Governor Sarah Palin lowered flags to half-mast. David is remembered for his conviction that "the history of this country is not known. Young people don't know it. Old people die with it. I don't want to die with it. I want the young people to have it."

In November 2011, Thomas O'Brien released his book Gwich'in Athabascan Implements: History, Manufacture, and Usage According to Reverend David Salmon.

Timeline:

1837: In center of the Gwich'in, Alexander Murray based, Fort Yukon.
1815: King Salmon born.
1840: John Bell of Hudson's Bay Company made Fort McPherson.
1845: William Salmon born.
1846: LaPierre House built.
1847: Fort Yukon built.
1851: Smallpox epidemic at Fort Yukon.
1862: Rev. Robert McDonald at Fort Yukon.
1867: Sale of Alaska; Hudson's Bay Company departed Fort Yukon.
1891: New Rampart House after Alaska-Canadian border clarified.
1893: Circle City founded.
2004-2007: David Salmon, First Traditional Chief.

∽

Chapter Four

The First Salmon Cannery in Alaska, John Peratrovich

In 1998 as I began researching the impact of the Yugoslavian Diaspora in gold rush Alaska, I discovered Elizabeth Peratrovich Day February 16 on the Alaska calendar. I contacted Elizabeth's daughter-in-law Nettie Peratrovich, a very articulate woman who began teaching me from the moment I met her.

One day in Anchorage, Nettie and her husband Frank Peratrovich Jr. invited me to their home for dinner, the beginning of several days of interviewing. Frank Jr. said that before the south Slavs influenced the Alaska interior, his grandfather John Peratrovich was developing Alaska's first salmon cannery in 1878 in southeast Alaska, two years before gold was discovered in Juneau and six years before the gold rush hit the Interior.

On Klawock's first cannery's label: Josie, Mary (Skan) Peratrovich, John, and Mabel Peratrovich, circa 1900, Klawock, Prince of Wales Island.
Courtesy of Frank Jr. and Nettie Peratrovich.

"Because John Peratrovich eventually had three wives and sixteen children, the name Peratrovich in Southeast is almost as common as Smith is elsewhere!" Nettie said. Among his many children, John Peratrovich reared two of Alaska's more notable leaders: Roy, a civil rights activist, five-time grand president of Alaska Native Brotherhood and married to Elizabeth Peratrovich; and Frank Sr., territorial and state senator, senate president, and first vice president of the Alaska Constitutional Convention in 1955.

As we visited, Frank Jr. remembered the story of his grandfather, father, and uncle, trailblazers in Alaska's development.

My grandfather John Peratrovich, a Croatian-Italian fisherman called "Dago John," was born on the Dalmatian coastline about 1859. He jumped ship from the coast and landed in San Francisco. As an expert seiner, he began looking for work. Word got around the canneries that John Peratrovich knew how to mend seine nets.

TLINGIT

25

In 1868, a trading post and a salmon saltery were opened in Klawock on Prince of Wales Island. In 1877, the cannery was incorporated into the North Pacific Packing and Trading Co., the beginning of the canned Alaska salmon industry.

During the summers, the local Tlingits who wintered to the northwest in Tuxekan used Klawock as a fishing camp.

In 1876, as North Pacific Trading and Packing Co (NPTPC) was planning on taking over the saltery, they were most interested in getting the local Natives in Klawock to make and mend their own seines, rather than sending the nets back and forth to San Francisco. NPTPC hired Grandpa as a net hanger. As the cannery planned its hand-pack system in Alaska, they asked Grandpa to take equipment needed for setup and to establish the cannery in Alaska. (Family legend has it that on the way to Klawock, the ship wrecked in a storm at the Seal Islands north of Afognak Island. John was rescued by Sugpiaq Eskimos. A Russian revenue cutter took John on to Sitka.)

When Grandpa arrived in Klawock about 1876, he went across the bay to the peninsula, later called Peratrovich Island, to begin the conversion from saltery [or primitive cannery] to the NPTPC cannery. The local Tlingit chief asked the seventeen-year-old seiner to show the people the art of seine netting. From the beginning Grandpa worked well with the Native people. The chief had a forty-two-year-old daughter, Catherine Snook Skan. From an earlier marriage to John Skan, she had his two teenage stepdaughters, Mary Skan

Left side of same family photo on following page: Front, seated: Grandma Tecumseh (Catherine Snook Skan Peratrovich Collins); seated w/ baby: Mary Skan Peratrovich with Mabel One; Standing behind Grandma Tecumseh, L–R: Georgie; Rosanne holding Evelyn; Josie holding Al. Left side: Ann and Jennie and others. Photo is circa 1911–12, Klawock.

Courtesy of Frank and Nettie Peratrovich

and Nellie Skan. In Tlingit matriarchal culture an older woman traditionally married a younger man so Catherine and Grandpa were married. In 1877, their first son Jack was born, followed by James, Nick, and Robert. The Tlingits in Klawock, unlike subsequent Southeast canneries, were employees in the local cannery. As the cash economy with the gold rush began to invade Alaska, Klawock's cannery employment helped to preserve its people. In other towns, not hiring locally, the ethnic tension became so high that miners in Juneau were crying for some form of civil government. Former customs collector M. D. Ball of Sitka was elected by local delegates to travel to Washington, D.C., taking with him a petition asking for formal recognition as Alaska's representative. Congress refused to seat him and would not respond to his plea for Alaska self-government. However, in 1884 the Organic Act made Alaska a district with an appointed governor and officers.

Over the years Klawock took care of itself. As Grandpa worked in the hand-pack cannery, he received shares as well as pay. He often made business trips back and forth to San Francisco. At some point, Libby McNeil and Libby took over the North Pacific Trading and Packing Co. cannery.

As Grandpa traveled, he visited his Slavic friends throughout Southeast, one of whom, Vincent Baranovich, had a still. On trips Outside, some of Grandpa's children accompanied him. [One family story says that John and one of his daughters were once planning a trip to Croatia, but he ran out of money in San

Right side of family photo from preceding page: John Peratrovich with young Roy on his lap (future husband of Elizabeth Peratrovich and father of Roy Jr, Loretta and Frank Jr.). Behind John Peratrovich: Jack's wife; Jack holding Robinson; Nick's wife; Nick holding Alex; Robert holding Helen; James. (Frank Peratrovich Sr was away in the Navy.) Photo is circa 1911–12, Klawock.

Courtesy of Frank and Nettie Peratrovich

Klawock, Prince of Wales Island, 1885.

Courtesy of Frank and Nettie Peratrovich.

Francisco. His daughter said that as they traveled to California she was told to sit on "the trunk that was full of money."]

During one trip while Grandpa was gone, his wife Catherine took up with another man, Tecumseh Collins, and she eventually divorced Grandpa. After the divorce, he married his wife's first stepdaughter, Mary Skan (1864–1926) with whom he had nine more children: Josie (portrayed on the early salmon label), Frank (territorial and state senator and vice president of Alaska's constitutional convention), Mabel One (also on the early salmon label), Sarah, Jennie, Ann, Roy (my father), Mabel Two, and Bertha. Uncle Frank and my father Roy were Grandpa and Gramma Mary's only sons. With Catherine's other stepdaughter, Nellie, Grandpa also had two more children: Roseanna and George. All of Grandpa's children were born when Natives were not considered citizens. [Citizenship wasn't extended to Alaska Natives until 1924.] Today, Grandpa's progeny number over 680.

Grandpa became the principal person in the salmon cannery. In 1900, a picture of him, my Gramma Mary, and their first two daughters, Josie and Mabel One, was on their Family Brand salmon label. But when Mabel One died, the label was retired. It was too painful a reminder. According to Tlingit customs, as Catherine and Grandpa's first four boys, Jack, James, Nick, and Robert, grew up, they tattooed their family name and an eagle onto their arms. When Grandpa went to San Francisco once a year, he usually took Robert.

Like a second mother, Dad's oldest sister, Josie, grew up taking care of all the kids. Grandpa built a large beautiful home for his wife and children and their mothers, where the children lived until they wed. After marriage, the adult children built homes close to his.

When Uncle Frank was only five, Grandpa's cannery burned. In his desk, he had kept the proof of his company shares; when they burned, he lost control of the cannery. His grandson David did rebuild it and his son Bob ran it.

In November 1915, David was rowing Grandpa in their boat between the cannery and Klawock village when the boat capsized. Although Grandpa was rescued, the exposure triggered a virus in his kidneys. When he was fifty-six, he died. My father, Roy, was only seven and became the man of the house.

Seven of Gramma Mary's daughters went to Chemawa Indian School in the Lower Forty-eight, but few returned. Like his sisters, Uncle Frank went Outside to boarding school at Haskell Institute, Topeka, Kansas. On a sports team tour he met the legendary football hero Jim Thorpe and later, he played against him on the football field. Uncle Frank also served in the Navy.

Uncle Bob's cannery also burned, and after Grandpa died in 1920 he rebuilt it. Bob also had a grocery store, the movie house, and the only power plant in town. At nine p.m. everyone knew Bob had gone to bed because he turned off the diesel run generators and with it, everyone else's power. Bob was quite the gentleman dresser, wearing three-piece suits every day.

Dad told me about the hardships he endured growing up. Uncle Frank was not around after his father died. He was away in school or in the Navy. Dad hunted deer for the family and brought home salmon. He sawed large firewood logs alone, chopped and stacked it. There was no time to play. No one ever helped except one day Uncle Bob saw Dad trying to get the saw to bite into a huge log laying down on the beach. Bob was in his three-piece suit but he jumped down to the beach, took off his jacket and helped Dad saw that log. Dad never forgot that. In 1924 Demmert's cannery was built. Dad used to wash dishes at that cannery across the bay to make a little money for his fatherless family. He was usually the last one to leave. One weekend when there was a dance at the Alaska Native Brotherhood Hall, he had one more impossible pan to clean. In desperation and when no one was looking, he threw the pot into the woods and rowed to Klawock for the dance. The next day nobody missed the pot!

Filipino employees would work for less than the locals, so the cannery brought them into town. In the bunkhouse at night, the Filipinos jammed on their musical instruments. Dad and his friends really liked the music. They salvaged some instruments the Salvation Army had discarded. The horns had sticky valves, which they fixed with string. From a horse in town, they borrowed some tail hairs. In the bunkhouse, Dad tied the hair to a steel bunk, anchored them to an upside-down metal tub and voila, he had

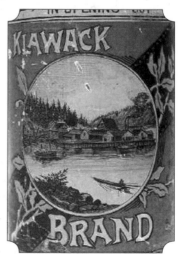

Klawock's first cannery's label, show photo of original cannery, 1890s.
Courtesy of Frank Jr. and Nettie Peratrovich.

Roy Peratrovich, youngest son of John and Mary Peratrovich, 1940, Klawock.
Courtesy of Roy Peratrovich Jr.

a bass guitar! The Filipinos taught Dad to play a ukulele as well. I don't know how he could with his huge hands. (He could lift an anvil by the cone with one hand.) Dad's favorite piece was "My Little Grass Shack in Hawaii." No one taught them how to play, they just learned by trying. Once on the Fourth of July, the town's local "marching band" paraded through town. Their bass drummer was deaf and blind but he loved banging on his big patched-up drum. When they got to the "Y" in the road the band went one way and Jumbo the drummer the other way. No one ever had the heart to tell Jumbo he went the wrong way. Dad also played guitar in a small dance band that played on weekends in Craig. He rowed around the coast to get the extra pin money.

When Dad was eighteen, his mother also died. However life had given him training for the battles yet to come. With the advantage of knowing Tlingit and his culture, Dad went on to become a fine speaker and a leader of his people.

Alaska's Civil Rights Act: Roy, Elizabeth, and Frank Peratrovich

Frank Jr. continued, sharing the story of his well-known mother and father.

Because we were part Yugoslav, my parents could eat in Montenegrin Mike Pusich's restaurant on Douglas Island—but he only made an exception for my parents. In the windows of restaurants and hotels in Juneau, there were signs, "No Indians or dogs allowed." (However those Slavs didn't care if you were an Indian, a Communist, or whatever, so long as you had that 'vich' in your name.)

Uncle Frank and my father Roy (born thirteen years after Frank) were both active in Alaska Native Brotherhood (ANB). Mother was also very active in the Alaska Native Sisterhood (ANS). One of their goals was to get the right to vote for Natives.

When Uncle Frank was in charge of distribution of food and clothing to widows and children under territorial Governor John W. Troy, Uncle Frank noticed that no Native widows and children came in. When he asked, the governor answered that Natives weren't allowed those benefits. When Uncle Frank replied he would quit, the governor reversed the policy. In 1945, Uncle

Frank began serving in the territorial legislature. Later he became first vice president of the Alaska Constitutional Convention, and in the 1960s he was the president of the Senate. A thoughtful man who spoke little, Uncle Frank was deeply respected. He fought to ban national canneries' fish trap monopolies, which caught unfair amounts of salmon and damaged the local seiners' harvest and sales. He included a provision in the new state constitution to outlaw the traps, and he won.

In contrast to the more serious Frank, my father was gregarious, a great jokester, and an excellent speaker. My mother, Elizabeth Jean Wanamaker, was born of the Raven moiety at Petersburg on the Fourth of July, 1911. Her parents were Presbyterian lay minister Andrew Wanamaker and his first wife, Jean (a wonderful person who understood English but could only speak Tlingit). The Tlingit name they gave Mother meant "the root of all women." Mother was serious, disciplined, stylish, and beautiful.

Frank Peratrovich Sr. running for the Alaska legislature, circa 1944.
Courtesy of Frank Jr. and Nettie Peratrovich.

Dad went to Chemawa Indian School in Salem, Oregon, where he played guard and was captain of the football team. His senior year in 1930, he left for Ketchikan High School where he met Mom. (Their school annual predicted they would get married.) After graduation in 1931, wanting to teach, they both enrolled at Bellingham Normal (today, Western Washington University) but they ran out of money. Thinking they could better save money, they got married. When that didn't happen, they returned to Klawock, where life for them was less expensive. Dad worked there as a fisherman, laborer, fireman, policeman, postmaster and as mayor. My older brother, Roy, was born in Klawock in 1934 and three years later, I was born in Juneau. In 1937 there were more Natives than whites in Alaska, and the average life expectancy for Natives was about forty-five. We Alaska Natives were at the bottom of the totem pole, on a level with a Third World nation.

Elizabeth Peratrovich's father, Andrew Wanamaker, (born 1886 in Sitka) circa 1919, Juneau.
Courtesy of Roy Peratrovich Jr.

31

In 1940, Dad was elected grand president of the Alaska Native Brotherhood (ANB), but he figured he couldn't do much good in Klawock for the Native people. We moved to Juneau in late December 1940. Roy was seven, I was four, and Sis was less than a year old. (Mom used to recall the hair-raising airplane trip coming into Juneau with our pilot Tex Beneke, who later became one of the owners of Alaska Airlines!) Roy was one of the first Native children to go to public school there; previously all the Native children had to attend the Bureau of Indian Affairs school in the village. Renting in Juneau was difficult, but we became the second Native family in a non-Native neighborhood. I always had to wear a white shirt to make sure we didn't appear to be "dirty Indians." We were very poor, so Mom hand-knit and crocheted beautiful dresses to sell. Her passion was reading.

By acclamation Dad was reelected grand president of ANB four more times. (Later in 1945, Mom was elected grand president of Alaska Native Sisterhood.)

In 1941, my parents wrote letters to the vice president and to Gov. Ernest Gruening protesting the racist public signs in Juneau. They noted that Natives paid school taxes even though their children were largely disallowed from public schools.

My parents submitted an antidiscrimination bill to the territorial legislature in 1943, but it failed. A Native American attorney, Bill Curran, began working for them for free, spending long evening hours drafting the civil rights act in our kitchen at 815 Dixon Street, above the governor's mansion. Passage was expected to take years.

At the annual convention in 1944, the ANB prepared Resolution No. Two: Anti-discrimination, to present to the Senate. (While the United States was fighting Hitler's policy of white supremacy in Europe, it looked like Mom

Alaska Native Sisterhood, from left, second: Elizabeth Peratrovich, Grand President, 1945, Juneau.

Courtesy of Frank Jr. and Nettie Peratrovich.

Governor Ernest Gruening signing the Antidiscrimination Bill. L–R: Senator O.D. Cochran (Nome), Mrs. Roy (Elizabeth) Peratrovich (Klawock), Gov. Ernest Gruening, Rep. Anderson (Nome), Senator N.R. Walker (Ketchikan), Roy Peratrovich (Klawock).
Courtesy of Frank Jr. and Nettie Peratrovich.

was taking on white supremacy in the Alaska territorial legislature.) Sen. Allen Shattuck rose up indignantly and addressed the legislature, "Who are these people, barely out of savagery, who want to associate with us whites with five thousand years of recorded history behind us?"

My mom put her knitting down and came forward. "I would not have expected that I, who am barely out of savagery, would have to remind gentlemen of five thousand years of recorded civilization of our Bill of Rights.

"There are three kinds of people who practice discrimination," she said. "First, the politician to maintain an inferior minority group; second, Mr. and Mrs. Jones, who aren't sure of their social position; and third, the great superman who believes in the superiority of the white race." The Senate and gallery exploded with applause.

After the Antidiscrimination Bill passed on February 8, 1945, my folks went to Percy's Cafe (which catered to Natives) where my Tlingit friend Gus Adams was having a Coke. They were so excited that the bill had just passed that they had to tell someone! Gus never forgot it. On February 16, Gov. Gruening signed the bill into law, nineteen years before the nation's civil rights law. To celebrate passage, Dad and Mom danced beautifully at the Baranof Hotel. No Native had ever danced there; to avoid them, people cleared the floor.

The reality was that the civil rights law was good, but its enforcement was never funded. In case of infraction, no one had the money to go to court—and

Elizabeth Peratrovich wearing corsage, circa 1945.
Photographer, William Paul Jr. Courtesy of Frank Jr. and Nettie Peratrovich.

the chances of getting a jury of your peers were poor. It was a moral victory rather than a new litigated way of life. Even with the law passed, Native people returning from World War II and later from Korea had a hard time finding lodging in Juneau. That's how I got to know Cecil Barnes, a former marine in Korea and later, the first chairman of Chugach corporation. A lot of people (including the most decorated Native during World War II) stayed with us for as much as a month.

The biggest difference the civil rights law made was that discrimination could no longer be outright; however, it did become subtle. Hotels just used the excuse, "We don't have any more rooms." However, the law made it possible for Natives to go to public schools.

Mom also fought for the Japanese-Americans who were interned during World War II in camps outside Alaska. My wife Nettie Peratrovich met a young Japanese girl who asked if Nettie had known Mom. The girl said, "Elizabeth Peratrovich was the most wonderful lady in the world. She got so many of us Japanese kids out of the camps. In Alaska, our lands were also not taken from us." As an influential person and big leader in ANS, Mom worked with Governor Gruening to get the Japanese children who had been born in Alaska out of the camps. During the 1950s, Mom helped a Polish marine who jumped ship in Juneau. My folks fed him him and helped him get a job. (During the 1950s, that wasn't popular.) She got a bill passed through Congress that allowed him to stay. When she saw something terribly wrong, she tried to right it.

Nationally, Mom went as the first Alaska representative to the National Congress of American Indians, trying to get support for Alaska civil rights. In 1956, she attended the Institute for Race

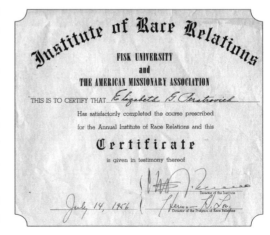

Institute of Race Relations from Fisk University certificate of Elizabeth Peratrovich's 1956 attendance, two years before her death.
Courtesy of Frank Jr. and Nettie Peratrovich.

Relations at Fisk University, where African-American clergy discussed how to integrate the church. Martin Luther King and several others who later became national leaders were also there.

Dad was the first Alaskan to receive a United Nations fellowship; with it, he went to Nova Scotia and studied their fishing industry. In 1952 he got a scholarship to study credit procedure at the Central Bank and Trust Company where he also took a business course at Denver University in Denver, Colorado. I remember Dad and I studying the material together at the dining room table. For the territorial government of Alaska and the Bureau of Indian Affairs, he first served as a special officer, then credit and finance officer, followed by being head of the tribal operations program in the state, based in Juneau. In 1955, he became a loan examiner for the Bureau of Indian Affairs (BIA) in the regional office at Anadarko, Oklahoma. In 1968 Governor Gruening announced that Dad was the new BIA superintendent of the Anchorage District, with responsibility in southcentral and in the Aleutian Islands.

Dad was open and very straightforward. Along with Barney Gottstein, he was on the first Alaska Human Rights Commission. When he was the area tribal officer for BIA, he would call Governor Egan, and let him know what wasn't right. Egan would say, "Roy, you gotta remember you're talking to the governor of Alaska." Dad just said, "Bill, don't pull rank on me now." If politicians ignored Native-related issues, based on the Native vote Dad could negotiate.

In 1958, when Mom died of cancer, few yet knew the name Elizabeth Peratrovich. It was at least twenty years before her name would become widely recognized. In the late 1980s, a university student researching the Alaska civil rights bill kept coming across the name Elizabeth Peratrovich. After he

Frank Peratrovich Jr, two unidentified. Far right: Roy Sr. and after she'd become ill, Elizabeth Peratrovich, mid-1950s, probably Oklahoma.

Courtesy of Frank Jr. and Nettie Peratrovich.

published his research paper, the Alaska Native Brotherhood and Sisterhood pushed the legislature to set aside a day beginning in 1988 to honor my mother, Feb. 16. On Feb. 16, 2003, the Municipality of Anchorage renamed a park at Fourth Avenue and E Street "Elizabeth and Roy Peratrovich Park." June 30, 2008, my brother Roy, a retired engineer and well-known sculptor, presented his sculpture, "Flight of the Raven," dedicated to our parents in Peratrovich Park.

Peratrovich family (fourth in from right, back row: Roy Peratrovich Jr., Loretta Peratrovich Montgomery, Diane Benson, Frank II, and Nettie Peratrovich) at dedication of Flight of the Raven, Peratrovich Park, Anchorage, June 30, 2008.

Courtesy of Roy Peratrovich Jr.

Timeline:

1878: First salmon cannery in Alaska, Klawock, Prince of Wales Island.

1884: Organic Act; Alaska becomes a federal district with a General Agent of Education to establish schools for Native and non-Native children.

1924: Indian Citizenship Act included Alaska Natives as US citizens.

1945: Antidiscrimination law through Roy, Frank and Elizabeth Peratrovich.

1955: Alaska Constitutional Convention; Frank Peratrovich.

1988: Elizabeth Peratrovich Day, February 16.

2003: Elizabeth and Roy Peratrovich Park, Anchorage

∞

Chapter Five

Francis "Frank" Haldane: Tsimshian, Metlakatla

Like the Haida, the Tsimshian migrated from Canada to Alaska, but more recently, in 1887. The Tsimshian sought a place to practice their Christian faith and settled on tiny Annette Island.

I met Francis Haldane after seeing flyers at the university announcing his public speaking on culture. Wanting to learn more, I called him in Anchorage in 2006. He kindly agreed to an interview. We met in his home where he and his wife shared their beautiful Alaska art collection with me. Settling back in his kitchen, he began telling me the story of his people.

A full Tsimshian of the wolf clan, I was born June 21, 1926, in Metlakatla, which is a fishing village fifteen air miles southeast of Ketchikan, where it rains and blows a lot! "Tsimshian" is a modern term, evolved from the 'Ksian'/ Skeena River, meaning "always misty, always rainy." Originally from British Columbia, the Tsimshian are unusual in that we have four, not two, clans: Eagle, Killer whale, Raven, and Wolf.

Francis Haldane wearing woven cedar hat and wolf clan button robe, Anchorage, 2006.
Judy Ferguson photo.

A Scottish lay missionary of the Anglican Church, William Duncan, first evangelized the Tsimshian at Fort Simpson, British Columbia. Because our Tsimshian names seemed impossible to pronounce, they were changed to Haldane, Verney, Booth, Ridley, and many others. My great-grandfather, Matthew Haldane, and his son, my grandfather, Benjamin A. Haldane (1874–1941), were among the Tsimshian first proselytized in Old Metlakatla [near Prince Rupert, British Columbia.] When my grand-

TSIMSHIAN

William Duncan, circa 1902, Curtis Studio, Seattle.
National Archives and Records Administration, 297274. Courtesy of Francis Haldane.

father was thirteen, he came with Duncan's mass migration to Alaska.

In the mid-1800s, William Duncan learned the Tsimshian language, then taught Christianity and modern-life skills to the Tsimshian at Old Metlakatla. They became self-sufficient, building their own boats—trollers, gill netters, and big seiners—as well as modern homes. They built and ran their own cannery and constructed an elaborate "cathedral."

In 1881, a disagreement arose over Duncan's refusal to administer some of the church's required guidelines, and consequently the Tsimshian homes were confiscated. The Church of England sent Bishop Ridley, who ruled against Duncan, accusing him of building his own empire.

About 1886, Duncan traveled to Washington, D.C., where he asked President Grover Cleveland for land on Annette Island in Alaska for the beleaguered Canadian Tsimshians. By 1890, 823 residents had arrived at "new Metlakatla," Alaska. The following year, Congress declared Annette Island a federal Indian reservation. The pioneers built their own sawmill, homes, an elaborate church, a school, and a cannery. Duncan ran the self-supporting cannery and gave shares to the community. The cannery—painted white, with stainless steel—was spotless, hosed down after every shift.

Whatever skills Duncan did not know, he quickly learned, and he taught the people, who were fast learners. To have a musical band, he was able to get a donation of twenty-eight different instruments which he then learned and taught others.

Duncan taught my grandfather, Ben (B.A.) Haldane, how to play the organ and piano, how to direct a band or choir, and photography. B.A. Haldane opened a studio in 1907 in his store, where he also sold dry

Francis' grandfather Ben (B.A.) Haldane, circa 1907, Metlakatla.
Photographer B.A. Haldane. Courtesy of Francis Haldane.

Metlakatla, town hall and church to far right; B.A. Haldane with camera and assistant in right foreground. Circa 1905.
National Archives Records Administration, 297865. Courtesy Francis Haldane.

goods, drugs, and groceries. His hundreds of century-old glass-plate portraits of Tsimshian people are now recognized by the world.

Duncan prohibited some Tsimshian practices, but he did not forbid all cultural expression or the language. Before Christianity, the Tsimshian believed that the individual's spirit never dies but continues through another human life. All creation also had a spirit and must be respected. For example, if a person were not respectful to the animals or trees, he created "bad luck," accumulating a debt. Forgiveness might be sought in service.

Southeast mythology illustrated the law of forgiveness repeatedly as well as offering entertainment, lessons, and clarifying mysteries. Raven was depicted as a powerful magician, a creator. The language expressed a way of life, family, tribe, nation, and identity. The protocol helped maintain domestic balance and harmony.

Duncan began well, but later he became dictatorial and would not allow Natives schooling beyond fourth grade. He refused to appoint a successor for his position. As he aged, the pioneers asked for Rev. Robert Tomlinson to take Duncan's place. Tomlinson's parents were missionaries and he also spoke Tsimshian. However, Duncan died without a successor in 1918, six years before my parents, Lucy Verney Haldane and Boyd Anthony Haldane, married in 1924.

I was born two years later. We always ate seafood, including oolichan (hooligan) and a sort of butter, oolichan grease. Oolichan, similar to smelt, mostly comes from the Nass River, near the Skeena River. To make oolichan grease,

Tsimshian have four clans: killer whale, eagle, raven, and wolf. Francis Haldane holding design of his wolf clan, Anchorage, 2006.

Judy Ferguson photo.

the fish were fermented, cooked, and then the oil came to the surface.

When I was sixteen or seventeen, I left Metlakatla for high school at Sheldon Jackson School in Sitka. While I was gone, the army built a large air base a few miles from Metlakatla. After being expelled from Sheldon Jackson, I was drafted into the Army Air Force, where I got into aeronautical communications. (Not only was my high school cut short, but I also missed out on two years of grade school, so I have a seventh-grade education.) From 1949 to 1960, I worked in aeronautical communications for the Civil Aeronautics Administration (later the Federal Aviation Administration, or FAA).

I began training in air traffic control when my instructor sized me up: "Haldane, I don't give a darn if you're a Native." I thought, "Uh, oh…" He went on, "I see you as an air traffic controller, but I see somebody not really believing in himself. If you issue a potentially harmful direction, I'll say, 'Click, disregard' and I'll give the right instruction to the pilot. Yes, those pilots have college degrees and fly big airplanes full of people. But they cannot, they will not, they better not, make a move without your approval. Down here on the ground, you are in charge. But," he warned, "if you don't believe in yourself, they'll know it, and they will feel uneasy."

I had been telling myself that being an air traffic controller was too much for me, was beyond my education. But after listening, I decided to give it my best shot.

By 1962 in Anchorage, I directed air traffic control and became crew chief, then first-line supervisor. Over the years, I have trained a lot of college kids, many of whom could not make it. I see if a person is willing to take a risk and to learn. Anyone—whites, blacks, Natives—can succeed if they get past the intimidation.

In 1983 I retired, eight years after the U.S. Coast Guard base on Annette Island also closed. Today, Annette Island Reserve is the only federal reservation for indigenous Alaskans.

According to historic Tsimshian protocol, the first moose I would get as a youth, I'd give to the elders. Today when I go home, still someone always brings me a fish. It's a powerful, beautiful practice and everyone benefits.

Francis Haldane, Army Air Force, circa 1944.
Courtesy of Francis Haldane.

Francis Haldane dancing with Lepquinm Gumilgit Gagoadim at Alaska Federation of Natives First Alaskans Elders and Youth Conference, 2012.
Bill Roth. Courtesy Francis Haldane.

In the mid-1970s, Jack Hudson, a schoolteacher and master carver, began teaching Native arts in Metlakatla. One of his students was David Boxley, who is also now a master carver. Dance groups have begun, including the Fourth Generation Dancers, my dance group. ("Fourth generation" dates from the introduction of Christianity to us.) Besides dancing I am also trained as a chemical dependency counselor, which I did for twenty years. For Southcentral Foundation, I both counseled and taught other counselors about alcohol and drug addiction, recovery, relapse, and prevention.

Our dance group, Lepquinm-gumilgitgagorum (pronounced "lepcan'm g'meelget gagorum—"Our Own Dance in Our Hearts"), representing all indigenous Alaska cultures, has performed in Washington, D.C., Bethel, and at the Alaska Native Heritage Center. We took first place at the 2007 World Eskimo Indian Olympics. In my parents' day, the drumbeat was "Assimilate as fast as possible." Today we celebrate reconnecting to our cultural roots.

Timeline

1887: Tsimshian migrate from British Columbia, Canada to Annette Island, Alaska.

1891: The United States Congress granted recognition to the new community by creating the Annette Islands Reserve, a federal Indian reservation.

Early 1940s: Large military airfield built on Annette Island.

Late 1940s: Airfield became U.S. Coast Guard search and rescue base.

1971: After Alaska Native Claims Settlement Act only Annette Islands Reserve remained an Indian reservation in Alaska.

∞

Chapter Six

Ada Haskin: Inland Tlingit, Skagway; Skookum Jim's Cousin

Generally Tlingit live on the Alaska southeast coast; however, their home extends across international borders into the Yukon Territory and British Columbia. Their extensive trade routes, as well as intermarriage, caused a few relatively large populations of Tlingit to settle around Atlin, Teslin, and Tagish lakes near Carcross. The first time I saw signs displaying the word, Tlingit, *in the Yukon Territory, I thought it was a mistake but later I learned the history and heard it from the people.*

Ada Haskin's cousin "Skookum" Jim Mason whose discovery sparked the Klondike gold rush, 1898, Yukon Territory.
Courtesy of Ada Haskin

Online at Wikipedia:

> *The greatest territory historically occupied by the Tlingit extended from along the present border between Alaska and British Columbia, north to the coast just southeast of the Copper River delta. The Tlingit occupied almost all of the Alexander Archipelago, except the southernmost end of Prince of Wales Island and its surroundings, where the Kaigani Haida moved just before the first encounters with European explorers. Inland, the Tlingit occupied areas along the major rivers that pierce the Coast Mountains and Saint Elias Mountains and flow into the Pacific, including the Alsek, Tatshenshini, Chilkat, Taku, and Stikine rivers. With regular travel up these rivers, the Tlingit developed extensive trade networks with Athabascan tribes of the interior, and commonly intermarried with them. From this regular travel and trade, a few relatively large populations of Tlingit settled around Atlin, Teslin, and Tagish Lakes, whose headwaters flow from areas near the headwaters of the Taku River.*
>
> *Delineating the modern territory of the Tlingit is complicated because they are spread across the border between the United States and Canada, by the lack of designated reservations, other complex legal and political concerns,*

42

and a relatively high level of mobility among the population, as well as overlapped territory with various Athabascan peoples. In Canada, the modern communities of Atlin, British Columbia (Taku River Tlingit), Teslin, Yukon (Teslin Tlingit Council), and Carcross, Yukon (Carcross/Tagish First Nation) have reserves and are the representative Interior Tlingit populations. The territory occupied by the modern Tlingit people in Alaska is however not restricted to particular reservations, unlike most tribes in the contiguous 48 states. This is the result of the Alaska Native Claims Settlement Act (ANCSA), which established regional corporations throughout Alaska with complex portfolios of land ownership rather than bounded reservations administered by tribal governments.

Two hours from Atlin, British Columbia, I visited with Ada Haskin as she sat knitting on a comfortable sofa in her Skagway living room. A likeable woman, she began patiently explaining a life that had been far from easy.

I was born in Whitehorse, Yukon Territory in 1924, the child of a Tlingit father and a Han [Athabascan] mother. In my early thirties, I married Fred Haskin and moved to his home in Skagway, seventy-five miles southwest, where I live today.

Ada Haskin, knitting a gift in her Skagway home in 2006.
Judy Ferguson photo.

Long before the Gold Rush, the Chilkat Tlingits caught fish and picked berries in Skagway. They controlled the mountain passes, traveling into the Interior on the Chilkoot and the Dalton trails for trade. In Angoon, inbreeding was once a concern, so my paternal grandmother and two other women traveled by canoe to Skagway and walked over the Chilkoot Trail to Tagish, where my grandmother met her new husband.

A few years later, my cousin Skookum Jim [Mason] was with his brother-in-law, California prospector George Carmack, when gold was discovered at Bonanza Creek on August 16, 1896. Originally Carmack was credited with the discovery of gold that set off the Klondike Gold Rush of 1898, but later my cousin Jim was correctly recognized.

Ironically, my grandparents and cousins camped in Dyea near Skagway, and packed for the prospectors over the trail to the Klondike. As non-Native merchants arrived from Juneau, our people traded moose hides for needed equipment and food.

From Atlin, British Columbia to Skagway, the land was Tlingit. [In 1901 Canada and the United States both claimed Skagway and Dyea. President

Theodore Roosevelt appointed an international tribunal who decided that the area was American.] A sign on the ridgetop marked the international border. I remember a story that once, after buying from the Juneau traders in Skagway, an old woman hid her parcels in her dogs' packs. When the goods were discovered, immigration officials tried to make the woman pay duty. Today, customs tax still makes it difficult for us to take gifts across the border to our potlatches, but still, we have dances. Once as I passed from Canada back into Alaska, the border security guard told me, "Ada, you folks can always come and go as you want. Don't let anyone tell you differently."

Johnnie Johns, Mud Lake, 1917.
Photo by Angela Sidney.
Courtesy of Ada Haskin.

Until 1942, there was no road to our home in Tagish, Yukon Territory. The train brought us goods from Skagway, stopping at Carcross en route to Whitehorse.

When my father, Johnnie Johns, was only in fourth grade, his father died. He had to drop out of the local mission school to help his family. He hunted for his sisters, and when he was seventeen he talked with a white man about guiding hunters professionally. Dad sent for horses out of Vancouver, British Columbia. They rounded up wild Canadian cayuses, loaded them in boxcars, and sent them to Carcross, where Dad picked them up. Ultimately, Dad became one of the top ten guides in North America. A self-made man, he ran an outfit with about ninety horses that ranged free. He was very intelligent and very kind. You'd have thought that he went to a university, he was so articulate. He took wealthy hunters to the ridges near Mud Lake (also called Marsh Lake) north of Tagish for Dall sheep. For two days, we rode horses to the peaks and camped there in a canvas wall tent. Once a hunter from South America asked Dad when he first arrived in the north!

When I was two, my mother died. I thought my mother had left me. I didn't understand what "Your mother died ..." meant. From my first two years, I dimly remembered my mother, but when she didn't return and others kept putting me here and there, I thought that no one liked me. Years later, I understood. I was raised by my grandma, Mariah John, and by my dad. To speak with Grandma, I could only speak Tlingit, which I have from birth.

Ada Haskin's grandmother Mariah John, 1951.
Courtesy of Ada Haskin.

When I was six, I walked up to the mail carrier's dog team, but they jumped me. The dogs began chewing my calf, my arm, and head. At the government hospital, they tied the muscle together in my calf. After the surgery, they put me in traction daily. How I hated it! I spent five months in the hospital, where they kept the Natives all in one room, no matter their situation.

Even though I had begun at the white people's school in Carcross, I couldn't go there anymore. When I got out of the hospital, my dad put me in the mission boarding school, where I stayed for six or seven years. They called us "savages." If I drew a totem pole, they said I was drawing my "pagan gods," whatever that meant.

The food there was terrible. When I was around twelve, the principal, a married, ordained minister and a father of six children, began molesting the older girls. I was frightened. But I finally told my dad. He typed a letter to the government, who must have fired off a letter to the principal because suddenly, I was told to leave school. That was the end of my education. Without a white father, I was not allowed to go to the other school, the one for whites.

During World War II, my dad's business suffered. No hunters came, but during the summers there were fishing parties. In the fall, we harvested wild grass at the lake with a horse-drawn cutter. We dried, raked, and piled the grass into haystacks.

Throughout the winter, the horses pawed through the snow for feed, but some needed extra. Every few days in the winter, Dad harnessed a team of two Clydesdales, hooked them to the hayrack, and I drove them seven miles over the thick lake ice to the piles, where I forked hay into the wagon. Then, using only bridles, Dad and I rounded up the horses that were thin. In the wild pastures, I rode bareback, herding as many as twenty-seven lean horses home for extra feed.

In the fall, we had also put up stacks of whitefish. Throughout the winter, we chopped a hole in the ice for our water and for cooking dog food daily. Over a fire in a sectioned

Johnnie Johns, 1984, Carcross, Yukon Territory.
Courtesy of Ada Haskin.

45

metal barrel, we boiled water, fish, oatmeal, and cornmeal. In early winter, Dad caught fresh whitefish in a net under the ice and sold them. He trapped around Carcross, up the lake, and in the mountains. For months, he was gone buying fur for Hudson's Bay Company.

When I was fourteen, Dad married again and had two more children. When the marriage failed, Dad, Grandma, and I raised the children.

One day, dad got a bad flu. We had no phone; I ran to the telegraph operator and told her we needed a chartered plane. The plane landed on the ice, and the storekeeper eased dad into the plane. I was left with my blind Grandma and three-year-old brother. I had to pack water, cook for the dogs, dump our slops, feed the horses,

Ada's big game guide father Johnnie Johns on cover of The Colourful Five Percent of the Yukon and Alaska, Read In All the Better Cabins *autographed from her father to her.*

Courtesy of Ada Haskin

get wood, make kindling, and fill our Blazo lanterns. I don't like the dark, so I had to get all my work finished before nightfall. I was glad when Dad got better and returned home.

After the road to Tagish was built, Dad started a hotel at Mile 272, and called it Johnnie's Place. I helped run it until I married Fred Haskin from Alaska and we moved to Skagway. Here we raised our family and still live here today. On ground where his great-grandfather once walked, my son, Buster, worked until recently at the Skagway Traditional Council, set up two years ago by Richard Stitt, self-governance coordinator for Tlingit and Haida in Juneau.

Dad died when he was eighty-nine. His beaded jacket from Old Crow still hangs in my closet and pictures of him as one of the nation's top hunting guides are on my wall.

Timeline:

1897–1900: Klondike Gold Rush

1898: Skagway, largest Alaska city; White Pass and Yukon Railroad; telegraph, Seattle–Sitka

1924: Natives become U.S. citizens

1935: Tlingit-Haida land claims

1971: Alaska Native Claims Settlement Act

2000: Richard Stitt set up the Skagway Traditional Council.

∞

Chapter Seven

Jilkateet, Marion Dennis Twitchell, Tlingit

The Tlingit are the northernmost of the Northwest Coast tribes. A hunter-gatherer, matrilineal society of southeast Alaska's temperate rainforest, they developed trade routes with their neighbors that were used by prospectors and Native packers during the 1890s Klondike Gold Rush. Today the Klondike Gold Rush National Historical Park includes portions of the White Pass Trail and the Chilkoot Trail, which leaves from the historic townsite of Dyea and runs to Bennett Lake, from which prospectors could raft to Dawson City, Yukon Territory. In 1998, the one-hundred-year anniversary of the gold rush, Canada and the United States combined

Marion Dennis Twitchell in her Tlingit button blanket robe with beadwork by her grandmother and standing near snowshoes made by her grandfather, Skagway, 2003.
Judy Ferguson photo.

Klondike Gold Rush National Historical Park and the Yukon's Chilkoot Trail National Historical Site into the Klondike Gold Rush International Historical Park.

After my first Tlingit friend, Maria Joseph of Haines, passed away, I met some of her family in Skagway in 2003 including a kinsman, Jilkateet, Marion Dennis, who shared their people's history.

I was named Jilkateet, Marion Dennis, when I was born in 1951 to Silas R. Dennis Sr. (Gooshdaiheen) and Dorothy Dennis (Tuwaxsee) in Skagway. I was named after my grandmother, "Mary" Marion Daanawaak Dennis. (Our family name of "Deigoosh" was changed by the white man to "Dennis.") My origins are Chilkoot.

At one time, my great-uncle Nahku owned Long Bay or Nahku Bay, which borders the mountains into Dyea. About 1900, my grandparents Sam and Sarah Dennis, originally from Haines, owned 160 acres in Dyea as their Native allotment land.

Tlingit include two tribes, Eagle and Raven, and disallow marriages within the same tribe. My father was the Eagle tribe, Killer Whale

TLINGIT

47

Tlingit packers, Dyea, near Skagway. Circa 1900.

Courtesy of Lance Twitchell.

clan. Because tribe and clan are passed through the matrilineal line, his children were Raven tribe, Sockeye clan.

The historically ferocious Tlingits believed in an eye for an eye, which served as a deterrent to trespass. Stories were used as a way to guide the people. If someone in the community was a child molester, parents warned their children that the person was a witch. The sea otter, the *kooshdaa ka*, was a kind of bogeyman. My people had a class system that included slaves, many of whom were Haida.

In every Tlingit family, the children were brought up by others more than by the parents. To prevent coddling, especially of male children, my uncles' words were considered more important than those of my dad's. In our culture, women also have a lot of influence.

In 1898, both my grandfather Bert and his father, Sam, were packers based out of Dyea on our Chilkoot Trail. Bert was very young and could only pack fifty pounds, while Sam, who was strong and broad-shouldered, could pack one hundred pounds. Paid very little, they freighted the prospectors' goods required to enter Canada during the Gold Rush.

I spent hours listening to Bert. He was born in 1881. The young packer lived to be ninety-two and died in 1973. My grandparents were well known during their era, but Skagway was a tough place racially; Natives had to blend.

My grandfather taught me, "According to white man's way, you're a princess; walk with your head high." Dad said, "You have a good name. When you go out that door, bring it back in the same condition." I taught my son, Lance Twitchell, the same admonition. My father believed the walk is better than the talk for demonstrating good leadership.

Dad was strict about not lying, cheating or stealing. While I was growing up, Dad would start a story and then, one by one around the dinner table, we'd add to it. His story might be about a man who lied or stole, teaching us

Indians who'd been in a two-day blizzard walking into Sheep Camp on the Chilkoot Trail towards Dyea, circa 1898.

Courtesy of Lance Twitchell.

that it was wrong. One of our favorite stories was about his father, Sam, who once found a field of diamonds. He traded a gem with his pastor, but he was never able to find the field again. Mom loved reading, and before bedtime, she gathered us around her to read to us. Until the early 1960s, we didn't have television. When we finally got it, I hated it. It took us away from each other.

My son Lance (Xh'unei) loved to listen to his grandfather; today (2003) Lance is the president of the Skagway Traditional Council.

Growing up, Lance was sort of oblivious to culture. When he attended school in Mankato, Minnesota, he began to learn there about indigenous culture. My mother began encouraging Lance to attend university. During the summers, he returned home and spent time with my father, whose health was deteriorating due partly to working in an oil terminal.

Dad talked to Lance about traditional leadership and Tlingit community. He taught him it was rude to talk about yourself and that the focus should always be on the harmony of the group rather than the interests of the individual. For example, he said, if he were offended by someone, he'd be slow to address the issue, finding a lateral way to communicate the grievance.

As Lance began to study the Tlingit language, Dad laughed affectionately at his attempts. Lance made it his goal to learn our language well enough so that Dad no longer laughed.

In 2000, in an emergency election of the Central Council of the Tlingit and Haida Indian Tribes of Alaska, Lance was made president of the newly created Skagway Traditional Council. It is not a corporation but a tribe, made up originally of fifty tribal members. In 2003 we had 150 members.

Richard Stitt of the Central Council in Juneau set Lance and other young leaders up in their communities, establishing local councils and providing contacts to get a very few computers, printers, and desks. We began trying to find what programs might be available; it was suggested that we try environmental grants. (Many people don't realize how much of Alaska—certainly Skagway—is polluted.) We learned to write grants, and in the last five years, we have really grown.

As our council documented our tribal history, we acknowledged that today traditional racism has simply mutated. While we have a good relationship with the Klondike Gold Rush National Historical Park, not only do we have to seek permission to impact the trail, but others make money off our trail; we never see a dime of it.

But some things are changing. The National Park Service asked us, "Does the park satisfyingly represent the history of this area?" "Absolutely not," we answered. For years and years, Skagway's history has amounted to a narrow ten-year window: White Gold Rush history. That is so negative for Natives. For us, 1898—with its deluge of White prospectors and their diseases—is the year "the world was turned upside down," the year of the Great Death.

Alaska's high rate of alcoholism and drug abuse is largely glossed over, not addressed. Like Skagway's blocks of beautiful tourist shop facades, it is ornamentation, while underneath, the buildings themselves are rotting.

In 1997, just before Dad died, he and Lance were eating cake together. Just

Left: Marion Dennis Twitchell's grandmother Mary Dennis, late 1950s.
Postcard by Dedman's Photo. Courtesy of Marion Dennis Twitchell.

before falling asleep, Dad pushed his cake toward Lance and said, "It's your turn."

Today Lance teaches our language and culture as an Assistant Professor of Alaska Native Languages at the University of Alaska Southeast.

In the *Juneau Empire* in 2012, Lance said the following.

The past 200 years have been devastating; from boarding schools to disease to social discriminations, we are now left with the aftermath of successful attempts to destroy languages and cultures.

Our languages have developed in specific places for thousands and thousands of years. Within them we see patterns of migrations, grammar that allows us to see the world differently.

Recent surveys leave us with this estimate: there are fewer than 250 peo-

ple who can speak a Southeast Alaska Native Language. That is three languages combined. Tlingit has about 200, Haida has about a half-dozen, and Coastal Tsimshian has about 30. This means that the clock is ticking quickly for each of these languages. This also means that we have some important decisions to make. Maybe we have been fooled into thinking that progress moves us towards an English-only world. But in fact, we have a tremendous amount of power and the decision is right here before us: Listen. Speak. Do it every day. Change the future and the world—before the language is gone forever.

(Xh'unei) Lance A. Twitchell.
Courtesy of Lance Twitchell.

Timeline:

1804: Baranov rebuilds trading post, Sitka.

1867: Purchase of Alaska from Russia.

1874: First white man in Chilkoot Pass for gold.

1878: First canneries: Klawock, Sitka; Sheldon Jackson Junior College established at Sitka.

1885: Treadwell mine.

1897–1900: Klondike Gold Rush.

1898: Skagway, largest Alaska city; White Pass and Yukon Railroad; telegraph, Seattle–Sitka.

1904: Last great Tlingit potlatch, Sitka.

1912: Alaska becomes a territory; Alaska Native Brotherhood formed.

1924: Natives become U.S. citizens.

1935: Tlingit-Haida land claims.

1971: Alaska Native Land Claims Settlement Act

2000: Richard Stitt of the Central Council of the Tlingit and Haida Indian Tribes of Alaska set up the Skagway Traditional Council.

Chapter Eight

Richard Stitt: Central Council Tlingit and Haida Indians of Alaska, Alaska Native Brotherhood, and William Paul

In 2002, I met Nettie Peratrovich, a Haida and former Bureau of Indian Affairs superintendant of the Nome District, daughter-in-law to civil rights advocate Elizabeth Peratrovich. Nettie encouraged me to visit the Alaska Native Brotherhood where indigenous political empowerment first began. I made an appointment to see Richard Stitt at

Richard Stitt, self-governance coordinator for the Central Council Tlingit and Haida Indians of Alaska, 2002, Juneau.
Judy Ferguson photo.

the headquarters of the Central Council Tlingit and Haida Indians of Alaska in Juneau.

A graduate of the first class from Mount Edgecumbe High School in 1948, Richard went on to get a bachelor of science degree in microbiology and public health in 1960 from Seattle Pacific College in Seattle. He served as a sergeant in the Marine Corps during the Korean War from November 1950 to November 1953. He was a member of the Alaska Native Brotherhood, Camp No. 2, Grand Camp Executive Committee, and a board member of Sealaska Corp. When I met him he was a self-governance coordinator for the Central Council Tlingit and Haida Indians of Alaska. His Tlingit name was Tsuneil, Naaw da sayk of the Tlingit Nation, Eagle Tribe, Clan Kaa x'oosihittaan (Eagle/Wolf), Clan House Kaa x'oosi Hit, Thunderbird Wolf crest, and he was a cousin to my first Tlingit friend, Maria Joseph.

The 1867 Treaty of Cession with the Russians spelled out that the inhabitants of Alaska "with the exception of uncivilized native tribes, shall be admitted to the enjoyment of all the rights, advantages, and immunities of citizens of the United States. . ." The Native peoples of Alaska were not second-class citizens. They were simply not citizens at all. As the treaty put it, "The uncivilized tribes will be subject to such laws and regulations as the United States may, from time to time, adopt in regard to aboriginal tribes of that country."

In 1915 the territorial legislature said that every Native "who has severed all tribal relationship and adopted the habits of civilized life" could become a citizen.

A Native was eligible for a certificate by going to a local school to be examined by a majority of the teachers. "Such examination shall broadly cover the general qualifications of the applicant as to an intelligent exercise of the obligations of suffrage, a total abandonment of any tribal customs or relationship, and the facts regarding the applicant's adoption of the habits of a civilized life," the law said. The schools at that time were geared to promote assimilation of Natives into the white culture, so the teachers seemed the best able to make such judgements.

After the teachers approved the application, a Native person had to have at least five white citizens who had been in Alaska at least one year testify that they knew the applicant for at least a year. The witnesses also had to say that the prospective citizen had met the requirements of the law.

Then the certificate, after being endorsed by five citizens, had to be presented to the district court. To achieve citizenship, the Native had to say he was living "separate and apart from any tribe of Indians" and had "adopted the habits of civilized life."

This Alaska action had its roots in the federal Dawes Act of 1887, where Indians born within the United States could become citizens if they removed themselves from their tribes and "adopted the habits of civilized life." One of the supporters of the Alaska law was the Alaska Native Brotherhood (ANB), formed by Southeast Natives to promote citizenship for Alaska Natives, education, and the end of aboriginal customs.

http://www.akhistorycourse.org/articles/article.

A robust Tlingit from Klawock on Prince of Wales Island, Richard extended his hand and welcomed me warmly. When I asked, he handed me a booklet, *A History of the Founders and Past Grand Presidents of Alaska Native Brotherhood, Grand Camp*, presenting the leaders and the purpose for ANB.

We began by returning to the era before minority hire, before the Alaska Native Claims Settlement Act, and before the modern civil rights movements, when Alaska Natives were not yet even American citizens, when citizenship for Natives depended on becoming "civilized." They were told that to be civilized meant they should "embrace the Christian faith and speak English fluently." In 1912, ANB's founders organized to pursue citizenship, to become politically empowered.

In the late 1800s, Sheldon Jackson, the representative for the Presbyterian church and the U.S. commissioner for education, arrived at Klukwan near Haines. There, he assigned a Tlingit/Caucasian couple, the L. F. Pauls, to build, preach, and teach. Their son, William F. Paul, went Outside to school and became a lawyer. In 1924, he became the first Native in the Alaska Territorial House of Representatives.

William L. Paul (1885-1977), Tlingit attorney, leader in Alaska Native Brotherhood, which pressed for voting rights, desegregation, and social services, as well as advancing the first Tlingit and Haida land claims in Alaska.

Courtesy of Richard Stitt and the Central Council Tlingit and Haida Indians of Alaska.

"As ANB crystallized," Richard continued, "William and his brother, Louis, fought for the Native right to vote. They wrote the foundation for the ANB, which solidified their political clout." He smiled wryly. "Few wanted to tangle with the ANB. "The brothers believed in the rule of law as opposed to violent rebellion. They lobbied for legislation that led to the first land suit, the *Tlingits and Haidas versus the United States*, asking for restitution of tribal lands based on the new Jurisdictional Act of 1935." Richard pointed to William's photo. "He lobbied for the 1934 Indian Reorganization Act that recognized tribal authority. That act led also to the formation of many Native stores, canneries, and new fishing boats throughout Alaska.

"One of William's sons, a law student named William Jr., discovered in 1939 that according to international law which is recognized by the United States that Natives legally still owned much of Alaska. This offered hope to us that we had not lost our land after all."

Thoughtfully, Richard said, "In the mid-sixties when the Iñupiaq of the North Slope began fighting the world's largest oil corporations in defense of their land, they turned to eighty-one-year-old William Paul Sr." [In fact, Alfred Starr of Nenana enlisted William Paul's help long before the Iñupiaq lawsuit.] "William in turn looked to Fred, his other son. Taking a different tack, [possibly after conferring with Tanana Chiefs Conference] Fred proposed that they fight not just for money, but for land and money [by going through Congress, not the court system as the Tlingit-Haida had been pursuing].

Leaning back, Richard said, "It's a credit that the ANB believed in due process: in education and going through the legal institutions. With society's early infractions, such as the denial of citizenship to Natives, disallowing aborigines from filing a mining claim or attending public schools, barring Natives from the Pioneers' Home, denying them aid to dependent children and the elderly, disallowing them from many public places, not permitting them to work with the Civilian Conservation Corps, had the ANB not re-

From the 1930s to the 1950s, about 70 villages set up Indian Reorganization Act (IRA) constitutions, similar to state constitutions, under this law. The largest of six IRA reserves created in the 1940s was the Venetie Reserve in the northeast Interior, covering 1.4 million acres.

In the end, the proposed reservation policy was a failure, but the legacy of the IRA movement is important - it became, along with traditional Native governments, one of two types of Native authority recognized by the federal government.

http://www.akhistory-course.org/articles/article.

❧

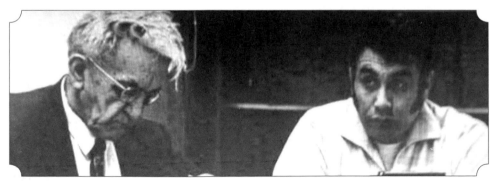

William Paul and Richard Stitt in Alaska Native Brotherhood executive meeting, February 1970.

ASL-Groups-NativeLeaders-5. Courtesy of Richard Stitt and the Central Council Tlingit and Haida Indians of Alaska.

sponded through the legal framework, can you imagine what a violent response there could have been?"

"ANB began the process of rebuilding the vestiges of Native ancient sovereignty, which is a consideration for the twenty-first century." He smiled.

Timeline:

1795: Russian Alexander Baranov bought land near today's Sitka from Tlingits and built Mikhailovsk which was destroyed. Baranov restablished on Castle Hill in today's Sitka, New Archangel, the capitol of Russian America.

1850s: Tlingits never conquered and continued to war.

1867: Russia sold Alaska to the United States. Tlingit said Russia couldn't sell what it didn't own; only owned Castle Hill.

1882: After sale of Alaska and while it was governed by American Revenue Cutters, through a cultural misunderstanding, Angoon was shelled by Revenue Cutter *Corwin*.

1885: Dr. Sheldon Jackson general agent for education in Alaska.

1896-1898: Klondike gold rush

1912: Alaska Native Brotherhood (ANB) founded first modern Alaska Native organization.

1912: Alaska a territory with a legislature.

1924: Indian Citizenship Act included Alaska Natives.

1929: ANB filed a lawsuit in the Federal Court of Claims against the United States government for the creation of the Tongass National Forest and the Glacier Bay National Park without consent of indigenous people of Southeast Alaska. The ANB was told that only federally recognized tribes could sue the United States over aboriginal land claims. The ANB petitioned Congress to recognize the aboriginal people of Southeast Alaska as a tribe.

1935: Tlingit-Haida Jurisdictional Act, an act of Congress, still referring to southeast as "Russian America," recognized the Tlingit and Haida people as a single tribe, and authorized the Tlingit Haida to sue.

1936: Indian Reorganization Act included Alaska Native governments.

1945: Antidiscrimination Act passed.

1968: Court of Claims awarded Tlingit Haida $7.5 million for extinguishment of aborginal title to all but 2.6 million of their 20.2 million acres however Tlingit Haida decided to join the Alaska Federation of Natives in seeking higher indigenous land claim compensation through the Alaska Native Claims Settlement Act.

∞

Chapter Nine

Johnny Goodlataw, Ahtna Elder, Kennecott, Chitina and Tazlina

Chief Goodlataw. Taken near Tarral (1908)

Chief Goodlataw, near Taral, 1908.
Courtesy of John Goodlataw

Ahtna land stretches from the southern Copper River, west to the Hanagita valley, east to Cantwell, north to the headwaters of Indian Creek and the Tok River, to near Tanacross' Mansfield Lake. Marked by the snowy volcanic cones of Mt. Sanford and Mt. Drum, intersected by the plunge into the red banks of the Copper River valley fed by the Wrangell-St. Elias glaciers, the land drains into the island-strewn Prince William Sound. Originally called Atna or Atnatena Athabascans, the 1890 census said of them, "their geographical position within reach of the principal southern tributary of the Yukon River [the Tanana], as well as [the watershed] flowing into Cook Inlet and Prince William Sound, rendered the small Ahtna nation with considerable importance long before the coming of the white man." Their trails have been traveled for twelve thousand years. To other groups, the Ahtna were called the "Ice People Who Live on the River of Life."

Generations before the 1907-1911 building of the Copper River and Northwestern Railway (CRNW) through Wood Canyon, the small Ahtna village of Taghaelden/ Taral stood at the intersection of Taral Creek and the Copper River. In 1796, Russian explorer Tarkanov wintered there. In 1900, Joe Goodlataw, father of Mae Marshall and Johnny Goodlataw, was born at Taral. Joe and his brother, Chief Goodlataw, and their cousin Cap grew up hunting, trapping, and fishing near Spirit Mountain in the Chugach Mountains.

Five years after Joe was born, the J.P. Morgan/ Guggenheim-owned Kennecott Corporation cut a 196-mile rail corridor with 129 bridges connecting the Wrangell-St. Elias mine to Cordova, to access a mill. At a cost of $20 million, they built across canyons, around glaciers, installed phone lines and hired thousands of workers, resulting in $200 million in copper ore. Ron Simpson remarked in his Legacy of the Chief, *"the copper corporation and railway forever changed the lives*

AHTNA

COPPER RIVER NATIVES, ALASKA

Postcard of Johnny Goodlataw's uncle Chief Goodlataw standing on a double-ender sled in Copper Center, 1920s. (Swastika, seen in background, was used in some Native American cultures. Related to the Athabascan, Navajo used it in healing rituals.)
Courtesy of John Goodlataw. Photographer: P.E. Kern, Skagway and Valdez.

of the Ahtna 'tuu Ts'itu." Simpson continued, "In 1910 many of these Copper River Indians gathered at Chittyna Village at mile 131 CRNW to witness the coming of the mammoth locomotives of the CRNW." Joe Goodlataw's cousin Cap worked for the CRNW.

About 1923, Joe married Mary Council of Chitina. Three years later, Mae (Marshall) was born, the third of Joe's thirteen children by two wives. Joe's fifth and Mary's last, Johnny, was born in 1934, a year before his mother died of tuberculosis. Two years after Johnny was born, the CRNW closed its copper production; the trains quit running and Chitina began to decline.

In 2006 sitting at his Tazlina fishcamp, Johnny Goodlataw, his wife, Irene Nicoli, and his sister, Mae Marshall, shared their story.

Johnny began, "Them old days, everyone walked." Mae added, "When I was small about 1928, the families who trapped and hunted off the highway had to move for school to what became the Native village of Chitina. The BIA gave so much acreage per plot for each family to build. Eventually the village amounted to three hundred people. At the BIA school, we had a nice German lady-teacher, Madeleine Belahant, who taught us health, how to keep clean, to raise a garden, to smoke and can fish, and to preserve food. Every spring we planted a garden together. When we harvested in the fall, we stacked up vegetables like cordwood in the school and distributed them throughout the winter to the village. No one went hungry." Johnny added, "she made and sold bread for fifty cents a loaf, had goats and chickens. She bought nothing. We even canned the goat milk. Because there was a lot of alcohol in the village when I graduated from eighth grade, she shipped me right off to Mt. Edgecumbe. (I was her favorite.) I really liked Edgecumbe."

Using his Model T, the first in the village, Joe Goodlataw freighted the mail from Chicken to Fairbanks for Don Sheldon. (A round trip from Chitina to Fairbanks took seven days.) Once when he broke down near Black Rapids, he had to walk all the way back home to Chitina for parts. Shortly after, he began grading the road for the Alaska Road Commission (ARC) from Tazlina to Valdez. In case of breakdown, he always towed his pickup behind the grader. Johnny remembered, "Once when he was grading the gravel road from Tazlina to the old town of Valdez, he let me ride with my lunch, candy, and pop in the cab of the towed pickup. In Valdez, he dropped me off at the El Nathan home and then picked me up again at 5 p.m. We'd go camp, and then the next morning, we'd do it all over again. I'll never forget that."

Johnny's dad also bought him a 1928 Model A, ton-and-a-half pickup to cut firewood for twenty dollars a cord for the village of twelve houses. "Big money, them days," he said. "Can of milk was twenty-five cents." Using a crosscut saw and ax, he climbed up the riverbank, chopped logs, rolled them down onto the river ice, and sawed them up for the village, even at seventy below.

He also trapped his dad's old trapline at Taral. "A top lynx was worth about thirty-five dollars," he remembered. "We sold to the local store or to fur buyer Dean Wilson.

"Once when we were out tent trapping at seventy below," he continued, "we banked the tent with snow and used a five-gallon gas can for a stove, but we overloaded it. About 1 a.m., we woke to flames engulfing the tent. In the dark, we grabbed some half-burned mukluks, socks, and jacket, ripped open the door flaps, and started running down our back trail and back over the river ice. At 5 a.m., we finally made it home with frostbite all over our faces and sweat soaked, but we got there."

Remembering what it took to stock the larder, he said, "Once a month, I went by dog team to the Chitina Cache store, run by a white man, Melvin Chase, to haul our groceries. By spring when the snow was blown off, it was really tough to get a load back home." But by the 1960s, Johnny's

Joe Goodlataw
of Tazlina

"I don't know how these young people are. Not like the olden days. School education don't do any good to them. I didn't go to school, myself. Only one year or so. Old time, they have 5 or 6 people in the house; explain how to make a living, how to do the work. They showed how to make snowshoes, sleds. All the young girls - the old ladies teach them how to tan skins. How to make moccasins out of hides. They can't do this anymore now. Nobody knows how to do this. Now they can't make nothing. For many, many thousands of years ... y showed young people. Now they can't do it anymore. They started drinking. And .. You can't tell them nothing. They can't do without it."

Johnny's father Joe Goodlataw.
Copper River Country Journal,
September 7, 1995.
Courtesy of Lisa Yoshimoto.

Irene Nicoli Goodlataw and Johnny Goodlataw, Tazlina, 2006.
Judy Ferguson photo.

father, Joe Goodlataw, was running his own gas station and café at Lower Tonsina.

Johnny's wife, Irene Nicoli, was born in 1945. A year before she died, she described growing up the traditional way in Tazlina. "My dad, Gene Nicoli, died when I was three. My mom was Ena Nicoli. Since I was little, I crosscut sawed firewood even at seventy below, and I pulled it home on a dogsled. We lived on the old road to Copper Center, which in 1975 was the main road." She remembered, "I used to haul spring water from across the river on a yoke with buckets. After the spring dried up, I got it from the river. We didn't have no car, them days," she continued. "My uncle, Henry Allen, made me a little pack-board. We also sewed canvas dog packs. We caught our fish here at the Copper River, where our culture camp is today. We used to get about three hundred fish, smoked and dried them, from 6 a.m. to midnight every day. Each night we packed the dried fish a half mile back home. When I was pretty little," she added, "we used to walk to a cabin at Dry Creek and trap muskrat. I have eaten lots of rats. When we got a moose, I always packed a quarter. I have worked hard all my life."

Johnny Goodlataw, also Tazlina Tribal Council's president, has driven a truck since 1974. Every summer now, he teaches the younger generation in a culture camp down the Copper Valley School Road on the Copper River. While the tree sap is still flowing, June 9 through 22, as many as two hundred people gather at the Chickaloon-Tazlina Culture

Johnny Goodlataw with fishwheel he made for Wrangell-St Elias National Park and Preserve.
Courtesy of Johnny Goodlataw.

60

Camp, living in tents near Johnny's fishwheel. He explained, "We eat black meat (seal) and seal oil. I'm the only one with a beautiful spot on the river. When I started I didn't even know this was my own grandfather's traditional fishing spot."

Jessie Nicolai, "Gramma" George, "Gramma" McKinley, Sophie Lincoln, Fannie Steinfeld and Irene Goodlataw's mother Ena Nicolai, 1950s, Bible conference.

Lisa Yoshimoto photo.

He continued, "In 2004 I made a fish wheel with four baskets for the Eyak Corporation. I also made one for the local Ahtna Cultural Center at the Wrangell-St. Elias Park. At our culture camp, the kids peeled the poles for the wheel. Using roots for lashing, we built a fish trap with a funnel inside and a trap door on top. We dedicated it to the Ahtna heritage. Today, we have five girls, twenty-four grandchildren, and thirteen great-grandchildren. We teach all our grandchildren to catch and cut fish and make campfire. When my grandson, Joshua Goodlataw, was eleven, he could take care of fish camp by himself. He knew how to run the power plant and cut and hang fish. I enjoy teaching our younger generation our traditional use of the land."

Johnny Goodlataw's last culture camp was in 2011. March 27, 2012, at seventy-seven, he passed away.

Timeline:

1796: Tarkanov winters at Taral.

1907-1938: Copper River and Northwestern Railway.

1928: Native Village of Chitina.

1971: Alaska Native Claims Settlement Act.

1980: Alaska National Interest Lands Conservation Act (or ANILCA) created the Wrangell-St. Elias National Park and Preserve.

∞

Chapter Ten

Reclaiming the Land: Priscilla Billum Mahle, Ahtna

Long before the 1960s movement for indigenous land claims, Priscilla Billum Mahle's grandfather filed for his land, a necessary precedent for Ahtna's later territorial claims. I first met Priscilla at the Alaska State Fair in Palmer in 2005. As we talked, she said she'd like to tell her family's story. Before I left Anchorage, I visited Priscilla in her home where she shared her story.

Doc Billum and Old Glory on Copper River near Lower Tonsina, circa 1912.
Anchorage Museum of History and Art (AMHA) B94.22.254;

I am the great-granddaughter of the famous Ahtna Athabascan sleep doctor, Doc Billum. I was born in 1939 in the village of Chitina to John Jr. and Molly Billum. With relatives from Southeast to the Tanana Valley, I am Ahtna, Salchaket Athabascan, as well as Tlingit from Yakutat.

The Copper River Ahtna used to trade copper nuggets with Yakutat. They walked there on an old trail following the Bremner River. It was said that when they bought Yakutat for $300 in copper, they also brought back the woman who became my grandmother.

In 1867 when the Russians were leaving Alaska, some of them told my family, "We won't be returning; a different people will be managing Alaska now. When they arrive—to protect your land—draw them a map to show them your indigenous borders."

My great-grandpa, Doc Billum, became a six-foot-two shaman, but when he was young, he and his family walked—the only way—all the way from the Salcha to Copper Center, a long way then. A group of Ahtna lived around Copper Center but due to the starvation time of 1898, they had to split up. One band went to Willow Creek Lake. Doc took his people southeast toward Chitina, and the third group went northeast, to Copper Center, looking for food.

AHTNA

Doc was known to sleep and dream and then to awake with a vision. Once he dreamed he met a strange people coming up the Copper River. He heard them speak in a foreign language with each other on a tributary of the Copper River. When he woke, he spoke in that language, English, which he had never heard before. Then speaking in Ahtna, he said, "A people are coming, and they will sound like this." In 1885 when Lt. Allen's party, the first American officials to explore up the Copper River, the English-speaking lieutenant met with Chief Nicolai. Like my great-grandpa had dreamed, they talked on a tributary of the Copper River.

Chief Nicolai, circa 1898.

AMHA.

Later, in 1898, as prospectors arrived with the Gold Rush, killing game, catching fish, and bringing disease and alcohol, that became our time of starvation. Once when Chief Nicolai of Taral was desperately hungry, he led the whites to a vein of copper, the Nicolai Prospect, in exchange for food. Speculators for the Kennecott Copper Corporation soon began developing the Kennecott Mine. Over a period of twenty-seven years, they extracted $200 million in copper, a lot of money in those days. Chitina was established along the Copper River. In 1911, the railroad began operation, connecting Strelna, McCarthy, and Kennicott by rail.

At Lower Tonsina on the Copper River, my great grandpa, Doc Billum, ran his ferry along with his son Ts'inaeen, John Sr. Not too many people had boats, but he did. Their usual customers were miners, prospectors, and their horses. He would ferry Chief Nicholai from Taral to Chitina, which was abandoned when the chief died. Doc was recognizable by his top hat. He helped both Native and non-Native, and he was nicknamed after a famous white physician of that era, Dr. Billum. In 1927, when Doc was working at the Copper Center Lodge, he caught the flu. He died, and he was buried near Lower Tonsina.

In 1938, the Kennecott Mine shut down; the next year, when I was born, the railroad closed.

The 14-storey Kennecott Concentration Mill. The five mines are north and northeast.

By Sarah McKred

Priscilla Billum Mahle, Anchorage, 2005.

Judy Ferguson photo.

In the 1930s and after World War II, heavy equipment began to be used in Alaska. Once, while nursing a hangover, Dad sat on a hill watching the new Caterpillars and their crane operators make the new roads. He sat there watching closely for three hours, then came home and told Mom, "I know how to run those Cats now." Later when a road commission job came up, he said that he knew how to run a V-8. After showing he could do it, he had a job always after that. He worked on the road by Tangle Lakes, Eureka, and around Paxson. During the winter, the boss always called Dad in. Soon he had enough to pay one hundred dollars for three lots, including a two-story house in the white section of Chitina.

My dad never went to school but he was very smart, and he had a memory like an elephant. He used to talk about the old days and tell us stories about the raven, the fox, and the night owl. One really scary story was about the satyrs who were half moose: tet'seneey. They had a pointy head and ears, and their bottom half was moose. During the summer when they were awake, the satyrs kidnapped women and children. Once, they took a girl in their big canoes to Southeast for their winter hibernation. The girl waited until they all fell sleep. Then she took one canoe but cut up the others. In the snow, she walked back to Liberty Falls. When she was close, she looked back, but she saw two of them tracking her. Quickly, she slid behind the falls, and left the satyrs crying. She returned to her people and told them how the satyrs had only three fingers on each hand, and then she showed them their evil smile. At that moment, Dad would make the satyrs' bad laugh and o-o-o-o, I'd be so afraid that I wouldn't go outside at night. My sister, Ella, who moved to Arizona, later said that the Navajos talk of a similar creature but their satyr is half-horse. Yes, Natives use stories to make their children listen, to obey, and to keep them safe. They also have strict laws.

Anthropologists say that the Navajos came from the Athabascans but my dad said we came from the Navajo area. According to an old story, a group of rejected Navajos and Apaches arrived here once, stayed, and intermarried. In fact, we speak the same language family as the Mescalero Apache and the Navajo.

Every day, my mom used to gather us together. Over the years, she read us the entire Bible seven times. I knew the children of Israel's history, how He made Himself known. My people always talked about one creator. Once

Doc Billum and his family including Doc's son John Billum Sr wearing sunglasses and trapper's hat; Douglas Billum wearing hat with snowshoe in it, Lower Tonsina, circa 1910.

AMHA, B71.14.25. .

I asked my Dad if he ever heard an Ahtna story about a flood. "Yes," he said, the raven made a bet with the Creator that he could fly over all this water. "Go ahead," God said, looking out on nothing but water. The raven flew and flew until he almost dropped. Finally he said, "I can't do it." In the story in Genesis, Noah sent out a raven, but he never came back. (I think Dad said that God made a little treetop for the raven to land on.)

I don't think our people smoked fish, but they dried them and made a wonderful dried fish soup. My dad trapped at Mile 114-119 near Spirit Mountain. He was a hunter, and went Dall sheep hunting in the Kotsina Mountains behind his fish camp at Horse Creek, eight and a half miles from Chitina, across the river. My mother gathered berries. In the spring and fall, she dug up a certain kind of tree root near the riverbank. She'd cut and fry it up, but we ate it raw too. I haven't had that in ten years, since she was gone.

We had a lot of hard times too. When I was eighteen months old, my mother was building a fire in a screwed-to-the-floor stove. She put me on a high stool, but I fell, and I landed right on a screw. It cut my head wide open and damaged my nerves, eyesight, hearing, and neck. A little over a year later, I was sent with other Natives on a boat to the children's hospital in Tacoma, Washington. I saw a girl crying because I couldn't hear her. She started playing with me so I wouldn't be so lonely. When I was only three, I had reconstructive surgery on my head. Three years later when I was six, I returned home from Tacoma to three of my ultimately five sisters, and my two brothers. We had a big house in the white section of town.

My Uncle Alec was sick with tuberculosis, and he was staying with us so mother could take care of him. I was a little girl, and I came into his room. I saw a glass of water on his nightstand, and I started drinking from it. I remem-

Right to left: Marnie Billum, Evelyn Finnesan, Priscilla Billum, Sally Finnesan, Ella Mae Billum, Shirley Ann Billum and brothers Harold and John Billum, circa 1952, Chitina.

Courtesy of Priscilla Billum Mahle.

ber a young man who could barely get up crying out, "No! no!" He died right after that.

One day while my mom was visiting in the village, my eight-year-old sister, Marnie, was watching Ella, me, and Shirley. When Marnie went outside, I began striking matches. I didn't know what they were. Then I blew them out and threw them into a pile of laundry. Suddenly smoke and fire erupted. We had two five-gallon cans of gas in the back, attached shed, which exploded. My sister, Shirley, got me out, and Marnie made sure everyone was out. Dad had a lot of guns; he lost everything. When my uncle Frank Eskilida called Dad, who was working in McCarthy, his first question was, "What about my children? When there was no answer, Dad's heart almost stopped and he yelled, "WHAT ABOUT MY CHILDREN!?" We had to move to the village, where seven of us lived in a one-room shack. It was a hard time.

When I was seven or eight years old, I got tuberculosis in my spine. My sister, Ella, my mother, and I, we all got sick. When mine became inactive, I went to Mt. Edgecumbe for a long-delayed back surgery for injuries from my childhood accident. To prevent my becoming a hunchback, I had to lie in bed with heavy casts that restricted my hips for the first of two years. When I finally tried to walk, the floor felt really hard. After I returned home, I felt like a stranger; I didn't fit in.

Our people have always valued clan over family. My dad was the Eagle clan and my mom was Raven. Since we are matrilineal, I am Raven. According to the Tlingit, Ravens are over Eagles. But here in the Copper River valley, it's the opposite: Eagles are over Ravens. My dad said princes and chiefs came from the Raven clan. I met a woman here from the Eagle clan; she brought me a raven, berries, and fish. I asked her if it was true that chiefs and princes came from my clan, and she said, "Yes." Then I figured the clans' inverted importance here must be due to local jealousy.

Some of Ron Simpson's *Legacy of the Chief* is fiction but the characters are not. The Hudson Bay blanket the chief was wearing in the cover photo was given to him, as is traditional, by his opposite clan, by my great-grandfather Doc Billum at a potlatch.

When I was nine in 1948, I started school under Mrs. Madeleine Belahant at the Chitina BIA school. A year later she retired, and Mr. O'Brien, a Chicago schoolteacher who was also very interested in Indians, replaced her. My grandpa was quite old, but he still got around pretty good. Mr. O'Brien used to tell him about Chicago.

Three years earlier, Congress had adopted the Indian Claims Commission Act to consider unresolved Indian claims against the United States. Mostly, our people were not aware that they needed to file claims on our indigenous land. In 1949, Mr. O'Brien asked Grandpa to draw a map of the land they had always used. So he drew a line from Bremner River down Cordova-way. (The people had walked on a trail along the Bremner to Yakutat where they traded copper nuggets. Yakutat people remember when the people of Chitina used

John Billum Sr.
Ahtna Kanas.
http://www.ahtna-inc.com/

to come, and some can even still do a three-hundred-year-old Chitina dance.) Mr. O'Brien asked my grandfather to draw a border around the land we always used. He drew a line from the mouth of the Bremner River near Cordova, up the Copper River, all the way to Cantwell, over to McCarthy, and to Kennicott.

About 1951, the signed claim by my grandfather, John Billum Sr., and Charles O'Brien, along with the map, was sent by certified mail to the BIA in Washington, D.C. His claim became legal with the assigned docket number of 187. After my grandfather died in 1954, the claim deferred then to my dad, John Jr.

In the early 1960s, an attorney in Washington specializing in Indian affairs wrote my dad, saying he could get the Billum family twenty-six million dollars in compensation as well as title to the land. Dad responded, "That land was used by all our people; we'll see what they want to do."

At the same time, the Copper Center Alaska Native Brotherhood [ANB] (particularly Markle Ewan and Oscar Craig) began addressing the federal government regarding Ahtna land claims. In 1962, Markle and Oscar traveled to the village of Tanana to participate in the reorganization of the Tanana Chiefs Conference. Stan McCutcheon, a lawyer representing Tyonek, told Dad that claims the Natives were sending to Congress were being disregarded with the statement, "They have no previous filed land claim." (Possibly those rejected claims were filed after 1954, a cutoff date.) Finally an attorney in Washington wrote the ANB at Copper Center, urging, "Go see John Billum; he has a recognized legal claim on file." In 1967, Markle Ewan, a close friend of my dad's, came with my uncle, Frank Hopson, to see my father where he was working in Lower Tonsina. They said they needed his land claim to make a blanket claim for the Ahtna.

The ANB sent Markle and Frank because they knew that Dad could not say no to them. On the basis of my grandfather's legal filing, the Ahtna indigenous land claim became possible. Stan McCutcheon said, "Had your people not had that claim, they would have had nothing." My father, who never went to school and could not write, needed no one to tell him what the right thing to do was.

Back right: Kenny Albert, Northway, Markle Ewan, Gulkana; front: Oscar Craig, Copper Center, 1963, Tanana Chiefs Conference, Tanana.
Courtesy of Al Ketzler.

Chief Nicholai traveled into the beautiful Hanagita valley where people now have fly-in cabins today. I wanted Dad and the people of Chitina to put in a claim for Kennecott but my dad said, "What would we do with that old mine?" but he did mention it to attorney Robert Goldberg. However, not long after that the state claimed the mine.

A man is honored when he lays down his own interest for that of his people, so I share the story of my grandfather, John Billum Sr., and my dad, John Billum Jr. I come from a long line of historical, indigenous people.

Timeline

1796: Tarkanov winters at Taral on Copper River.
1867: In Treaty of Cession, Russia sells Alaska to U.S.
1885: Lt. Allen, first American up Copper River; meets Chief Nicolai.
1898: Klondike gold rush.
1900: Chitina Mining and Exploration Co. Richest known concentration of copper in the world.
1903: Guggenheim and J.P. Morgan's Kennecott Copper Corporation.
1911 to 1938: Copper River and Northwest Railroad hauls ore.
1951: John Billum Sr., Doc Billum's son, files first Ahtna land claim.
1962: Oscar Craig and Markle Ewan at first Tanana Chiefs meeting.
1971: Alaska Native Claims Settlement Act.
1980: Alaska National Interest Lands Conservation Act (ANILCA) creates Wrangell-St. Elias National Park and Preserve.

∾

Chapter Eleven

The Middle and Upper Tanana Valley: From Wilderness to the Twenty-first Century

To depict the evolution from western pre-contact to current, I have set key persons against the backdrop of the Tanana Valley from circa 1800 to 2012. At Healy Lake, we follow the Sam and Healy families through the Kirsteatter and Saylor descendants; we experience Dot Lake through David Joe and Chief Andrew Isaac; Mansfield Lake-Ketchumstuk-Tanacross, we see through Chief Andrew Isaac's sisters Laura Isaac Sanford and Isabel John; Tetlin through Charlie David and fur trader John Hajdukovich; Nabesna-Northway through Oscar Albert and finally, experience a potlatch and today's challenges through former

Old Chief (Wo'ish) Healy, son of Chetai Ts'eeg circa 1919, Healy River Trading Post.
Healy River Trading Post
UAF-1988-35-10
Courtesy of Paul Kirsteatter.

Tanacross Tribal Council President Jerry Isaac, now Tanana Chiefs Conference president.

The middle and upper Tanana River were first directly impacted by non-Natives as recently as 1898, but they were isolated until the building of the AlCan Highway in 1942.

For centuries throughout the Alaska interior, scattered bands of Athabascans followed the food supply. Those near the Canadian border were the Upper Tanana Nabesnas (later called Northway). High in the hills separating the Copper and Tanana rivers, the Mentasta Ahtna were a gateway between the coastal and the Interior groups. Downstream, more Upper Tanana families lived at Tetlin and Last Tetlings. Tanacross people originated generally from Mansfield Lake and Ketchumstuk. Their close cousins, the Healy band, followed the caribou over the ridge tops.

East of Delta Junction, today Healy Lake is accessible only by air, boat, or snowmachine. Called a gateway to North America by retired anthropologist John Cook, the lake was reputedly part of the

TANACROSS

corridor from the ancient land bridge and showed human habitation throughout eleven thousand years.

Lee Saylor who was married to a daughter of the Healy Lake tribe, Stella Healy, and is the father of three Healy Lake chiefs: Patrick and Ben Saylor and JoAnn Saylor Polston, has archived many indigenous stories. His wife Stella was the daughter of Chief John Healy and the granddaughter of Old Chief Healy. Lee's late mother-in-law, Jeanie Healy, told the history to Lee who explained the following from his North Pole home in 1998:

> *Chief Chetai (elder) Ts'eeg, whose name meant 'tall, old man,' sired the Healy family. Apparently he ruled with an iron hand. Ts'eeg was a pretty tough old man. Like others, he had to conserve gunpowder which, in that era, came dearly. The patriarch who fathered another family, the Sam dynasty, T'sek (pronounced "Ts'eyh,"), was a powerful medicine man in the Healy-Fortymile Middle Fork rivers to Joseph village in the hills. His name meant 'ochre paint,' referring to an orange pigment used on snowshoes and face paint found in the Tanana valley. T'sek was Margaret Jacob Kirsteatter's maternal great grandfather.*

Healy River and Ketchumstuk people; photo taken by telegraph line construction worker. It is titled "Joseph Village Fortymile River Band." Back, l-r: second: Old Sam. Possibly Old Chief Healy. Saul from Ketchumstuk who later married the chief's daughter Mary/ Hootna. Far right: bearded man, possibly Tseyh (Tsek), father of Little White Man, Old Sam, Sam's brother and Josie. Front: woman holding child is Belle Sam holding Jeanie Sam Healy, circa 1901. [In regard to the name, Joseph Village, it may refer "Chief" Joe (Joseph Joe). Chief Joe had a sister Haxtala who married a "Joseph" from the Salcha who later died in a caribou stampede on the middle fork of the Fortymile River. They had two sons, John and Joe Joseph. The latter was Jerry Isaac's maternal grandfather. See Jerry Isaac chapter.]
Identification and story from Lee Saylor. Photo from Farnsworth Collection.

Both families lived on an island separated by a slough from the north bank of the Healy River, an ancient site that has since washed into the river. The traditional annual cycle of the Healy Lake people included Joseph village with its access to the Fortymile River.

Old Sam and Belle Sam holding Jeanie Sam (Healy), Agnes (or Maggie) at their Middle Tanana skin house and cache that holds a birchbark toboggan and dried meat, just out of reach of the dog, 1903. Identification by Lee Saylor.
Born With the River
Craig Mishler. Farnsworth Coll., UAF.

(Early traders Arthur Harper, Jack McQuesten, Al Mayo, and John Jerome Healy operated trading posts at the mouth of the Fortymile.) Joseph village was the Healy band's base. The people traveled from the Gerstle, Johnson, and Robertson rivers, across Billy Creek, up to the Fortymile River headwaters near Joseph, to the other side of the Volkmar River,

up the south fork of the Clearwater River, up to Jarvis Creek, and back down to Healy Lake. Besides Joseph village, Chief Healy had another site twenty-five miles upriver from the lake, Kay K'eyh, "Ground Hog" village. The Joseph/Healy Lake people sometimes went to Nuklakyet (Tanana) to trade or farther down the Yukon River and returned after freeze-up.

The people lived on caribou and whitefish.

Probably taken at "Chief" Joe's house at Sam Point on Healy River (Mendes Chaag'.) Agnes, Chief Joe's wife, in doorway behind Old Chief Healy, circa 1918-1920. Once when Chief Healy, Cataba, and Old Sam were boys, they got the chief's father, Chief Chetai Ts'eeg's, muzzle loader. They loaded it with a double charge of gunpowder which later landed Tseeg on his derriere when he shot a moose. Lee Saylor said, "I imagine some boys were in big trouble."
Drane Collection, UAF-1991-46-720.

Ada Luke in her father, Frank Luke's arms; Lucy Sam Luke; Margaret Kirsteatter's grand-mother, Belle Sam and her second husband, Old Sam; Lena Sam, and unidentified, late 1920s, Healy River. Lee Saylor remembered that Old Sam, the son of Tsek and the younger brother of Little White Man, once walked to Circle City to get canned milk for his starving daughter Jeanie Healy. In 1920, the Sam family moved to Sam Creek. In 1938, they moved to Healy Lake where they died in the 1943 epidemic.

Courtesy of Paul Kirsteatter.

They would find an old burned area, preferably with a gully, stack up burned trees on either side and hope to funnel migrating caribou down into a drift wood coral. When the caribou began coming, the women and children built fires and ran the animals into the corral, letting a few leaders slip out the far end. When the flow was established, they set snares in the corral's holes. As soon as an animal was caught, they cut the caribou's tendon and then quickly reset the snares. When they had all the animals they needed, they finished off the downed caribou.

Before T'sek's era, before musket loaders, during the time of bow and arrow and spear (circa 1835), there was a massacre eight miles north of Delta Junction on the north side of the Tanana, possibly at the bluff in Hansen Hollow in Big Delta. On the Tanana River slough, there were twin brothers with a camp. They were known to be so fast and agile that their name, Na' thee dek, meant 'chips exploding from a burst rock.' It was said they could run straight up a mountainside. In everything, they backed each other up. However, they had a younger brother who liked to make trouble, get into fights, and kill people. But no one dared challenge him because he was the favorite nephew of Ch'inchedl Chitai (Chief Big Nose). Ch'inchedl, who headquartered between George and Sam lakes at Nose Hill village, was a wicked war chief. During feuding times, he hired out as a mercenary to the warring clans. One day, his favorite nephew was down at the Big Delta Tanana slough fighting his older brother, one of the twins. The other twin had had enough of this troublemaker, and he jammed a spear into him, killing him.

When the favorite nephew did not come home, Ch'inchedl sent his men out to look for him up and down the river. When they reached the camp at Hansen Hollow, the twin brother told them what he had done and said the young man deserved it. On hearing that his nephew was dead, Ch'inchedl returned to massacre the camp of some thirty people at the Hollow. The Na' thee dek twin brothers grabbed their young brother and ran. They sprinted alongside the bluff, jumped a lead in the ice, while tossing their baby brother between them as they ran to keep up their pace. By the time they reached Black Hill by the Gerstle River, they could no longer keep running and carrying their brother. They decided to make a mercy plea and decorated him with dentalium beads, their ch'inxuu, *and their spare weapons. When Ch'inchedl's war party approached, the twins cried out, "It is we you want. You can have everything. Take him and raise him as your own." In response, the henchman split the young boy's head in half and took the beads. The Na' thee dek went on to Tetlin, but everyone there was too scared to give them asylum. The brothers continued down the Copper River and finally settled in the Eklutna area. There was never again a permanent village in Big Delta. (Jack Justin of Nabesna once said that Delta was referred to as "a place of bad spirits.")*

In 1885, the Lt. Henry Allen party were the first to explore the Tanana River valley.
Fred Wildon Fickett papers, UAA-hmc-0108-series8b-1.

In 1867, twelve years before trader John Hajdukovich was born, Russia sold Alaska to the United States. From 1865 to 1867, explorer William H. Dall reconnoitered Alaska on the Russian-American Telegraph Expedition. In his journal, Dall wrote, "No white man has dipped his paddle into the Tanana's waters, and we only know its length and character from Indian reports." Later, in 1883, Lieutenant Frederick Schwatka wrote, "The Tanana is eight hundred to nine hundred miles long . . . [It is] the largest wholly unexplored river in the world and is certainly the longest of the western continent," published in his *A summer in Alaska, a popular account of the travels of an Alaska exploring expedition along the great Yukon River, from its source to its mouth, in the British North-west Territory, and in the territory of Alaska.* In 1885, Lieutenant Henry T. Allen snowshoed up the Copper River, pulling a sled. He and his two companions were the first white men to cross the Alaska Range and gaze down into the Tanana River valley.

Lt. Billy Mitchell of WAMCATS, *Fort Egbert, 1903.*
Courtesy Rika's Roadhouse.

In 1896, gold was discovered at Circle on the Yukon River. A corridor was needed to reach the gold fields. In 1898, Lieutenant Joseph C. Castner searched for a passage from the Goodpaster River to Circle but he almost died doing it. Finally, starving and in rags, his company heard an ax pounding in the woods. Ten Natives and their children were camped at the Goodpaster's mouth. They fed Joseph Castner and his men and conducted them to a lower Tanana band of Natives to guide them on to the coast.

As with this family clan, there was a chief. Over him, there was a greater chief from the larger bands. DeLois Burggraf of Fairbanks explained, "Historically, the major job of a chief was to maintain peace and to ensure that there was access to game not only for the local band but also for the neighboring groups. If a visitor came to see a chief, he always brought tribute, which was banked for others in time of need. The currency was fur, game, and skill. Interior Natives used to congress at Nuchalawoyya, Tanana, where the rivers meet. When there was enough tension to require it, they had a big gathering. They did all they could to avoid war because war meant genocide, down to the last woman and child of the defeated tribe. By definition, only one tribe could survive."

But all this was about to undergo a change. During the global depression of the late 1890s, news of gold in the Fortymile and the Klondike was reported in Seattle. International businessmen started a public relations campaign appealing to the global poor. Adventurers boarded ships bound for the beaches of Skagway and Juneau. Overnight, gold camps sprang up, becoming hotbeds of crime. To connect and govern this chaotic "ice box," the army began establishing a military presence. Forts Liscum in Valdez and Egbert (Eagle) on the Yukon became points of entry into Alaska. However, the isolated forts had to communicate with each other and with the outside world. In 1898, a message sent to Washington, D.C., took a year to arrive. Consequently, in 1900, Congress funded the largest construction project of its time, the Washington–Alaska Military Cable and Telegraph System (WAMCATS.) Troops ar-

Guide for Lt. Billy Mitchell, Joseph Joe or "Chief" Joe, holding Alec Joe, father of David Joe, with his second wife Agnes, George Lake, circa 1919.
Drane Collection, U.A. Fairbanks, 94-046-494.

rived in Alaska to cut trail and lay telegraph wire. However, with poor climate conditions, the project dragged. A desperate Brigadier General Adolphus W. Greely of the Signal Corps in Washington, D.C., dispatched Lieutenant William L. "Billy" Mitchell to lay wire through 1,497 miles of uncharted wilderness.

Southwest of Fort Egbert on the Middle Fork of the Fortymile, Lt. Mitchell met Chief Healy, the head of the Healy Lake Athabascans, (born in 1849 at Joseph Village on the Middle Fork of the Fortymile

William and Jane Newton with children, Madge, Hal, Kathleen and unnamed missionary, Healy River, circa 1917.
Courtesy of Barbara and Ronan Short and Kathleen Newton Shafer.

River), at Joseph. Chief Healy offered Mitchell a guide, Joseph Joe, whom he referred to as "Chief Joe," although he was not a chief. Chief Healy instructed "Chief" Joe to guide the army down the Goodpaster River, which was away from the Fortymile caribou herd, but was also a longer route.

At the head of the Goodpaster, Mitchell established a base camp, Summit. At the midpoint, he built Central station. At the Goodpaster mouth, near a band of Natives who came from the villages of Chena, Wood River, and the Salcha mission, he built the WAMCATS headquarters.

Before Mitchell's trail was finished, however, there was a gold strike at Fairbanks in 1902. Although his trail was off-limits, stampeders still hit the trail hard. They came tramping down from the Klondike and the Yukon rivers, down the Goodpaster, and up the Tanana. Mitchell had opened the door, and the prospectors stuck their foot in. Hundreds of white miners swept past a people living in nomadic wikiups. The new culture rippled into the river valleys and over the mountains, opening the era the Natives called "when the world was turned upside down."

In 1905, William Newton of Newcastle, England, moved to the Healy River where he built his trading post, the Healy Development Company. Newton brought his thirty-five-year-old bride, Jane Thompson, who raised their three children as a prototype of British life in the wilderness. During the sixteen years that Newton traded there, there were famines and epidemics. In 1911, wildfires depleted the caribou. The crisis was exacerbated because few steamboats could navigate the shallow upper Tanana, causing one hundred pounds of flour to cost as much as twenty-five dollars. When an epidemic hit Healy Lake, Jane nursed some of the sick in their tents. In a letter home, she wrote, "It's terrible what the government does not do for these people."

Two years after the Fairbanks gold discovery, John Hajdukovich arrived on the steamboat *Cudahy*. The steamboat went aground twenty miles outside the village of Chena. Cold and wet, John walked into Fairbanks. He quickly found that all the good ground was staked, and he struck out for the head of the Wood River.

In 1906, when gold was reported up the Goodpaster River, John and seventeen other prospectors boarded the sternwheeler *Florence S.* and went up the braided Tanana River to McCarty's (later, Rika's Roadhouse) at Big Delta. From there, the men used pole boats, twenty-four-foot, narrow craft that they propelled by shoving a long pole against the river's bottom. This was extremely difficult, going upstream against the current.

Gus Jacob, the son of Old Charlie, a medicine man of Ketchumstuk, and Gus' wife, Agnes Sam, circa 1911, Healy Lake.
Courtesy of Paul Kirsteatter.

The prospectors worked hard to penetrate the country. As they filled the valleys, they met Athabascan bands at the Goodpaster mouth and at Healy Lake. They competed with the Natives for firewood and for hunting and they also changed the local names. When Captain Northway made a pioneering steamboat trip to the Upper Tanana about 1909, he met Chief T'aaiy Ta' [Tah-ee 'tuh]. The captain renamed the chief after himself, Northway. The chief, his family, and their village lost their original name; some of the Nabesna groups became known not by their Indian names, but as Northway.

From 1903 to 1914, the head over the Salchaket and Goodpaster bands was Chief Jarvis. After he became a Christian at the Salchaket mission, he traveled up and down the river to oversee the needs of his people, but about 1914 he disappeared. His body was found upstream from Rika's Roadhouse at the junction of the Tanana and Delta rivers, at Blue Creek. Some said he drowned or maybe was even shot. The tragedy was compounded when his widow, Agnes, suddenly married Chief Joe. Naturally, mistrust arose between Chief Joe's Salchaket people and the Healy band. However when Chief Jarvis' body was found, Episcopalian missionaries examined him, as later documented in *The Alaskan Churchman*. Nothing indicating murder was found on his body, consistent with the story that he drowned.

Some time after 1910 or 1917, Chief Healy's Joseph village band shifted away from the Fortymile and Yukon rivers to base at Healy Lake, Healy River, Sam, and George Creeks. (People identified their lineage based on their base camp and their [matriarchal] clan name.) During that time, Margaret Jacob

*Little White Man Cataba, was known as the best story teller. He died in 1943 epidemic.
Next is his wife and the mother of Belle Sam and Chief Joe; Paddy Healy, Old Chief
Healy, John Healy, "Chief Joe" or Joseph Joe; probably Joe's first wife, Lucy, and Belle
Sam, circa 1908, Healy River. Personal note: this Chief Healy more resembles the tall
man in Joseph village photo than the Chief Healy and Agnes photo.*
Identification by Lee Saylor and Kathleen Newton Shafer. Courtesy of Paul Kirsteatter.

Kirsteatter was born in 1915 to Agnes Sam and Gus Jacob, first cousin to Chief
Walter Isaac (born 1883). After Agnes' husband Gus died, she married Paddy
(Patrick) Healy. When Margaret was three, her mother also died. Margaret was
taken in by her great uncle, Old Sam, and her grandmother, Belle Sam, where
she was raised like a sibling with her great aunt, Jeanie "Jenny" Sam Healy,
Lee Saylor's mother-in-law. Neither Old Sam nor Belle Sam spoke English;
Margaret grew up hearing her people's stories in their pure language.

Three years before Margaret was born, gold was found on a northeast tributary into Healy Lake at Kenyon Creek. White men began pouring through
Healy Lake and up the valley. Chief Healy watched the white men strip the
hills of firewood as they competed for cabin logs, game, and fur. The chief
fought the trend as some of the Native women began to become involved with
the white bachelors. Once when the old chief was at his remote camp Ground
Hog village, twenty-five miles from Healy Lake, a white man came walking up
the valley, "necking a load" (pulling it from his head). Sighing in futility, the
chief said, "I'm old man, medicine man."

Even Chief Healy's name did not remain untouched. Two prospectors, Pat
Doherty and Josh Ray, began calling him, "Healy." The chief with his whis-
kered, iron gaze reminded them of North American Trading and Transportation
Company head John Jerome Healy, also a man with a goatee and focused expression. The nickname stuck. Chief Healy, who resisted the white flood, was
caught in it. His real name—possibly "Chetai Ts'eegh" like his father—was all
but forgotten.

Margaret Kirsteatter's husband Paul Kirsteatter said, "As a medicine man, old Chief Healy sometimes saw things. When he was seventy-one-years-old, he told my wife, Margaret, 'In my dream ... all trees ... grass... will grow again at Healy Lake.'" Paul remembered that the chief further prophesied, "'There is one woman who will build the fire to start my village again.'" At that time in 1920, that woman, Margaret Jacob, was only a five-year-old child growing up with her grandmother. Paul remembered that as a child, Margaret loved to dance. Older folks would say she was worthless, but old Chief Healy would pick her up and say, "This little girl is going to rebuild my village!"

Children of Old Chief Healy and his first wife, Kwo'ish: Paddy, Mary (Hootna) and John Healy, 1927 potlatch Healy Lake.
Courtesy Paul Kirsteatter and Kathleen Newton Shafer.

In *Adventures in Alaska and Along the Trail*, H. Wendell Endicott (of Boston) described the Healy Lake potlatch of 1927. Endicott was a hunting client of big game guide John Hajdukovich. One evening John began telling the story of "the famous potlatch of 1927," held that July at Healy Lake. Wendell asked, "What is a potlatch?" John explained that in ancient times, the Tanacross and Upper Tanana Athabascans had been bitter enemies with the Ahtna, but over time, relations had warmed to the point of intermarriage. So, when a Tanacross husband died in his adopted Ahtna home, to underscore their appreciation to the Ahtna of their acceptance of the outsider, the Tanacross invited the Ahtna to a great feast and at its conclusion, they gave them practically all their worldly possessions, reducing themselves to poverty. But Endicott added, "Today the potlatch has grown in size and elaborateness and is more a feast of good will and entertainment."

Chief Healy was fifty-nine when his children Paddy, Mary (Hootna), and John Healy honored him. "Eight families had been saving maybe for fifteen to twenty years," John Hajdukovich remembered.

Endicott learned that the Copper Center chief was a "big Ahtna chief" (in 1927, the father of Katie John of Mentasta was the last traditional chief of the invited village of Batzulnetas (pronounced "Benzoolneetuhs"), Chief Charley Sanford). The chief had never responded to previous potlatch invitations. Undeterred, "Chief Healy made big plans and dispatched elaborate invitations

Dancing at the 1927 Healy Lake potlatch.
Healy River Trading Post Collection
UAF-1988-35-9. Courtesy Paul Kirsteatter.

to the chief at Copper Center." Special cabins, with imported planed floors, were built for the party.

Kathleen Newton Shafer of Newton's Healy River trading post remembered, "People came over the trails from the Crossing [Tanacross], Nabesna, and Tetlin for the potlatch. Automobiles were ordered from Fairbanks to go two hundred miles to Copper Center to bring the guests back to Big Delta. Two riverboats took the guests 150 miles upriver, with return trips guaranteed. Endicott continued, "The boats did not dock at the village but at the nearby bluff where Chief Healy and his cohorts stood erect and motionless. When the men of Balzulnetas arrived, they were greeted with rifle fire at the Healy River mouth." The rifle fire was not aimless, according to Endicott, but from an angle: it was pointed at a certain spot, making a trajectory, as if a sweeping arm were ushering its guests into its embrace.

"It was a celebration at Healy Lake like . . . before the invasion of the white men," the *Fairbanks Daily News-Miner* reported. Five hundred blankets, cream-colored with colored borders, at $13.50 each, rippled in the breeze off the old village hill, and fifty guns saluted the incoming guests arriving from as far away as the Copper River.

The *Fairbanks Daily News-Miner* continued: "Healy River consists of only seven or eight cabins and several families. The village gave away hundreds of blankets, fifty guns, and spread a feast each night for five days. Seventy-five Natives visited."

As soon as Chief Healy gave his guests a plate, a teapot, a cup, it was immediately theirs. He was more than up to it when after drinking tea or eating food, they threw the pot out the door or the plate on the floor. The host just appeared with another steaming pot of tea and another plate of food.

Endicott continued, "After rest during the day, at sunset, the Indians gathered in a circle and commemorated the dead in mourning songs. After the homage was paid to the dead, they seated themselves on the floor of the big meeting cabin, ready for the feast." Beginning with servings of moose head soup, followed by hardtack, dried meat, doughnuts, and canned fruit, the banquet proceeded slowly and was accompanied by "rituals less modern than the food. Then began the impressive Indian dances, which lasted for hours," he

Back, l-r: Jinny (Jeanie Sam) Healy, John Healy, Reverend Drane, Old Sam, possibly Paddy Healy, Agnes Sam Jacob Healy. Front: Harold, Madge and Kathleen Newton, Alice Jacob (Joe) and Margaret Jacob (Kirsteatter), circa 1919.
UAF-1988-35-26. Identification and courtesy of Lee Saylor.

said. "The tribal dance of the southern Indians from the Copper River differed from those of the others. A booming tom-tom from a moosehide drum beat steadily through the half-dusk. The four chiefs present sat together, looking on approvingly."

Each day this program was repeated. At times from the banquet floor, men would rise to make speeches. Hajdukovich explained, "The Copper River Indians talked slowly, so their friends might understand the slightly different dialect." They spoke of who was related to whom, of intermarriages: oral records of blood relationships. Since there were no written documents, it was a safeguard against intermarriage. "How else," Margaret's daughter, Josephine Beaver, asked, "could Natives from Copper River to Big Delta know who was a relative?"

The *News-Miner* continued, "All the gifts were presented on the last afternoon of the potlatch. When a man did not like the pattern of the blanket he got or the kind of gun presented to him, he would make known his desires and ask for the objects of his choice. Tanana Crossing, Tetlin, and Copper River Indians at once began selling and trading their gifts with the full approval of their hosts." After they had given away their blankets and guns, the Healy River people insisted upon giving their visitors parkas and almost all the food in the village. They even tried to press their cooking utensils upon the departing guests. "Chief Joe canoed from George Lake just for the celebration," remembered Jeanie Healy. "When the potlatch was over, he shouldered his canoe and walked home."

Much of the potlatch's expenses were funded by a loan from John Hajdukovich to the chief. Endicott wrote, "After it was all over and the guests were departing, old Chief Healy drew John aside. There was a deep smile of satisfaction upon the old chief's lips. 'John, they have it all,' he said. 'You have

John Hajdukovich, circa 1955.

Courtesy of Fairbanks Pioneer Museum.

helped me lots. . . . They have it all. If I die tonight, I die happy.'" In the spring of 1928, before Chief Healy died, he boated a cache load of furs to John to more than repay him. John said, "Don't ever underestimate a man. There is always a better one than you are."

From 1906 through the 1930s, the traders had been the connection between the Natives' subsistence culture and the white man's market, but those days were quickly fading. The 1930s brought governmental agencies and anthropologists to the isolated upper Tanana Valley. For twenty years, Natives and non-Natives had trapped, hunted, and traded furs side by side with no outside interference. The trader in each village was the local source of revenue and western goods. However, the modern world was slowly expanding into the remote Alaska interior.

In 1929-1930, Dartmouth College professor Dr. Robert A. McKennan flew to Alaska to study the purity of the isolated Upper Tanana-Athabascan culture. John Hajdukovich escorted him to the area. Of the visit, the *Fairbanks Daily News-Miner* wrote: "McKennan selected the Upper Tanana 'because Indians there have had less contact with whites than at other places.' His studies established a base study for Athabascan, the family of all Mackenzie and Interior Alaska Indians. McKennan traveled on a Harvard University fellowship. He entered the McCarty [Big Delta] country, traveling through the White, Chisana and Nabesna river districts to the various Indian villages. He spent the winter collecting data, including Native social and religious customs. All were able, more or less, to speak English, but it was necessary to carry on conversations with some of the oldest men through younger natives who had been educated."

Three years before John Hajdukovich died, Dr. McKennan autographed a copy of his book, *The Upper Tanana Indians,* "To John Hajdukovich, a fellow student of these Indians whose friendly advice and helping hand along the trail contributed so much to my study of the Upper Tanana. 30 July 1962, Bob McKennan."

When John had been guiding in the 1920s, he and his big game hunting clients, East Coast industrialists Wendell Endicott and Edward Mallinckrodt, they discussed "the noblest of solutions," according to Tanana Chiefs Conference president Jerry Isaac. In 1930, their idea resulted in the Tetlin Reserve. John felt that a federal reserve, implemented by government resources and under federal control, would best equip his Native friends for survival in the modern world. They envisioned a school, a clinic, and a post office, all sustained by a village economy. They drew up plans and petitioned to have 625 square miles of public land at Tetlin withdrawn from public domain as a federal reserve managed by the Office of Indian Affairs. The Tetlin Reserve would be developed by the Natives and overseen by the federal government. Hajdukovich, Endicott, and Mallinckrodt imagined a fur ranch, sustained with a farming crop in the village. They worked with Chief Peter Joe of Tetlin, who fully supported the idea.

In 1930, Earl J. Beck, the Bureau of Education's division superintendent, mushed with John to Tetlin to consider the need for a school. Beck was forced by temperatures of minus fifty degrees to spend two weeks with Chief Peter Joe's people at Tetlin, where he found John to be protective and quite fair with the people.

The following summer, Dr. Carlson Ryan Jr., the director of education in the Office of Indian Affairs, visited the upper Tanana by boat. He reported that the Native people, with John's and Jack Singleton's help, had built their own school and bridge using lumber they had "ripped" themselves. The people were clean and healthy. (Natives elsewhere were infected with tuberculosis and whooping cough, where even soap could be a rare commodity.) Further, Dr. Ryan observed that Jack Singleton had taught the Natives how to use a tractor, and together, they had made a garden out of four acres.

Many options for Native transition to the modern age would be under consideration during the 1930s including the Indian Reorganization Act and the possibility of more and larger reservations. The latter brought an outcry from the public who said that Lower Forty-eight reservations had been a failure. The proposal of a village industry as envisioned by John and his wealthy friends caught Dr. Ryan's interest.

In 1930, for the first time in twenty-seven years, John traveled Outside to see his friends Mallinckrodt and H. Wendell Endicott to discuss the Tetlin Reserve. Endicott had written a letter to President Hoover, which was delivered to the president just as he was considering the reserve. Everything fell perfectly into place, and an executive order was signed June 10, 1930. Consequently, four hundred thousand acres was withdrawn from public domain. Earnest Walker Sawyer, a special representative for the Alaska Railroad, announced that in five years he expected Natives to be trained in fur farming. Further, Natives were encouraged to form more reserves.

Mallinckdrodt donated five thousand dollars for a tractor, sawmill, farming equipment, and seed potatoes. However, both the Office

Chief Peter Joe, Tetlin, circa 1930.
Tetlin Photo Coll. UAF-1987-0114-56 Courtesy of Larry Mark.

82

Charlie David remembering his friend John Hajdukovich, 1998.

Judy Ferguson photo.

of Indian Affairs and the Bureau of Education claimed they were not authorized to oversee the operation.

Depressed fur prices and the onset of the Great Depression doomed the success of the Tetlin fur farm from its inception. Also, John was distracted when he had to repossess his trading business from his friend, Ted Lowell, and resume trading. Worse, Dr. Ryan was pessimistic regarding the Natives' ability to carry off the utopian ideas. His position may have been fueled by the local Episcopalian lay preacher E.A. McIntosh's opposition to the reserve.

In further sabotage, Ryan refused to give John a salary to supervise the farm. The industrial school, which was to be a fur farm, was dead before it began. The caterpillar and sawmill were sometimes rented for local construction, but the cottage industry never developed.

John had to turn from the interests of the Tetlin Reserve just to keep himself financially afloat. Jerry Isaac said, "It was the grandest sort of plan. I wish my forefathers had done that for us."

In 1936, cheap credit became available to the Alaska Natives through the Indian Reorganization Act of 1934. The subsequent loans to the Natives allowed them to compete directly with the traders. Chief Peter Joe of Tetlin organized a tribal council, procured a loan for a cooperative store, and got a freight boat.

John Hajdukovich spent his life protecting the Natives. He was also owed $23,000 with no prospect of remuneration. He proposed a Native-owned store that initially he would oversee. One of the store's purposes was to pay back the debt owed him.

Eighty-seven-year-old Tetlin elder Charlie David recalled a meeting held by Chief Peter Joe. In a four-hour meeting, twelve-year-old Charlie was devastated by the tug-of-war between the new politics and the betrayal of a gentle father figure. Although John was "allowed to remain in Tetlin," he could not run his business. According to Tetlin elder Alfred John, John's Native friends attempted to repay some of the money owed him by giving him blankets and guns, but it was far from what was owed. Unable to endure it any longer, Charlie David ran home and wept. After the meeting, the chief wrote to the Office of Indian Affairs, accusing John of importing liquor, and asked for his removal from the village where he had traded since 1918.

John had always adamantly opposed the easy profits of alcohol. Despite a 1932 agreement among the upper Tanana traders, one of the merchants,

Herman Kessler, brought in three tons of liquor, followed by fifty tons in 1938 to Nabesna, from where he shipped it to the other villages. When the cases of liquor began to arrive, Tetlin elder Alfred John, said, "We just thought it was bottles of pancake syrup." The Native leaders pleaded publicly, "Please don't bring in any alcohol." When John was sure all the traders were selling liquor, in protest he resigned as U.S. commissioner in 1936. However, this resulting lack of authority only removed the fear of him. The door for liquor swung further open.

On a visit to reconnoiter the situation financed by the *Association on American Indian Affairs Inc.*, an investigator Moris Burge reviewed the upper Tanana with John. In his final summary of the situation, he pushed for greater responsibility of the people and a larger game reserve, the latter which fueled the territorial ambitions of the Episcopalian lay minister at the Tanana Crossing mission, E. A. McIntosh, and Tetlin's new teacher, Fred A. Dimler.

Since 1912 when McIntosh arrived in Tanana Crossing to help supervise the Natives in building the mission, he was often in conflict with John Hajdukovich. At that time, he was quoted in the *Fairbanks Daily News-Miner*

Back, l-r: Old Sam's brother Little White Man (Kat'ba); teacher Mr. Fleischman; may be Alice Jacob Joe; unknown; Lena Sam Healy; Ellen Felix (Demit); Frank Felix; unknown; Arthur Healy. Middle row, l-r: Margaret Jacob holding Josephine; Jeanie Healy; John Healy; seventh and eighth adults: Emma Joseph and Mary Hootna Healy (Charlie); bottom left may be Eva Luke. 1940, Healy Lake first school.

Identification by Lee Saylor. Courtesy Lee Saylor and Jeanie Healy.

as saying, "The missionary is the father of the Natives, and they obey his rulings. The chief and six counselors rule the village under the supervision of the missionary." Further, McIntosh and Dimler encouraged Native leaders to testify: "Get John Hajdukovich out of the village."

In 1941, John told Mallinckrodt that he would no longer deal with the Office of Indian Affairs. He said that during just a few years, all of his and teacher Jack Singleton's twenty years of work had been undone. He said, "When we were chased out of Tetlin by the Indian Office, there was a population of over one hundred people: forty-five kids going to school. Twenty of them are in the graveyard now. Same situation—under the watch of the Office of Indian Affairs—exists wherever one goes."

Paul Kirsteatter, who was a great help to this history of Healy Lake, 1949, Gerstle River bridge.
Courtesy of
Paul Kirsteatter.

Throughout the 1930s, the Healy Lake people continued to migrate between Sam Creek, Healy Lake, and even George Creek. Consequently in 1937, it wasn't odd that the missionaries' detailed report stated that there were only thirty-four people in the Healy Lake village. In 1940 a teacher from Tanacross, Mr. Fleischman, taught school for the summer at Healy Lake. Old Chief Healy's son, Chief John Healy, wanted a year-round school. However in 1943, a severe epidemic swept through the lake. To cleanse themselves, people took steam baths, but it only spread the infection. Healy trading post manager Stan Young could not keep up with the burials, and he had to resort to shallow graves. Houses were filled with the dead. In the spring, Bert Hansen brought a doctor in by boat, but it was too late. Those who escaped fled farther up the river. Chief John Healy took his remaining people, including Margaret and Alice Jacob, to the new AlCan Highway, hoping that on the road system the small children could go to school. In a cabin at the Little Gerstle River, John Healy and several others began a small community.

Josephine, Margaret Jacob (Kirsteatter) and her sister, Alice Jacob Joe and David Joe, 1946, Healy River.
Courtesy of Paul Kirsteatter.

Paul Kirsteatter, born in 1922 in Illinois, began hauling construction materials on the AlCan in 1946. At the Little Gerstle bridge, he met Margaret Jacob and her daughter, Josephine. After Paul and Margaret married, she began learning English more in depth from Paul and by listening to the radio. In turn, she taught Paul to trap. At first they lived in Joe Joseph's old cabin at Healy Lake, but Paul learned quickly how to live off the land. Among the few surviving old-timers, he was well accepted.

As their family grew, Paul was gone a lot, trapping. He headquartered at Joseph village, and set steel through the Fortymile country back to Healy Lake. He and Margaret enjoyed occasional visits from Margaret's old friend, John Hajdukovich.

In 1955 when John Hajdukovich was seventy-six, he and seventy-one-year-old Moses Albert of Mansfield Lake went on a ten-day, cross-country hike. They took off from the Kirsteatters' home at Healy Lake, but they took the wrong ridge coming off Mount Harper. After days of wandering, they shot a caribou but in the process, John left his rifle on the summit. Using a cane, he pushed on sixty miles of steep mountains and through swampy drainages. Finally, they wandered into Healy Lake where Margaret and Paul were very happy to see them.

During the mid-1950s, Walter Isaac was chief over Mansfield Lake. He looked to Margaret as the natural leader of Healy Lake, and recognized her as chief. During the winters, Margaret made fishnets and skinned while Paul homeschooled their children: Fred, Linda, and Dorothy, at the elementary grade school level.

During the summers, Fred liked to sift through the dirt for artifacts. He began collecting some curious objects, obsidian projectile fragments. Dr. Robert McKennan of Dartmouth University heard about Fred's finds. McKennan's student, John Cook, examined the fragments. In a 1960s *Tundra Times* article, Fred's arrow and spear heads were reported as some of "the most important finds in North America" and indicated that Healy Lake may've been a human corridor for over ten thousand years.

Until Fred was ten, the Kirsteatters' subsistence life ran smoothly. "However," Fred explained in 1998, "during a large military maneuver in 1963, ten thousand GIs from the Goodpaster River and George Lake swarmed onto our frozen lake. They ran their tanks over the old Sam Hill Native cemetery and bulldozed our trapping trails. They stole our equipment, left litter, and we couldn't trap. The caribou, moose and fur-bearing animals were pushed out, and we were hungry. The state's Division of Lands told us 'to cease and desist our use of public domain property.'" The Kirsteatters realized how unprotected their land was. In 1964, they asked John Hajdukovich to contact the *Association on American Indian Affairs* (AAIA), which he did. After examination of the Kirsteatter claims, executive director Bill Byler, wrote to John that Margaret Kirsteatter's claim was an individual one rather than that of a village so AAIA could not help them.

Ben Saylor and his parents, Lee Saylor and Old Sam and Chief Healy's granddaughter, Stella Healy Saylor, 1970.
Courtesy of Lee Saylor.

Other intrusions were going on in indigenous lands throughout interior Alaska. Native resistance was coalescing with the reorganization of the Tanana Chiefs Conference and with the Alaska Federation of Natives. Natives had begun documenting their claims to the land. However the Healy Lake descendants were either dead or lived elsewhere during the winter. There were not

Margaret Kirsteatter and her great aunt Jeanie Healy with grandson Patrick Saylor and his mother, Chief John Healy's daughter Stella Healy Saylor, 1971, Healy Lake.

Courtesy of Lee Saylor.

enough year-round residents at the lake to be included in the Alaska Native Claims Settlement Act.

Fred Kirsteatter explained:

We were one of the few unrecognized villages. However in John Hajdukovich's 1951 file, there was a proposal for a reservation from the upper Tanana to the Little Gerstle River, which included documentation of the old Healy Lake village. We appointed my mother, Margaret, David Joe, and Lee Saylor as the Land Selection Committee. (I was back east at college, making contact with Congressman Don Young and Senator Ted Stevens.) We also based our claim on the Native Allotment Act applications of Healy Lake descendants, authorized by the traditional chief, my mother, Margaret. We traced all our surviving relatives. All winter by gas lamp, the committee studied Healy Lake area maps. We selected traditional-use, contiguous waterways as far as the AlCan Highway. A minimum of twenty-five people was needed to prove use and occupancy of Healy Lake to secure recognized village status.

To receive benefits and civic facilities, each village had to designate at least three townships for itself, eighteen square miles apiece. It was really tedious. All this research had to be done without any mail service, telephones, or two-way radios. We were really remote. Ultimately, twenty-five persons whose families originated at Healy Lake registered for Native land claims. After the village was finally recognized, Healy Lake became settled again, year-round.

In 1971, a tribal council was set up, the first since John Healy died in 1948, representing Healy Lake families and including Robert Lee, an Inupiaq originally from Kotzebue with an allotment at the north end of Healy Lake. He was elected village council president. Fred said, "My mom, Margaret, was declared Traditional Chief." David Joe, Josephine Beaver, and Jeanie Healy, frequently represented by Lee Saylor, sat on the council. Fred added, "After I returned from college, I took over a lot of the duties."

In 1974, Healy Lake was confirmed as an Alaska Native Claims Settlement Act village.

Patrick Saylor and his father, Lee Saylor, who was a great help to this history of Healy Lake, 2009.
Courtesy of Lee Saylor.

Chief John Healy had wanted a school since the 1930s and 1940s, but even by the 1970s it still did not exist. Dan Beck, former Delta-Greely school superintendent, said that in the fall of 1977, only five school-age children lived at the lake. "With a two-thousand-watt generator, we started the first Healy Lake school in the community hall," he said. "When one gallon of gas was used up, the lights just went out. We replaced it with a bigger generator, and we also supplied teacher housing." A certain enrollment quota was required to gain government funding for a school. Using his political savvy, Fred Kirsteatter secured housing, water, sewer, an airport, telephone, mail, and power

Fred Kirsteatter's funeral: l-r: Norman Joseph; fourth: Mary Evans. Women with flowers: Evie Erickson, Elanor Kirsteatter, (far back, mostly hidden: Gary Healy), Dorothy Kirsteatter Revette, Lisa Revette, Sarah Joe Gorrod, Dan Gorrod, Larry Luke, Alex Joe, Brian Erickson, Patrick Saylor, Ray Fifer, David Joe, unknown. July 19, 2012.
Identification by Lee Saylor. Courtesy of Sarah Joe Gorrod.

for Healy Lake. Descendants returned, which supplied the needed enrollment, and school construction began.

"Man, it was tough," Fred said. "Five of us building a city in the wilderness!" However, the woman whom Chief Healy had prophesied would one day rebuild his village died a year before the end of the school construction in 1999. Margaret Kirsteatter had indeed reestablished a village. "I did it," Fred said, "to honor my mom."

In 1998, Margaret Kirsteatter died. Fourteen years later, their son Fred died July 13, followed ten days later by Paul Kirsteatter on July 23, 2012.

The Grandson of Chief Joe, David Joe and His Sister, Sarah Gorrod, of Healy and Dot Lakes

Margaret Jacob Kirsteatter's sister, Alice Jacob, did not have it as good as her sister, Margaret. After both sisters lost their mother and were raised by their grandmother, Belle Sam, Alice married Alec Joe, who had a drinking problem. One day, Alice was told her husband had been sold bad alcohol. He died of a terrible stomachache at the Big Gerstle River bridge. After he died, Alice had to move into a tent with her three-year-old son, David Joe, at Dot Lake.

The grandson of the Native guide for Lieutenant Billy Mitchell, David Joe has lived in Delta for several years. In 2003 at the Delta Diner, David Joe shared his story.

Tanana Chiefs Conference called by Judge Wickersham in 1915 to consider indigenous land issues. David Joe's father Chief Joe "Na da tuts" is pictured in the front row, far left. Back row, l-r: Julius Pilot, Nenana; Alexander Titus, Hot Springs; G.F. Cramer, Thomas Riggs, Jr., C.W. Ritchie; Chief Alexander William, Tenana. Middle row: Jacob Star of Tanana; Chief William, Tanana; Chief Alexander, Tolovana; Chief Thomas, Nenana; James Wickersham; Chief Ivan of Coschaket; Chief Charlie [Charlley] of Munto [Minto]. Front row: Chief Joe, Salchaket; Chief John of Chena; John Folger of Tanana; Rev. Guy H. Madara; Paul Williams of Tanana, interpreter.
Wickersham State Historic Site. ASL-P277-011-072. ASL-PCA-277. Courtesy of Alfred "Bear" Ketzler Jr.

Alice and David Joe, circa 1946, Healy River.
Courtesy of Paul Kirsteatter.

After his first wife died, and only a few months after the death of Chief Jarvis, my grandfather Chief Joe married Agnes, the widow of Chief Jarvis, the former head of the Salchaket and Goodpaster River bands from 1903 to 1914. He and my grandmother moved to George Creek, where they had my father, Alec.

Between George Lake and Sam Lake [Sand Lake on modern maps], north of the Tanana River near a bluff called Nose Hill, there was a village named for its chief, Ch'in Chedl. The chief led a raid on the Kluane Lake Indians in the Yukon Territory. In retribution, Kot'tzeeg, the chief of the Kluane, wiped out Ch'in Chedl's village on the upper Tanana. Around the old site, I have found long, shallow trenches and lots of cache pits used for storing food. There are also remains of homes: holes dug down into the dirt with sleeping benches. Saplings were arched over the holes to stretch caribou hides over for shelter, wikiups.

In 1915, the Salcha band elected my grandfather as chief and to represent them at the Tanana Chiefs Conference, called by Judge Wickersham to discuss the coming of the railroad and the protection of our indigenous lands. The conclusion of the conference was, "We want to be left alone. As the whole continent was made for you, God made Alaska for the Indian people. All we hope is to be able to live here all the time."

According to Auntie Jeanie Healy, my grandfather Chief Joe was considered a wealthy man; he always carried a gold watch. His wealth was credited to having found a frog's nest, which he always had in his medicine bag. Some people felt that he was mean, but the stories may have come from a mix of jealousy, suspicion, gossip, as well as some truth.

He paddled a canvas canoe to the famous 1927 potlatch at Healy Lake. When it was over, he packed his canoe back over the foot trail to George Creek. Over the next four years, possibly wanting to top Chief Healy's potlatch, he killed and dried ten moose. He was building a community hall in 1932 when he got sick with dysentery, possibly from typhoid. He died in Tanana where his grave is today.

I was born August 31, 1942, in a tent at fish camp at Healy Lake to Alice and Alec Joe. The night I was born, my maternal grandfather, Old Sam, heard a baby cry. Aunt Margaret told him that Alice had just had a boy. Old Sam cried, and then he died the night that I was born.

Dot Lake School: front, l-r: Linda Joines. Second row: Peter Charles, Daisy Felix, Clara Charles, Hazel Charles, David Joe. Back: Stella Charles, Anita Gavin, Susan Joines, Ivan Charles, Agnes Felix, late 1953.

Walking Among Tall Trees, A.F. Gavin.

In May 1943 epidemic devastated the Healy Lake people. Three of my sisters died. My dad, mom, and I joined Chief John Healy and the few survivors at the Little Gerstle River.

When my father was only twenty-eight in 1944, he died at the Gerstle River bridge. Not long after, my mom got sick with tuberculosis. She was sent to the hospital at Tanana for a year while I lived with my Uncle Paul and Aunt Margaret Kirsteatter and her daughter, Josephine, at Healy Lake. It seemed like forever. When Mom returned, we lived in a tent at the Little Gerstle from 1947-1948. In the mornings from under my blankets, I could see my breath like a white cloud. From her sleeping bag, Mom would stick firewood in the little Yukon stove, causing a frost shower. I spoke only Athabascan and I had never lived in a house. Mom cut firewood with a cross-

David and his nephew Logan with David's adopted parents, Jackie and Fred Vogel, and his sister Sarah Gorrod, circa 1981.

Courtesy of David Joe.

cut saw and trapped lynx and muskrat for meat and fur. She and Margaret sewed furs and traded them for groceries with Rika Wallen at her Big Delta roadhouse.

After that, Mom and I lived with Abraham and Mom's great aunt, Eva Luke, at Clear and Sam Creeks, west of Dot Lake, for two years. During that time, my mother and Abraham Isaac, Chief Andrew Isaac's brother, had my little sister, Sarah, born June 1950 at Sam Creek. Sarah didn't know her father well as she grew up. Mom, Sarah, and I lived in the tent from 1950 to 1952.

At that time, Fred and Wanda "Jackie" Vogel arrived at Dot Lake. During the construction of the AlCan Highway, soldiers had built tarpaper and rough lumber buildings, which Uncle Paul and others later sold to civilians. The Vogels bought several and used one for a Dot Lake roadhouse and another for a school. Jackie was a Christian. I entered school under Mr. A.F. Gavin at age

91

nine along with ten other kids: the Charles, Lukes, and Isaacs. I began learning English.

I wasn't used to being inside and they couldn't keep me there. In 1952, the Vogels gave us a building, and we began living in a house. It was a big change; we were always warm and we had plenty of room.

In 1957 when I was fifteen, my mom got pneumonia; she was taken to the hospital in Fairbanks. Her case was pretty advanced plus care was delayed and she died in the corridor. That was the end of my world. I had to grow up fast. Fred and Jackie became our parents. Fred Vogel became a Christian, and he began ministering at the nondenominational Dot Lake chapel that he had just built. Before I left for Mount Edgecumbe in 1961, they opened the Dot Lake children's home (taken over later by Jackie's sister, Ruth, and her Athabascan husband, Carl Charles). After I left, Sarah lived at the children's home and at other times with Aunt Margaret and Uncle Paul until they adopted her when she was fourteen.

In 1961, I went to Sitka to begin four years at Mount Edgecumbe boarding school. Our school annual had an acronym: TAHETA, standing for the six main indigenous cultures of Alaska: Tlingit, Aleut, Haida, Eskimo, Tsimshian, and Athabascan.

Going to the boarding school was good for me. At the drop of a hat now, I can live like an Indian or like a white. I can speak my language when elders need clarification about some English they don't understand. Many of my best friends are white. Through the white culture, I learned the skills necessary for modern living. I achieved a good career and have had a much easier life than the old, nomadic one.

At home, Uncles Andrew Isaac, Paul Kirsteatter, and Abraham Luke taught me hunting and trapping. They had me sit in icy streams and sometimes whipped me with willows, a protocol for prepping a boy for manhood.

That wasn't the only battle I had to fight. Later when I was thirty-two, I joined the Operating Engineers and worked at Coldfoot, but I had a problem with alcohol. I got fired

David Joe, Chief Andrew Isaac and his wife, Maggie Isaac, and David's sister Sarah Gorrod, circa 1990.

Courtesy of David Joe.

but I had another job waiting for me at Franklin Bluffs. I went downtown in Fairbanks and ordered some drinks at the Cottage Bar. I drank one, but I thought, "You're really stupid. You could have a good career in construction, or you could go nowhere." Although I had been a hard-core drinker, I pushed it away, and I have had no alcohol since 1975. I tell kids, "It's easy; you just quit."

When I was young, I was sometimes treated like a second-class citizen. My mom would tell me, "Whites live a different way of life; they don't understand. Don't be belligerent. Be patient; they'll come around and see who you are." So I made that my way.

In my era, a man's word was good. Money was left on a gas pump or cache for payment of goods. If you ran out of gas and saw a fifty-five-gallon barrel, you'd pump gas and leave the money. Everyone knew to leave it alone. We took care of each other not for profit but because it was the way. But change came in the 1960s Vietnam war era, which brought new people. Until that time, Alaska operated on the honor of a man's word and respect for his property.

However, in those days, there was no protection for Native lands. Periodically, I began driving my uncle, Tanana Chiefs Conference First Traditional Chief Andrew Isaac, to meetings in Anchorage and Fairbanks to testify regarding the pending Alaska Native Land Claims Settlement Act.

At Healy Lake, we had secured Native allotments, but we wanted to get village status. We needed a minimum of twenty-five people to prove use and occupancy of the lake. By gas lamp in 1971, my cousin, Chief Fred Kirsteatter, my Aunt Margaret Kirsteatter, and I studied Healy Lake maps, tracing and documenting all the surviving relatives.

After thirty years of working with the Operating Engineers 302, I retired. Today, the union rep passes my name on to young Native men as an example of what can be achieved.

My son, David Alexander Joe Jr. (Alex), and I once hosted a potlatch for his kindergarten class in 1998, thanking the Delta Elementary School for having him. Sonny Luke did the drumming. We gave out kindergarten-size blankets, handkerchiefs, and five dollars each. "And Dad taught us how to bead," Alex added. In the winter of 2005, my son, Alex, and I lived near Healy Lake; that winter, he attended the Healy Lake school, first dreamed of in 1943 by Chief John Healy.

At the end of the interview, Alex, who resembles his grandfather, Alec Joe, began tugging on his dad's sleeve, wanting to go to rent a video before it became too late. Always using words that heal, David modeled a sentence in Athabascan for me, "Bring ice cream and a video to Grandma's:" "Nada video ice cream sunsh'ah see inahs." With that, David slipped his arm around his young son's shoulder, left the shadows of his past life, and stepped into the dark of that September evening.

Ketchumstuk, Mansfield Lake/Tanana Crossing: Chief Andrew Isaac, Laura Sanford, and Isabel John

I first met Andrew and Maggie Isaac of Dot Lake in 1968, four years before Tanana Chiefs Conference made him First Traditional Chief in 1972. A warm, humble, and naturally dignified man, he and Maggie frequently visited their daughter's husband's family, the Emericks, in Big Delta, my home.

Thirty-seven years later in Tok, I met with Chief Andrew Isaac's sisters, Laura Sanford and Isabel John, at Laura's home. They began sharing their life, from 1898 to the present.

Tanana Chiefs Conference original First Traditional Chief Andrew Isaac (1898-1991) of Ketchumstuk and Dot Lake, grandson of Chief Isaac.
Courtesy of Laura Sanford.

Our people, the Daendeh Athabascan, traditionally traveled from the Canadian border northwest to the Delta and Goodpaster rivers, south to the Copper River. [In Hudson Stuck's *Ten Thousand Miles on a Dogsled*, Stuck said he was surprised to realize that the people of Tanana Crossing didn't speak the language of the Lower Tanana and the middle Yukon. Stuck realized that unlike the people of the Salachaket that the Tanacross people were of the Porcupine and Peel River stock in Canada and had migrated to Eagle and over to Ketchumstuk.] My brother, Chief Andrew Isaac, Aandoo', was born in 1898 in a camp between Joseph village and Ketchumstuk. Our sister, Isabel, was born at Ketchumstuk, one of our long-term sites. After disease destroyed most of the population, our survivors moved to Mansfield Lake, where I was born in 1928.

After St. Timothy's Episcopal Mission was built at Tanana Crossing in 1912, my people began to move there from Mansfield. Relocated

Andrew Isaac's grandfather Chief Isaac, originally from Cos Jacket or Chena, married first to She'ye and then, Edna and written about in Hudson Stuck's Ten Thousand Miles with a Dog Sled. *Mansfield Lake, 1909.*

Courtesy of Jeanie Healy-Lee Saylor.

94

today on the highway side of the river, the village is Tanacross now, twelve miles northwest of Tok near the Alaska Highway. My brother and sister were born as our nomadic people made the transition from subsisting on five million acres to a life in the village.

Andrew was born on a ridge in a snowbanked shelter made of spruce trees. He remembered our grandpa, Chief Isaac, born about 1848, making him a little bow and arrow. Grandpa may have been from Joseph village, and his wife was from Copper. After their chilen were raised, Grandma died. Grandpa trapped out of a moss house and another cabin from batten boards and birch bark. He stored goods for a big potlatch in a cache for years, but a fire destroyed everything. He got sick, so he returned to Mansfield, where my father, Titus, and my brother, Andrew, took care of him. My grandpa asked Joe Joseph to bring the preacher up by boat, poling and paddling, to pray for him. When he arrived, the preacher told my grandpa, "Now you are going to leave us. You have three sons and grandchildren. Do you want a church and school for your people before you die?"

Titus Isaac, father of Andrew Isaac, Isabel John, and Laura Sanford, 1920s, Tanacross.
Courtesy Jeanie Healy and Lee Saylor.

My grandpa knew other villages were getting those and said yes. After Grandpa died, the Native people built the church, a house, and the school.

Arthur Wright [father of Don Wright, renowned for winning Alaska Native Land Claims and also father of famous dog musher Gareth Wright and Al Wright of Wright Air Service] was the missionary, followed at the mission by a Mr. McIntosh.

Andrew Isaac working on fur trader John Hajdukovich's freight boat, circa 1921.
Jeanie Healy-Lee Saylor Coll.

Tanana Crossing was a big village then. When the next chief, Walter Isaac [Jerry Isaac's grandfather], got sick, he asked my brother, Andrew, to become chief.

Andrew remembered seeing his first white man in 1904, just after First Lt. William "Billy" Mitchell penetrated our wilderness with the telegraph line from Eagle through the Fortymile River country, down the Goodpaster River to points west.

As we were growing up, we used Billy Mitchell's telegraph wire to heat tea. We tweaked the wire to hang a teapot over a fire.

Isabel John sister of Andrew Isaac cooking dog food, 2003, Tok.
Judy Ferguson photo.

Sometimes we used it to dry meat or as a clothesline. My sister, Isabel, born in 1922, said she used to wear thin caribou-skin pants. Our mom, Annie, tied them with a string to keep them up. Isabel was ashamed for that. Our grandma also tanned a little caribou, a little lynx. She'd make that rabbit skin soft and we'd have a scarf and not freeze. Native people, when they traveled, made a baby pacifier from the upper pad of a caribou's knee. It's a tough, fatlike cartilage. They push a little stick through the fat. The baby rode in a blanket on the Mother's back and sucked that pacifier. Our mom used to flesh hides for hours. Once she left for lunch and Isabel took her two-handled skinning knife and pulled it down across the caribou hide and cut it! She ran to Grandma fast! When Grandma used to take us fishing, we used a long willow with a hooked branch: no string and no regular hook. My grandma called to the fish, "Oh, lonesome, lonesome? Come closer, come up!" Then we'd pull a fish out!

When we were young, we lived near Mansfield, hunting and trapping. Our wall tent was on the trail. The fur buyer, John Hajdukovich, used to stop for tea. He carried the best goods: good-quality washtubs, washboards, and stovepipe. Our brother Andrew used to work for John, as a wrangler on his big game hunts as well as on his riverboat.

Matthew Paul used to run Herman Kessler's tent-frame store next to Matthew's cabin. But they never had canned fruit, just dried stuff. The only canned goods he had was butter. We used rice and raisins for dessert. We didn't have powdered milk.

We lived far from the Tanana Crossing school. Sometimes I attended classes, but Isabel did not. The teacher used to rap our hands with a ruler if we spoke in our own language. We were just learning English. We were a shy people; we could only say "yes" and "no."

Donations of clothing intended for the Natives from Lower Forty-eight churches were used to pay for work done at the mission. The pastor would say, "Split and stack firewood in trade for clothes." The teacher commanded, "Fill a four-pound can of blueberries—not green ones. Then, you can select some clothes." If I am kind of tough today, that's why. You remember how they used to treat us. I never thought that I'd live like white men: to have running water, to have my own stove, all I have to do is turn it on.

I remember the first medical operations in Tanana Crossing. Dr. Schaible of Fairbanks flew in and set up an operating room in the school. A bunch of kids got their tonsils taken out. But not me. I [was] just a big crybaby. But my brother, Andrew, who was [an] adult, had a lump between his ribs. "Doctor," Andrew began, "this lump bug me." "Well," Dr. Schaible said, "if it bugs you, let's take it out." Shheeee, that Dr. Schaible took that lump out right there in the school. Afterward, my brother walked kind of funny down the path back to his cabin.

Laura Isaac Sanford (1928-2010), Tok, 2003.
Judy Ferguson photo.

After 1942 and the building of the AlCan Highway [Alaska-Canada Highway], we could go to town to the doctor or to trade our furs. Our wilderness was no longer isolated.

After statehood, in 1964, the state planned to sell recreational lots on traditional Native lands at nearby George Lake. As Interior Natives began to reorganize the Tanana Chiefs Conference, Andrew testified here and in Washington, D.C., for protection of our traditional lands through the Alaska Native Claims Settlement Act. He fought for our subsistence way of life but said that as a people, we must also get an education.

When I was young, I almost went to school at Mt. Edgecumbe, but as I waited to catch the bus to leave, I thought, "I am the last one at home, and my parents, Titus and Annie, are old." I wondered, "Who's going to melt their snow water and chop their wood?" So I stayed.

Our kids grew up here among white people, learning computers. I teach them my way, and if white man's way doesn't work out, they can turn back.

An Isaac Family Lineage by William E. Simeone

Chief Isaac who asked Archdeacon Hudson Stuck to have Episcopalian missionaries come to the upper Tanana originated either from the village of Tanana or from Chena. Andrew Isaac said that his grandfather Chief Isaac moved first to the Goodpaster River mouth, then to Boat Bottom at the head of the Healy River, over to Joseph Village, and eventually appeared in Ketchumstuk in the 1900 and 1910 census. He married a woman from Ketchumstuk and had at least three children: Walter Isaac, Follet Isaac, and Titus Isaac. Chief Isaac died about 1912.

Walter Isaac married Maggie Demit of Ketchumstuk, daughter of a man named either Dambet or Jack Demit. Walter and Maggie Isaac had Oscar Isaac, father of Jerry Isaac. Eventually Walter Isaac became chief of Tanacross.

Jerry's father, Oscar Isaac, was married to Martha Joseph, the daughter of Salina (Paul) Joseph and Joe Joseph of Salchaket. Martha Joseph's maternal uncle was David Paul.

Walter's second son, Follet Isaac, married a woman from Ketchumstuk but she died in the 1918 flu epidemic. He moved to Nabesna and married a woman named Pauline or Polly. Initially Follet was a medicine man; he later became a Christian.

Walter's third son, Titus Isaac, married a woman named Annie Esau, they had Andrew Isaac, Isabel John, and Laura Sanford.

∽

A paraphrase of Chief Andrew Isaac's biography at http://www.tananachiefs.org/Chief_Andrew_Isaac.shtm:

Born April 16, 1898 in between Joseph Village and Ketchumstuk in a camp, Chief Andrew Isaac was named Aandoo' by Chief Harry Luke, his grandfather Chief Isaac's relative.

Educated by many, Chief Andrew Isaac learned all aspects of the Athabascan lifestyle.

In 1904, he met his first western person. Episcopal Archdeacon Hudson Stuck who came through speaking a foreign language, English.

One day when he was a child Chief Andrew Isaac was accidentally shot by his friend. He remembered the prayers he had learned. He lost so much blood that he was near death. But in four days, he made a miraculous recovery. He became a follower of the Lord the rest of his life.

This near death was followed by many epidemics including the flu which killed two-dozen people in one week at Lake Mansfield. Chief Andrew Isaac was one of the first to catch it but he survived.

Beginning at age eleven, Chief Andrew Isaac worked as a packer in the coal and gold mines, followed by manning freight boats and pack trains for John Hajdukovich. Since Chief Andrew Isaac was known to live an honest, healthy and respectful life, his uncle Walter Isaac appointed him as Chief of the United Crow Band in 1932.

He played a large role in the Alaska Native land claim settlement, testifying both in Anchorage in 1966 and later, in Washington, D.C. He believed the Athabascan people should never sell their land.

> *In 1972, he was appointed First Traditional Chief of the Athabascan people by Tanana Chiefs Conference. In 1979, he was awarded an honorary doctorate of the humanities by the University of Alaska Fairbanks. The Indian Health Service clinic in Fairbanks was also named after him. Chief Andrew Isaac, his wife Maggie Isaac and their four children moved to Dot Lake in 1946 where he lived until a year before he died at 93 on March 23, 1991.*
>
> ∽

Today our Native children don't know how to dry fish or to tan hides. They listen to how our life was and ask, "Are you for real?" We could get fifty caribou a day. We divided them up among ourselves, saying, "You take that, we take..." Caribou isn't too big; we could pass hunks around easily. Everybody always ate. My mom and dad knew how much meat we needed for the winter. They stripped the meat off, the fur, and the hair. They make moccasin. They tan a skin all the time and get sinew for winter. They were all busy; the ladies, busy. We were not sick but healthy; we travel all the way through the year.

To teach our young, I carry an album of photos. If a child questions my stories, "Are you sure?" I point to a photo of my grandma skinning her moose hide. I have kept this for our children to remember and to know.

Old-time Christmas in the Interior, Oscar Albert

In 1998, at Nabesna/Northway elder Enna Northway Albert took me to the home of her brother-in-law Oscar Albert where he shared memories of their life in the upper Tanana in the 1930s. Oscar began:

Three years after the last of the international gold rushes, Chisana, began, I was born October 8, 1917, on Moose Creek near Nabesna. During the rush, Captain Northway's steamboat used to stop in at Moose Creek, selling and buying goods. When I was born to Peter and Elsie Albert in a tent on a drainage of the Black Hills, the muskrat and beaver-infested lakes were icing over. A people of the hills and lakes, our band trapped highland and marsh animals: marten, wolf, wolverine, lynx, fox, beaver, and muskrat. We got moose any season, dried it, and put it up. People helped each other and they were happy.

Before the AlCan highway was built, the Tanana wilderness could only be reached by boat or dogsled. John Hajdukovich had a store in Nabesna and used trading boats. His cousin Milo, C. D. Flannigan, and Herman Kessler were the other traders in our area.

We put in thirteen- to fourteen-hour days driving freight boats for Hajdukovich and Kessler. At night, we parked and slept on the boat. We got five dollars a day, thirty-five dollars a week. If we ran out of food on the trapline, we went to Hajdukovich's caches and signed for goods or sent word to John in Big Delta.

Christmas was a big feast. The first time we heard about God, "Blind Grandma" (Sah Cho'), Chief Frank Sam's mother, asked her granddaughter, Lily Northway, "Do you know God?" and she taught her to pray.

Oscar Albert listening to his old friend and fur buyer John Hajdukovich telling the history of the upper Tanana in 1963 on tape. Northway, 1998.

Judy Ferguson photo.

Herman Kessler taught us about the birth of Christ. Those who lived near St. Timothy's mission at Tanana Crossing (Tanacross) heard of Christmas traditions since 1910 and 1915. Families near the Canadian border were more remote.

To celebrate Christmas, we mushed in from our traplines. The men cut and gathered firewood. For weeks, the ladies sewed new slippers. Under the frozen ground, we dug for muskrat caches, a sweet tubular grass called muskrat candy, a cattail. In the community cabin, we diced this, mixed it with stored greens, and fried both in moose fat. With a celery flavor, the cattail was delicious with cranberries and blueberries. We made moose head soup and kept it simmering on the wood barrel stove for the villagers, along with rice and biscuits. Hajdukovich mushed in three cans of Christmas candy while Kessler freighted in loads of dried meat.

On Christmas Day, we traveled from house to house with a willow

Oscar Albert, 94, passed away November 30, 2011. One of 19 children, Oscar Albert's siblings included his surviving sister Ada Gallen.

He supported his large family as well as feeding 16 dogs and trapping no matter the temperature.

Oscar will be missed for his sense of humor, teasing, joking and giving special nicknames. Oscar loved to drive and drove until he was no longer able to. He continued to enjoy life in the passenger seat.

You could always count on Oscar to lend a helping hand to anyone, often opening his home to people who needed a place to stay.

∽

Dean Wilson's father, Dale Wilson, trapping partner with Oscar Albert, 1947, Northway.

Courtesy of Dean Wilson.

hook and long stick, pulling a sled behind. We tapped on each door. If grudges were held, hands were clasped in friendship. When the willow hook was presented, the household slipped money or meat onto the prong. Each family member put on fresh clothes and joined us at the community hall, where Christmas dinner waited.

After a dinner of soup, meats, greens, and berries, we picked up our fiddles. Tetlin schoolteacher Jack Singleton taught us the two-step. For six or seven days, we danced, played games, and ate pie through New Year's Day.

I never went to school, but I always trapped in the Black Hills. About 1927, I worked in the Kennecott copper mine at the Nabesna Glacier. I married Mary Luke and we had fourteen children, eight of whom lived; of those, five are alive today. To support this large family as well as feeding sixteen dogs, I trapped no matter what the temperature. Sometimes I packed a 150-pound sack of muskrats; I sure don't like to pack that one! The traders paid us twenty-five cents for a small "rat" and fifteen dollars for a big lynx. The biggest year, 1932, we got fourteen or fifteen dollars for a super-blanket beaver. In those days, everything was cheap and you could buy a lot for five dollars.

Around 1940, I met Dale Wilson, father of well-known fur buyer Dean Wilson. A trapper from Washington state, Dale and I decided to trap together. In the fall, Dale caught a steamship to Valdez and then met me at Big Delta, where we rode up the Tanana to Nabesna, dodging slush ice. He stayed in one of my cabins until his family later joined him.

When the war started, suddenly men showed up to build the new highway. Sure surprised us.

I took a physical for the army but I never served. At Christmas after the war, the army, wearing scroungy Santa outfits, passed out gifts to us, up and down the new AlCan. That was first time we ever heard about Santa Claus. I worked

Chief Walter Northway's daughter Enna Albert, helps tell Christmas story, Northway, 1998.

Judy Ferguson photo.

on the new Northway airstrip in 1940. In 1946, the old village of Nabesna was relocated at today's Northway, just off the new "highway." But our family stayed in our home place at Moose Creek, three miles off the road, over the flats. Our eight children grew up in the Black Hills and at our home cabin. That year, I got a car and so did everyone else. All the time we were on that road. Lots of liquor came up that highway too.

Northway potlatch, 1942 or 1943. Chief Frank Sam who preceded Walter Northway as chief, back, right.

Courtesy of Rika's Roadhouse.

Disease came with the men who built the AlCan, and in 1950, tuberculosis infected us. My sister-in-law, Enna, who was sick, remembered Hajdukovich telling her, "Seven times just before sunrise, breathe deeply, soak the sun in on your front and on your back for a half-hour every morning and afternoon, and then always walk, walk, walk." Enna got well, but I lost my mother, my brother, and my sister.

> *In 2008, Stacey Carkhuff of Project Jukebox University of Alaska Fairbanks interviewed Ada Gallen of Northway about the impact of the AlCan Highway on Northway:*
>
> *Polly Hyslop: When the soldiers met with the Chief, what did he say? Ada Gallen: They got permission from Frank Sam and Walter Northway but they can't do nothing. They glad to get road. We usually walk. They used to walk to Tetlin, and Tanacross. They walked to Dawson to get their groceries. With their dogs wearing dog packs, they'd start in May and come back in August: three months. They packed their stuff, caching loads along the way, doing it in laps. That's why they were glad to get the road. Yea, we got shoes,...Yea, we got a new house. Stacey Carkhuff: Who owned the first car in the village? Ada Gallen: Oscar Albert. We go all over! We just jump in: kids and all. He had a big pickup too.*
>
> ∞

In 1956, when my daughter Verda was ten, she joined her older sister in Northway and began going to the school. There were children there of all ages as well as adults in first grade taught by Mr. Pringle in the one-room school. My daughter remembered her first ice cream at the cafe in the 1950s.

Today, employed at Tetlin National Wildlife Refuge, Verda points to our Black Hills, remembers her childhood, and explains the land of the muskrat lakes to our visitors.

Struggling to earn money, we could only afford dinner at Christmastime, not gifts. Con Miller, the later owner of the Santa Claus House, wearing a Santa Claus suit, began making trips, driving his old car up the AlCan. He sold clothes and gave out candy. We didn't exchange gifts until the 1960s, when jobs became more available.

In 1960, I got the first snowmachine in our area. I began living on the road at an old village site, Fish Camp, outside of Northway.

After the settlement of Alaska Native land claims, there was more work. But life, including our Christmas celebrations, was never again like it was before the AlCan. No, you're not gonna see that kinda time no more.

Former Tanacross Tribal President and Tanana Chiefs Conference President Jerry Isaac

The following 2005 interview preceded Jerry Isaac's current position as Tanana Chiefs Conference president. The perspective and information during his tenure as Tanacross tribal president is relevant to and limited to the era before 2006, when he became TCC president.

Over a period of thirteen years, Jerry has graciously shared with me stories of his early life, his evolution as a leader, his struggles as Tanacross tribal president, the deaths of his son and his wife, and now, his work as president of Tanana Chiefs Conference.

Two sons of Chief Isaac: Chief Walter Isaac and third man, Follet Isaac with David Paul in the center, Tanana Crossing, circa 1919.
UAF-1991-46-564.
Frederick B. Drane Collection

All my life I had to ask someone for permission: my parents, teachers, and the government. I was afraid to take a risk if "Daddy" might not be there with a bag of money to bail me out.

One day a man from Oklahoma, Bill Hayden, who was married to a Cherokee, came to Tanacross and challenged me to look at the big picture. Under Bill's teaching, I began to change from a dependency-minded Native American to a responsible tribal member wanting socioeconomic independence. I saw that Tanacross could enter the business world and could become successful.

I am the great-grandson of Chief Isaac written about in Hudson Stuck's book, *Ten Thousand Miles with a Dog Sled*. He first asked the archdeacon for a church and a school for Tanana Crossing. He knew that the people would adapt eventually to a new way of life. His son Chief Walter Isaac of Ketchumstuk was my grandfather. He bare-

Jerry Isaac, Tanacross, 2005.
Judy Ferguson photo.

ly spoke English but his wife, Maggie, who seldom spoke English, managed to memorize the entire Nicene Creed. Their oldest son Oscar Isaac was my father. I was born in 1953 in old Tanacross [Tanana Crossing] on the north side of the Tanana River. We Daendeh people originated from Mansfield Lake. My father didn't speak English well; he and his generation rode the unique era from wilderness-dependent to a cash economy.

Joe Joseph, my maternal grandfather, was born about 1880 in Salcha. He met my grandmother Selina when he was freighting for John Hajdukovich. My grandfathers lived the transition from dog team to aviation. Joe Joseph strongly advocated preparation for the new way of life.

I was born nine years after the Alaska Highway [formerly the AlCan] intersected our land; I grew up twenty years before the Alaska Native Land Claim Settlement Act and its modern Native corporations. I grew up in a twelve-by-twenty-four-foot, often cold, one-room cabin shared by twelve people; we hauled water and used a slop bucket as well as an outhouse.

Concepts of saving and managing money were not natural to a people for whom survival was always tenuous, a tribal society who shared feast and famine alike.

When I was three, my mother, Martha Joseph Isaac, was taken away for a year and half for treatment of tuberculosis. In those days, my father was drinking. I missed my mother, and I was cold and bewildered in a house managed mostly by my grandma. Two of my siblings were also gone, in treatment for TB.

When I entered first grade, the first day I was so nervous that I twiddled my pencil above my desk. Irritated, the teacher grabbed my pencil and then rapped my hand, really scaring me. When I had a tonsillectomy, for ten days I had to leave the village and live in Fairbanks; it collapsed my whole world. I didn't even want to eat.

I was a bad student. I couldn't learn through the standard, linear teaching method. To me, everything was interconnected. My vocabulary was poor, and communication was a nightmare. I had to learn how to learn for myself.

As a youth, I told people that all I wanted to do was to drink beer and listen to my Jimi Hendrix tapes. I didn't like the notion of "progress," and I rebelled against the establishment and capitalism. I fought for simplicity, and I slept wherever night might find me.

For high school, I went away to Chemawa Indian School in Oregon. Because of the school's Native American focus, I began to feel proud. I returned home with a feather in my hair.

Joe Joseph, Jerry's maternal grandfather, (1885-1976) circa 1915.
Courtesy of Jerry Isaac.

In 1976, Arlene Demit and I began a family, so I had to go to work. When I was only twenty-three, my cousin, Betty Denny, asked if I would run for tribal council. Immediately, I had a fire in my belly to correct the social conditions in my village—unemployment, alcoholism, dysfunctional families—and to procure a higher standard of living.

After I became tribal council president, an unpaid position, much of my time was not my own. In 1989, I began complaining to the Administration for Native Americans because the expertise promised for training Native leaders had not been forthcoming. Oklahomans for Indian Opportunity dispatched Bill Hayden to Tanacross. Bill and our tribal council began making a long-

Jerry's father, Oscar Isaac, 1953.
Lee Saylor-Jeanie Healy.

range plan. He taught us tribal self-sufficiency. He admonished me, "Don't tell me why you can't. You have land, a unique culture, and you live in a prosperous state. You have the Indian Self Determination Act, Housing and Urban Development, the Environmental Protection Agency, and Bureau of Justice grant possibilities. There are many business opportunities out there. Get the money and buy the help." When I asked, "What if we fail? Cause everything has to interface perfectly…" He retorted, "You don't build—to fail."

Between 1989 and 1996, I was slowly mentored and converted from being a dependency-minded Native American to an independent sovereign, wanting socioeconomic independence for my village. With that positive mind-set I knew that Tanacross could go into the business world, and we could succeed.

In our village, we started out with nothing. We were unskilled Natives. We came from socially, economically, and politically impacted disarray. We had to take what came and live with it; we had no choice. And that resulted in a low self-esteem. I have asked myself repeatedly, "How can I help my people find the bridge from the past to the present and orient to a life with new rules?" It's a Catch-22 situation. I can't force employers to hire my people. And there is a great struggle within many Natives today to find a healthy, profitable way to make it in today's world. Many are not comfortable in the Caucasian work-place. Others can adapt but are concerned with not losing their cultural uniqueness, their lifestyle. In

Arlene Demit Isaac, circa late 1990s.
Jerry Isaac Collection. John Rusyniak photo.

1995, Tanacross had sixty-eight percent unemployment. The tribal council had to provide social services, mediate the people's needs, and offer scholarships, all with a budget of sixty thousand dollars and one staff person. No accounting was done and no records were kept. All finances went through the Tanana Chiefs Conference, costing us an additional twenty-five percent of our yearly budget. I wondered how so much money could be flowing through the upper echelons but yet the people themselves were still riddled with gambling, drug and alcohol addictions, abuse, historical intertribal feuding, unemployment, domestic problems, and poverty. Also, we as a tribal government had not delivered our people's most basic need: jobs.

From 1997 to 2005, we pulled our funds from the Native American Housing and Self Determination/Interior Regional Housing Authority. I wanted to use that money as leverage for funding sources that required local fiscal matching. Using contract vehicle under Public Law 93-638 [the Indian Self-Determination and Education Assistance Act of 1975, Titles I and III], along with money from the Bureau of Indian Affairs [BIA], we began delivering social services directly to the people. We turned our attention then to a bigger piece of the pie: general contracting.

The capitalist bureaucracy created the cake as well as the tools on the table. Governmental social programs preach independence, but they engender dependency for welfare's continued existence. Despite the rhetoric, social services, grants, and other government aid are not likely to disappear. But in spite of these crutches, we must learn the tools of capitalism. There is, however, an inherent cultural conflict. For instance, if I visit a village, I will be hosted and

Dihthâad
Lake Mansfield

Tanacross and beyond, Lake Mansfield Dihthaad.

Courtesy of Jerry Isaac.

no payment will be asked of me. But I will donate a gift or I will do something for my host family. Similarly in the potlatch tradition, a family saves for years to gift those who are honored at the ceremony. By contrast, capitalism is based on gaining, not on giving. What we as Natives face in the modern era includes more than an issue of work or skill or of location: it is a reversal in life perception and of lifestyle.

However, no one is going to give monetary control to an unproven people. An unskilled man faces what seems like an insurmountable mountain: how to create jobs, apply for grants, negotiate contracts, and lobby. I knew there was more out there; I had to find how to bring it under our control and further, how to translate it into a holistic approach. I went to an Anchorage bank that would risk loaning money to a village with no line of credit.

After starting contract vehicle, we began general contracting. But none of us were qualified. In September 1998, we decided to hire outside professionals. It was a hard choice, but we needed the expertise. Using general contracting, we would have a village-based industry. Tanacross' traditional use areas and sacred sites were not far from the National Missile Defense System near Fort Greely. Also—someday—the Alaska Railroad or the natural gas pipeline might go through tribal lands. It bothered us for billions of dollars to flow past our Upper Tanana people but still we might wind up with nothing.

Grants are limited by conditions and are temporary, but I knew that a stable business could provide a cash cow for my people. However, without bonding—having no track record, liquid assets, or large capital backing—first, we had to team with bonded partners. In 2002, Tanacross' newly created business, Dihthaad Global Services [DGS], partnered with Doyon Universal Services and Arctic Structure to build the National Missile Defense Program's four-million-dollar, four-hundred-person camp. Dihthaad Global Services (DGS) had five members on the board and two tribal council members. Through Bechtel National, Inc, we were given the GMD Test Bed housekeeping and janitorial work contract. Through Fluor Alaska, Inc., DGS received the million-dollar GMDTB security contract, for which we also requested Delta Junction local hire. We knew that we must develop successive businesses, paced to bloom as each previous one phased out.

If you want something, you put in time, blood, sweat, and tears. We could've lost our shirt, but having people willing to be accountable for the risks is an intrinsic part of business. Indeed there was another risk ahead but one that I did not see coming. In 2003, my son, Damian, was killed in a tragic accident.

After the death of my son in 2003, and during a very black time, I wrote the following:

Jerry, Damian, and Arlene Isaac, Tanacross.
Courtesy of Jerry Isaac.

I have struggled all my life with addictions; my self-discipline has been on again, off again. Our son and his other siblings grew up unable to depend on consistent, available food, and attention. They were born into a family with a long familial and tribal history of serious addictions. As I have attempted to lead Tanacross, my family has paid a deep price. I have tried to help Tanacross heal, to step up to a higher level but the infighting, the bickering, and the disrespect is deeply ingrained. As the tribal council president, I was dedicated to advance the tribe. I was unpaid, and I was always in demand.

November 24, 2004, I returned from a trip Outside, after another long bout of alcoholism. My blood alcohol level was 2.9, very high. I almost died. I hope that this will serve as a warning to young leaders. For four days I was in a detoxification center in Seattle. I felt weakened almost beyond repair but I did re-evaluate. I wondered why I have sacrificed so much in my life to try and save a people who don't seem to want to be saved. When I was in my darkest hour of need, my brother-in-law came and prayed with me. Strange, how the Lord sends His messengers at the right time to reinforce my purpose, my commitment, and my goal.

As my life has evolved, I have taken up a calling, laid it down, and then, picked it back up again. In my early days, I fought forest fires. My spiritual life has been my strength. The fire triangle illustrates the basics a man must have. For fire, there must be oxygen, fuel, and heat. Conversely, for a man to be a productive citizen, he can't be hungry or without hope. Employment gives people a purpose, a reason to improve, and an orientation. I knew that my only credentials were love, care, and respect for my people, to help them from dysfunction and bankruptcy to spiritual revitalization.

Much of my life, I have been heavily influenced by political liberal thinking but often that view boils down to self-indulgence and complaining. I used to flail against the word "progress," but today, much of what we Natives eat we have to buy. Like anyone else, we cannot live without money. I don't blame "what the white man did," or my parents, or try to dodge responsibility for my own addictions on the woes of my childhood. If we are to go forward, we have to accept our own tindividual responsibility. At the same time, it seems like we are the most controlled, dependent people in the world. That mindset is so deeply ingrained and so infectious. Even though millions of dollars come into the state to help the villages, there are still serious problems: drug and alcohol abuse of which I am also guilty. There is domestic abuse, unemployment, and unwed mothers and fathers. On BIA supplements, people aren't even making a living. Why do our people have to struggle when our regional, profit-making corporations like Doyon transact over 2.3 billion dollars a year?

After working for Tanacross for twenty-eight years, I ponder what I have done. I have tried to search with foresight so my people would not be caught unprepared. Due to longtime and continuing animosity among the people, the odds seemed sometimes insurmountable. Believing in fairness and equality, my standard has been to lead without racial discrimination. I tried to lead with a fascination in trying new things, knowing that times and seasons change. I knew there would be sacrifices for which I was not prepared and still am not. Although I don't read it often, the Bible has been the foundation for my ongoing devotion. I have led with my traditional drumming, singing, and dancing.

In old times, the need to work and its ethos disallowed today's temptation and depression. People were always occupied, active in some way, and only sat down for twenty minutes to eat or to relax. Due to the long winter darkness, they went to bed early. They didn't indulge in introspection. Suicide was so disrespected that I remember once when a man hung himself, he was cut down from the rope and his body was thrown away. Such was thought of that crime.

[After his son's death, Jerry Isaac found a way to begin leading his people once again. In 2005, he gave his thoughts on survival in the modern era.]

Not only is subsistence an intrinsic part of our lives but today, capitalism is a new key to our self-sufficiency. If we don't conquer these necessary skills, we contribute to our own demise. We must put a cap on our use of grants and learn how to invest money so it will grow. We need to develop successive businesses, one to pick up when the previous one has eclipsed its time: to be self-sustaining. I want to deal with banks on a mutual respect basis. It's a tough reality.

As Tanacross Tribal Council president, typical of the daily boondoggles I faced was the free home program. Only three of our 350 homes met the program's qualifications, but our houses had black mold and cracking, rotting foundations. In twenty years, the Regional Housing Authority never helped us build a new home, which was another reason that we chose to run our own show during that time. Like others, we need to pay taxes and to save money but our people are addicted to drinking and gambling. However, we have had nothing to look forward to—no jobs and no money. We are in the depths of debt. We have defaulted on our loans and have been foreclosed on. At that moment when I didn't want to get up and try one more time, my wife Arlene asked me, "Will this become a pattern for you, to go part way and then to quit?"

At that time, not knowing if we could get contracts to pay a staff again, I hired three men. One successfully negotiated a partnership for a demolition project in Alabama, where Dithhaad Global Services had seven employees. We also met with Coastal Security International out of Washington, D.C. from whom Dithhaad got the subcontract, and we employed several security guards.

As I face my own hurdles and those of my people, I encourage young leaders to avoid the pitfalls to which I have yielded. My father, grandfather, and their fathers' priority was always the continuation of our people. Throughout the long haul, we must take responsibility and fuel the economic, political, and social future of our people, to break trail into the twenty-first century.

In March 2006, Jerry Isaac was elected president of the nonprofit Tanana Chiefs Conference, which is responsible for forty-two villages and ten thousand people in 235,000 square miles: thirty-two percent of Alaska and only slightly smaller than Texas. The circumstances in each of these villages vary greatly. The more rural are quite dependent on subsistence. Those villages closer to urban centers have the greater possibility of running a business as well as living the traditional way of life.

The year 2006 was very hard for Jerry Isaac. He lost his mother, father-in-law, and his wife, Arlene Mary Demit. Three years later in her honor, Jerry hosted a potlatch that drew leaders from all over Alaska and Canada.

In spring 2011, Jerry was reelected as TCC president. In his 2006 acceptance speech, true to his course, President Jerry Isaac said,

"We shall forge a new direction for our people. I am aware of the real and serious fiscal issues that are facing us today . . . that will test our strength, understanding, patience, tolerance, and resolve. . . . We must craft our own agendas of planned approaches to overcome the challenges. From the banks of our rivers and streams, from our hills and mountains, from our traplines and fish camps, from our villages and our homes, we must set out to revitalize the dormant, untapped strength, and vitality of the spirit of our people. Let the direct command of our forebears prevail once more! Survival of our people, at all costs, through calculated adaptation to the present-day lifestyle, guided by our past. From the sacred and hallowed valleys of our countryside, from the shores of our lakes and the sacred beat of our drums,

let it be known that there is a new meaning to these very words: "WE SHALL SURVIVE!"

Gathering of the Tribes: Potlatch for Arlene Mary Demit, June 2009

Jerry Isaac lost his wife, Arlene Mary Demit, on November 9, 2006. According to Tanacross protocol, a memorial potlatch gives honor to the deceased and gifts to the family's other moiety [which is either of two kinship groups based on unilateral descent that together make up a tribe or society].

Tanana Chiefs Conference president Jerry Isaac thanks Doyon, Limited Board Chairman Orie Williams and Doyon, Limited, President and CEO Aaron Schutt for million dollar donation for construction of the new Chief Andrew Isaac Health Center, 2011.
Sam Harrel *Fairbanks Daily News-Miner*

In his book Rifles, Blankets and Beads, *William E. Simeone remembered the Tanacross community center where the Isaac potlatch was held. Simeone described a woodcut hanging on the wall of the original Tanana chiefs who met with Judge Wickersham in 1915. "These are the original chiefs who began negotiations with the government over land. The outcome of their efforts is symbolized by the American flag hanging on the wall. Also representative of Tanacross tradition are the gunhoks, two red, white, and blue dance sticks, hanging on the opposite wall. Together, these symbols represent the rights, equality, and power vested in citizenship that Native people demand in their quest to determine their own destiny."*

In early June, the Isaac family held a three-day potlatch to celebrate the life and heritage of Arlene Demit Isaac. Athabascan lineage is passed through the matrilineal line. Arlene's mother, Bella Joseph, was from a high-ranking clan, Nalt'sin, in Tetlin and her father, Fred Demit, was related to the Nalt'sin and was from Nabesna/Northway.

In Tanacross on June 11-13, 2009, chiefs from Nulato and Ruby on the Yukon River; from Minto on the Tanana River; Ahtna from Tazlina, Copper Center, Chistochina, Gakona, and Gulkana in the Copper River basin; Mentasta and Moosehide near Dawson; and Tutchone from Haines Junction, Yukon Territory came to pay tribute. Tanana Chiefs President Jerry Isaac, the son "of great chiefs," greeted the crowd. At potlatch, history is reviewed, relations strengthened, obligations met, and geographical and genealogical benchmarks reaffirmed. As ten courses for the meal were prepared, speakers from across the north began to share. Jerry Isaac introduced Don Stevens of Steven's Village. Speakers followed one after the other in natural rhythm, including Larry Titus of Minto; Nulato First Chief Miki Stickman; Daisy Stevens, a Gwich'in of Fort Yukon; eighty-year-old Markle Pete; Chief James Allen, a southern Tutchone from Haines Junction, Yukon Territory; Jonathan Solomon's sister Hannah Solomon Adams of Fort Yukon; Robert Charlie of Minto; and pastor Ben Neeley of Gulkana. Neeley, born in 1910, began by saying, "The Copper River Ahtna were once a great people. In 1912, Copper River people came to Mansfield Lake [the original village for Tanacross] for potlatch. We knew song and dance. Today, kids aren't interested in the songs and dances and our language is dead." Referring to the June 10 tragedy when nine-year-old Jasmine Ewan and six-year-old Elijah Ewan died in a house fire in Copper Center, he said, "Today we have sorrow in Copper River but in the book of Romans, it says, 'We weep with those who weep and rejoice with those who rejoice.' Today we come to weep with you." He continued, "Old time was different, but today the Athabascan people are a Christian people." Remembering a long-

Pastor Ben Neeley of Gulkana, born 1910, remembered, "In 1912, Copper River people came to Mansfield Lake [Tanacross] for potlatch." Tanacross, 2009.
Judy Ferguson photo.

ago "sorry song," Pastor Neeley shared the story of the drowning of a great chief. The ninety-nine-year-old pastor began spontaneously leading the Ahtna, Tanana, Koyukon, and Tutchone in singing their shared grief. The honored elder later led the young in the ancient release, echoed by vibrant young leader Don Stevens.

Don Stevens of Stevens Village shared song and dance, 2009.
Judy Ferguson photo.

Chief James Allen, who'd traveled from Haines Junction and Burwash Landing, said, "In my area, we're losing potlatch, and today we live more like the modern white society. It's good to see your kids dancing."

Daisy Stevens admitted she was nervous to speak publicly, but she soon launched into a sharing of her real friendship with Arlene Demit, remembering her "before she was a sparkle in Jerry Isaac's eyes." Daisy recalled when they were young and used to "hang out on Two Street. It was practically a kind of our own reservation! We owned it! But something happened!" She laughed, "What did we do?!"

Adding, "I think it might've had something to do with land claims." She continued, "Arlene was a very loving person." She grinned. "Tetlin [Arlene's mother's village] doesn't know it but being from Fort Yukon, I can understand your language!" Everyone laughed.

Robert Charlie of Old Minto Culture Camp encouraged the people. "We have two responsibilities: first, to get married, secondly, for our kids. Potlatch, he said, is a landmark and these monuments help us remember who we are. Too bad we aren't in the old time when the chiefs spoke freely at potlatch discussing issues. He continued, "*Chughet'sen* [a word Chief Peter John used to express Athabascan spirituality] means unconditional love. There is no greater word and that's our roots; don't forget that. You were born under that Athabascan umbrella."

In that tradition, Sharon Tyone of Tanana warmly greeted every person at potlatch, shaking hands, hugging, jumping seats when needed. She was a sparkle in motion.

As we waited for the banquet, host Jerry Isaac reminded us that in his grandfather, Follet Isaac's, day, the people

Kenny Thomas drumming as Jerry Isaac dances at his wife's potlatch, 2009, Tanacross.
John Rusyniak.

would wreak a particular payment when they had to wait for dinner. He told the story of his grandfather's potlatch when the impatient men threw the plates and utensils when dinner wasn't ready on time. Jerry grinned and promised, "Dinner will be ready soon so don't pitch your plates!" he laughed.

Soon while everyone remained in their seats, young people unfurled butcher paper down the aisles on which to set the condiments. Wave after wave of youngsters carried trays of freshly baked bread (bannock), hot moose head

John Isaac dancing with a gunhok, 2009, Tanacross.
John Rusyniak photo.

soup, followed by Copper River grilled salmon, pans of succulent moose vertebrae, rice and moose, three great salads, Jell-O, fry bread, raspberry-flavored Dream Whip in a cup, Alaska blueberries in syrup, followed by hot tea. Aluminum foil was provided for the stacks of food that guests would carry home. Simeone continued, "Wild food is preferred to most purchased food" and "moose meat is coveted" to serve at potlatch.

The clouds held back the rain as guests retreated briefly outside before the dancing. As the drums (*ch'elxal*) began to be lightly tapped and men warmed up their voices, Jerry Isaac, his sons and nephews—Herbie Demit, Jerry Isaac Jr., Galen D. Isaac, John O. Isaac, Travis H. Karshekoff, and Jacob T. Isaac—stood abreast in regal

113

Larry Jonathan, 2009, Tanacross.
John Rusyniak.

moosehide jackets and sashes presenting the beginning of the dance (*ch'uuljus*). After the introductory dance of the men alone, the young ladies, including Dawn Demit; Terri Smoke; Julia, Trixie, and Martha Isaac; Kaylinn Titus; Charmaine Isaac; and Karshawna Grant flowed into the hall, shuffling in the opposite direction in an inner circle. Dance sticks (*gunhoks*), and beaded, colored regalia signifying Jerry's father's Nalt'sin moiety [black and white], and his mother's Dikaagyu moiety [red and white] filled the room. Traditionally dances include "sorry songs," followed by "dance songs" and much later by a "potlatch song" sung over the gifts immediately before distribution. Jerry Isaac explained, "A memorial potlatch is about letting go. The combination of sharing in potlatch preparation, visiting, dancing, and humor help that process." He pointed out, "Colors in the hair, jacket and bandanas catch the eye and help soothe the wounded feelings. That vibrancy helps create a spirit of happiness."

Simeone explained that dancing and singing are part of the guests' reciprocal obligation. Simeone said, "The dancing helps expel the grief from the body. [However] the mourning changes as people playfully sing about life in Tanacross, dancing joyfully with long strips of 'calico.' With their feet planted wide apart, men hold a scarf and jab the air to the beat of the drum.—Women form a circle around the men and either stand still while moving their arms or shuffle in a counter-clockwise movement." Tanacross sibs [A kinship group consisting of two or more lineages considered as being related, as by common descent from an ancestor.] include the Dikaagyu (Jerry's mother, Martha Isaac),

Tc'a·z, Tcicyu sibs, Nalt'sin (Jerry's father, Chief Oscar Isaac) and Al si' dEndi. Simeone explained, "Bandanas are hung around the hall for dancers to take down and connect as a chain. The potlatch song is sung three times, 'the luck' is sent out and comes back."

In the early morning hours like a benediction, the potlatch song (*xw-tiitl ch'itiik*) was sung. Arlene Demit Isaac's heirs came forward, including sons Herbie Demit, Jerry Isaac Jr., and Galen D. Isaac, and daughter Angelene Bella Isaac. Jerry Isaac, representing the maternal lineage of the Isaac moiety

Jerry Isaac gifts one of his sons Galen Isaac, 2009, Tanacross.
John Rusyniak photo.

114

(Dikaagyu), presented their children with the traditional rifles and blankets to his wife's high-ranking Tetlin moiety, Nalt'sin.

During his wife's illness, he wrote a grieving song for her:

"Out there, in the vastness of this land over which I am appointed as the voice, the chief, the spokesman of this land, that greatness of responsibility, the recognition of that. What am I to do with it—that I may be rendered to help my wife convalesce? My dear wife."

For sixty days following the potlatch, Isaac kept eating, traveling, and working to a minimum as a part of the letting go process.

With chiefs from Yukon Territory, Yukon, Copper, Tetlin, middle and upper Tanana rivers, and Healy Lake, the gathering to honor the Jerry Isaac family echoed the wood engraving on the Tanacross Community Center wall: a gathering in the eternal flow of the chiefs of the land.

Tanana Chiefs Conference from the TCC website: http://www.tananachiefs.org/history_tcc.shtm

TCC's movement into the modern era began with the advancement of non-Natives into the Interior. Tribal leaders strengthened their loose confederation to protect traditional rights. The first land dispute came in 1915 when the chiefs organized to protect a burial ground in Nenana from the Alaska Railroad. As a result, the railroad avoided the cemetery.

Conflicts became an increasing problem; the threat of loss of Native land grew after statehood in 1959. The Alaska Statehood Act recognized Native land rights, yet the state administration began planning as though it did not. It had two plans that were of particular concern. One was to build a road to the Minto Lakes area northwest of Fairbanks and the Rampart Dam project. That project and another ill-conceived idea—creating a harbor at Point Hope on the northwest coast with nuclear blast—contributed substantially to the rise of the land claims movement.

A remarkable array of young, educated Native leaders began pushing the land claims toward a suitable outcome.

TCC includes: Yukon-Tanana Subregion: *Alatna, Allakaket, Evansville (Bettles Field), Hughes, Kaktovik, Manley, Minto, Nenana, Rampart, Stevens Village, Tanana;* **Yukon Flats Subregion:** *Arctic Village, Beaver, Canyon Village, Chalkyitsik, Circle, Fort Yukon, Venetie;* **Upper Tanana:** *Dot Lake, Eagle, Fairbanks, Healy Lake, Northway, Tanacross, Tetlin, Tok;* **Yukon-Koyukuk Subregion:** *Galena, Huslia, Kaltag, Koyukuk, Nulato, Ruby;* **Upper Kuskokwim Subregion:** *McGrath, Nikolai, Takotna;* **Lower Yukon Subregion:** *Anvik, Grayling, Holy Cross, Shageluk.*

∞

Chapter Twelve

Alice Snigaroff Petrivelli, Gentle Aleut Unangax̂ Warrior

Alice Petrivelli's people, the Unangax̂ flourished for thousands of years before the invasion of the Russians who began calling them 'Aleuts'. In the late 1700s, Russian traders forced the Unangax̂/Aleut into fur hunting; the results were devestating.

However when the missionaries arrived, they placed value on local cultures

Alice Petrivelli, Anchorage, 2002.
Judy Ferguson photo.

and encouraged indigenous leadership in parish life and missionary activity. This policy was intended to gain the loyalty of the people by the Church and State becoming protectors over the 10,000 inhabitants of Russian America but the result was a new, autonomous form of indigenous identity, in which many Native traditions survived in local "Russian" Orthodox tradition, in the religious life of the villages.

In 1824, Russian Orthodox missionary Ivan Veniaminov gave the people an alphabet. Seventeen years later, Aleuts in his area could read and write. Under his care, the church at Atka was built in 1830.

1824, Russian Orthodox missionary Ivan Veniaminov, St. Innocent, circa 1830.
Library of Congress.
cph.3c32144.

Over the years, the local Orthodox church became the people's pride and joy, a jewel that each of them contributed to building. Its spire with its Orthodox cross pointed to the blend of Slavic and Alaska Native cultures.

The most visible trace of the Russian colonial period in Alaska today is the presence of nearly ninety Russian Orthodox parishes with a membership of over 20,000 men, women, and children, almost exclusively indigenous people.

116

However, World War II nearly brought an end to the Aleut paradise. In 1942, the Japanese bombed the Aleutians. Under the pretext of protecting them, the U.S. government moved 882 Aleuts to camps in southeast Alaska. As a twelve-year-old, Alice Petrivelli lived through the tragedy of World War II.

At the suggestion of Nettie Peratrovich, I asked Alice to share her story. A small but strong-hearted woman, Alice described her life in the Aleutian Island chain before and after the World War II Japanese invasion.

Atka.

Courtesy of Alice Petrivelli.

Speaking from her home in 2002, she began, "We didn't know where we were going." Caught in government agency confusion, war, and racism, Alice and eighty-three other Aleuts lost their culture and their homes on Atka.

The Aleut have been on the chain for fifteen thousand years. We had a paradise, and few of us ever left. Treeless and open, laced with waterfalls and green hills, the islands were our second skin. During the summer, we harvested salmon, halibut, and cod as well as sea lion and seal. We salted, dried, and smoked them. In those days when the water was clean, we walked down to the beach at low tide for breakfast. We peeled kelp off the rocks and rowed our dories out to get mollusks and chitons. During the winter, we trapped fox.

In 1910, seal and otter hunting were stopped. Nineteen years later, I was born in Atka in 1929. When I was a young child during the 1930s, the United States began stocking our islands with fox. My father, Cedar Snigaroff, leased an island, Tagula, near Adak, where he trapped blue fox. He and my brother Poda took turns trapping, as they did with the village-leased islands. Poda ran the cooperative store as well. We averaged ten thousand dollars a year. The village, including my family, leased Amlia and Amchitka islands, trapping fox for everyone. Because we were isolated, we sold only to Mr. Harold Bowman of Kanaga Ranch Company based out of Atka and Seattle. The profits were divided to families depending on their size. We had all we needed: nature and real people. My father built us a home with indoor plumbing and hardwood floors. My mother died when I was five. I remember my father used to make us sit and listen to classical music on the Victrola. We had a beautiful Orthodox church filled with our own handmade icons. Life was peaceful and good.

In 1942, our way of life came to an end. After the Japanese bombed Pearl Harbor December 7, 1941, they bombed Dutch Harbor in early June, followed by an invasion of the island of Adak, 480 miles to the west, then Kiska, 240 miles farther west and then the westernmost island, Attu. The military and governmental officials said they feared for our safety, but the evacuations were done in wartime chaos, filled with racism. Governmental agencies were operating under crisis and lacked clarity; the navy ordered the evacuation of some of the Aleutians and Pribilofs. Taking as much as two months, each evacuation was handled differently.

Alice Snigaroff, far right, and other Atka islanders at the Killisnoo detention camp. Center is Ruby McGee, a teacher from Emporia, Kansas. Summer 1943.
Courtesy of Alice Snigaroff Petrivelli.

In June 1942, the *USS Hulbert*, a naval vessel, weighed anchor off Atka and demanded to transport us to some yet-to-be-determined refuge. The commander of the *Hulbert* dispatched a demolition crew to Atka to burn our beloved church and most of our homes. Our home, due to the indoor plumbing, and the home of Chief William Dirks were both spared. As planes took off during the night, we rode our dory through the tide, but we almost capsized. Sixty-two people and allowed no baggage, we boarded the *Hulbert*. Some of our people were left still on land, hiding from the Japanese. Concerned about those families, our chief asked if he might return to notify them. The commander refused and burned his dory along with everyone else's. Shivering and confused, we watched our homes burning; the light reflecting off the dark water looked like a bomb had hit. We left behind our food, our warm clothes, and our fishing equipment. We had no idea where we were going.

The navy wasn't sure where to take us; they were waiting on decisions between the army, the Alaska Indian Service, and Governor Gruening. Nonetheless, the evacuations continued. We were taken to Nikolski and from there to Dutch Harbor, where the *Delarof*, a military transportation ship built to carry five hundred, was waiting. Although the *Delarof* was already filled with Pribilovians, we boarded, making a total of eight hundred souls. In transit, men and women were allowed drinking water only once a day. The Indian Service decided to deposit us at abandoned canneries in Southeast. The Pribilovians were offloaded at Funter Bay, and we were unloaded at Killisnoo, a cannery south of Admiralty Island. The ship's captain felt sorry for us and gave each of us a pillow, a mattress, and a blanket. But we were left without food, drinking water, building materials, tools, or medical supplies.

We found a pond, but it was stagnant and we had to boil our drinking water. We had two outhouses for eighty-three people. Throughout the winter, the Tlingits in Angoon, who pitied us, provided us with salmon. Without our tools, we were helpless. Eventually, we got some army-surplus clothing and staples like powdered eggs, but it wasn't our Aleut food from the sea. Local people said that winter of 1942 to 1943 was the worst in fifty years. The walls of the cannery had cracks between

Alice Snigaroff in Wrangell, 1944.
Courtesy of Alice Snigaroff Petrivelli

the boards. Every day, my family and I huddled around a little stove. My sister, Vera, caught double pneumonia and nearly died. Of all the camps, we had the highest mortality rate. Eighteen people, twenty-two percent of us, at Killisnoo died. Many of them, our elderly, were our repository of honor and wisdom. I blocked out much of what happened during that time.

While we were in the camps, soldiers vandalized our remaining homes on Atka. When half of us finally returned, we found our properties destroyed, no dories, and no fishing tackle. In 1942, forty-two Aleuts on Attu were taken prisoner by the Japanese. After the war, the twenty-seven who survived the Japanese prison camp were not allowed to return home.

After the war, no one helped me. I worked to go to school in Sitka. But living among strangers, life was never the same. In 1949, I paid for my own return home. I was confused until I married, and I was bitter for longer. What was meant to protect us devastated our culture. We were treated like second-class citizens by the military, the government, and in newspaper articles. Today, some call it "the Aleutian trail of tears."

In 1988, the Aleutian and Pribilof Restitution Act was signed. To compensate for our losses, we were paid twelve thousand dollars each, while the Japanese-Americans, who were interned also during the war, were paid twenty thousand dollars.

I am the director and former president of the Aleut Corporation. In honor of the centennial of Vitus Bering, my daughter, anthropologist Patricia Petrivelli, and I attended a celebration in Russia's Commander Islands. For the first time since 1948, I heard Attuan, which is a dead language in Alaska today.

Generation after generation, the hatred goes on. I have decided if I forgive, I cleanse myself. These experiences have made me stronger. Strength, and not the bitterness, is what I will pass on to my children and to my grandchildren.

In 2003, sponsored by the Honoring Alaska's Indigenous Literature (HAIL) working committee with support from the Alaska Federation of Natives, Alaska Rural Systemic Initiative, Alaska Native Knowledge Network, and the Anchorage Museum of History and Art, Alice Petrivelli received a posthumous award for her father, Cedar Snigaroff, for passing on Unangax history in his own language in Niigugis Maqaxtazaqangis: Atkan Historic Traditions, *published in 1979 by the Alaska Native Language Center, University of Alaska Fairbanks.*

Alice Petrivelli contributed to When the Wind Was a River: Aleut Evacuation in World War II *by Dean Kohlhoff, 1995, University of Washington Press.*

Crystal Anastasia Duskin
Kdam Idigaa,
Unangax̂ dancer, circa 2006.
Courtesy of Crystal Dushin.

Timeline:

Unangax̂ Aleuts prospered more than 7,000 years before European influence.

1741: At Adak Island in the Aleutian Islands, Alexei Chirikov trades with Aleut men.

1772-1775: Permanent Russian settlement established at Unalaska.

1786: Russians took Unangax̂ /Aleuts to hunt the northern fur seals that bred in the Pribilof Islands and later moved families to the islands to live permanently.

1795: Orthodox monk Makarius baptizes many at Unalaska.

1796-1799: Russian-American Company established at Unalaska.

1804-1864: Iakov Netsvetov, Unangas Creole, the first Western Russian Orthodox priest, translates parts of the Bible.

1818: The Russian-American Company employs Natives only on voluntary contracts. Class of Creoles, persons of mixed ancestry, created.

1824: Ivan Veniaminov, Russian Orthodox missionary, arrives and learns the Unangax̂ / Eastern Aleut language. He develops an alphabet and writes a Unangax̂ /Aleut catechism, the first book written in an Alaska Native language.

1828: Iakov Netsvetov, a Creole and graduate of Irkutsk Theological Seminary, arrives at Atka, where he serves until 1844.

1830: Church in Atka built.

1835: Epidemics begin.

1841: All Aleuts in Veniaminov's district can write.

1865: Surveyors for the Western Union International Telegraph, including Whymper and Dall future authors on Alaska work in Alaska.

1867: Russia ceded Alaska to the United States for $7,200,000.

1965, 1969, 1971: Underground nuclear testing on Amchitka.

1971: Alaska Native Claims Settlement Act.

∽

Chapter Thirteen

Living On Scraps: W.C "TOD" Kozevnikoff of Tanana

In 2004 when I was publishing interviews in my Fairbanks Daily News-Miner *column, I received a call from Tod Kozevnikoff. A warm man with a wonderful sense of humor, Tod had a story he wanted to tell. Not only was it a candid story, but it also included two of the major events in the history of the village of Tanana: the building of Fort Gibbon and the impact of World War II.*

Tod was raised by his grandparents, Charlie and Nettie Erhart. When he was fourteen, he left home and began working at the Northern

Tod Kozevnikoff, Fairbanks, 2004.

Judy Ferguson photo.

Commercial Co., F.E. Mining Co., and the Alaska Railroad in Fairbanks. He returned to Tanana where he worked at the Tanana Hospital, from which he retired in 1983.

In a second career, Tod began working for Northern Oilfields, Doyon Drilling, and ARCO on the North Slope. After retiring again from oil work, he started working for Tanana Chiefs Conference as a remote maintenance operator in 2008.

His passion was spending his summers at his fish camp on the Yukon River; jamming with his friends at the Athabascan Fiddle Festival and spending time with his grandchildren, especially his great-grandson, Evan Titan.

I interviewed Tod in 2004 at the home he shared with his wife, Eileen. After his story was published, there was a negative reaction from one family member. In every personal memoir, more than one life is touched and as with any story, there are many perspectives of the same event. The following is Tod's voice, his story as he wished to tell it.

I grew up between the Tanana and Yukon rivers at Nuchalawoya, *where the rivers meet,* a traditional Native trading site.

In 1891 when the Church of England established a mission at the confluence of these rivers, Athabascans gathered for work and for teaching. Two non-Natives ministered to the small community—a deaconess who took care

KOYUKON

of the sick and an itinerant priest. The confluence also became the transfer point for steamboats.

Eight years later, Fort Gibbon was established. Neither soldiers or Natives were allowed to buy liquor there. However, with their access to the mission's clothing barrel, the Natives would loan civilian clothing to the soldiers. When

Confluence of the Tanana and Yukon rivers, Nuchalawoya. Far left near Yukon River: Tanana Mission Chapel; village of Tanana is to the right; circa 1907.
Walter and Lillian Phillips Collection, UAF-1985-72-53.

the disguised soldier left the liquor store, he paid the Natives waiting in the brush with a bottle, and a party began. At one time, there were as many as sixteen saloons around Fort Gibbon. In 1923, the itinerant Archdeacon Hudson Stuck wondered if the Native people would survive the corrupting influence of the military.

My maternal grandmother, Nettie Luke, was a small but mentally tough

Fort Gibbon, Tanana.

UAF 1958 1026 1234, Bunnell Collection.

Athabascan girl. As a young lady on snowshoes with only a dull ax, she cut willow branches and small spruce every day to keep her mother's wikiup warm. In the summer, she lined the family canoe, pulling the boat with a tether from shore, while her mother steered it. If a drinking party was around the bend, Nettie kept pulling, trying to keep her mother from stopping.

One trapping season, her mother loaned nine-year-old Nettie to a neighboring family. They used Nettie as a work dog and forced her to pull their sled,

123

L to r, third and fourth persons: Tod Kozevnikoff's maternal grandparents, Charles and Nettie Erhart. Little girl is Tod's mother's sister Violet. Early-1930s at Eightmile Island on the Tanana River near the village of Tanana.

Courtesy of Tod Kozevnikoff.

seldom feeding her. She had to break trail through deep snow up to her waist. In the spring, as the family was returning to Tanana, she broke into a run to escape her captors. Later, young Nettie married a teamster, an older man who freighted for the Army forts, named Charles Erhart. He was a relaxed man with a great sense of humor who, like many, made moonshine. My grandmother gave birth to and raised their daughter, the beautiful and willful Elizabeth. Concerned about controlling Elizabeth, my grandmother married her off to a steamboat deckhand, Ambrose Kozevnikoff from St. Michael, who was living in Tanana at the time. Kozevnikoff was the son of a Russian, Alex Kozevnikoff, a supervisor for the Northern Commercial Trading Co. and his Yup'ik wife, Tatiana. The result was my handsome father, Ambrose Kozevnikoff.

As a young man, my dad got the N.C. Company mail run contract from Tanana up the Tanana River to Manley Hot Springs. Each trip, he had to break trail and deal with overflow water, sixty-three miles to Manley. During the summer, he cut wood with a crosscut saw for the steamboats.

After my grandmother arranged the marriage between my twenty-five-year-old father and my seventeen-year-old mother, I was born in Tanana's old

Mail run to Tanana, circa 1912.
Rivenburg, Lawyer and Cora album; UAF-1994-70-3

Fort Gibbon hospital in 1937. My sister, Maria, soon followed.

My dad was Orthodox and my mother Episcopalian, but when all else failed, my grandmother Nettie believed in Justin, the local shaman. Once when I swallowed a big olive pit that obstructed my intestines, the Army doctor declared he could do nothing. My grandmother called for Justin. He conducted his medicine, and the next day, I passed the seed.

Despite the reprieve, two children and a husband proved to be too much for my young mother. When my father returned from the trail, our house was filled with arguing. Because she didn't want

Tod's parents Ambrose and Elizabeth Kozevnikoff, circa 1936, Tanana.
Courtesy of Tod Kozevnikoff.

me to report her activities during his absence, she sent me away with him on the next mail run. On that trip, I remember playing with the slot machines at Manley Hot Springs. When Dad realized that Mom was seeing an old school friend of his back at home, he began to drink more than usual.

Mom left our house and moved back across from the village of Tanana to her parental home at Eightmile Island on the Tanana River. Even though I was too young, before she left, she tried to farm me out to several families in the village and put me in school. When the teachers realized I was under age, I was returned to Gramma's at Eightmile. Finally my father sent for me and for my sister to live with him in Tanana. My grandmother put us in a canoe and paddled us across the wide confluence to Tanana. I wanted to return to my mother, but I did not know she was leaving Tanana with another man. When we arrived at our house in the village, my father was drunk. My grandmother threw a cup of cold water in his face and she left.

My sister was put in a good home, but I was left in our barren house with no food, a witness to my father's agony. He could maintain his job in the new radio tower at the Civilian Aviation Administration airfield station, but he seldom returned home to me and to sleep. I checked on my sister by peeking through the kitchen window of the house where she lived. I saw her washing dishes, after a meal.

I was four or five years old. I wandered the beach every day foraging for food. Daily, a neighbor with a fish wheel tossed fish viscera into his dog food

Lend-lease program during World War II, ferrying American planes to Russia to fight the Axis partners.

http://bravo369.net/warplanes-to-siberia-uncommon-allies

cooking pot. I skewered a few stomachs and roasted them over the fire. By day, I explored Fort Gibbon's old ruins and searched the beach for metal parts washed up by increased river traffic. If I found a scrap part, I took it to the kindly storeowner, who treated it like it was gold. He offered me candy and would start an often-repeated story with, "Did I ever tell you about … "

World War II jump-started our local economy. The lend-lease program offered American airplanes and aviation fuel to our Russian allies to help fight the Axis. Anyone with a boat or raft could get $1.50 or more per barrel of fuel when he delivered it from Nenana to Galena. Soldiers hemmed in a flotilla of 250 fuel drums with a wired-together spruce pole frame, to nudge it with an inboard launch down the Tanana. Once in the wider Yukon River, at the Tozitna River, soldiers combined the smaller rafts and made large flotillas of two thousand drums, which they pushed on to Galena. Frequently during a night supply run into the village of Tanana, a driver would mark his flotilla by setting a burning lantern on his raft to track it, ran his errands, and then caught up with the freight in the slow current. I spent my days pretending I too was driving a boat.

Center is Tod Kozevnikoff; to his left is Morris Thompson (who later became president of Doyon, Ltd,). To their side is a Byers Air Service plane, Tanana, circa 1950.

Courtesy of Tod Kozevnikoff.

126

A local relative who had been watching my way of life got word back to my grandmother. It wasn't long before my auntie came and took me home to Eightmile Island.

After I grew up, like my father, I worked on sternwheelers as a deckhand, and also like him, I tried to anesthetize my pain. For years, I lost myself in drinking bouts, which were laced with black depression. Today with that behind me, as a sixty-seven-year-old grandfather, I have begun to write. As a child, I knew the results of alcohol abuse, but without proper guidance, I was an innocent. I repeated the same alcoholic mistakes my father made. Children must be nurtured.

Today, the joy of our grandchildren fills our home. I hope to warn others that substituting "fun" for education, trying to heal life's pain with booze, only increases the problems. If I might be a signal in the dark, like the burning lantern on those flotillas of fuel drums, my story would be worth the telling.

Tod and Eileen Kozevnikoff, Fairbanks, circa 2007.
Courtesy of Tod Kozevnikoff.

Four years after our interview, on May 23, 2009, Tod Kozevnikoff passed away after a seven-year battle with cancer.

Timeline:
For thousands of years, Athabascan leaders gathered at Nuchalawoya.
1880: Tanakhotkhaik Athabascan village of 62. Arthur Harper established his Alaska Commercial Company.
1891: St James Episcopal mission established by Rev. Provost.
1897: Northern Commercial Company established below the mission.
1899-1923: Fort Gibbon built and operational.
1941-1945: Lend-lease (Public Law 77-11): planes to Russia to fight Axis.
1950s: The Air Force constructed a series of 18 radar sites throughout Alaska and a distant early warning (DEW) radar system and linked them with the White Alice long line communications system.
1962-late 1960s: After reorganizing, Tanana Chiefs Conference met at Tanana before moving to Fairbanks.
∞

My parents were Jacob and Alma Chullitlik Shavings. Where we lived in Mekoryuk on the north side of Nunivak Island, there was no school in those days; we lived in sod houses. In 1924, I, Qiiuran, was born in a sod house with six to eight inches of dried grass laid over a driftwood frame, covered with blocks of sod. Before the school was built, there were only three to four families in Mekoryuk.

During the winter, we wore a sealskin or reindeer skin parka. When it got cold, we put on sealskin pants. Sometimes we wore murre and other duck-skin parkas, which are pretty tough. For raingear, we wore anoraks of *oogruk* seal and walrus intestine.

Henry Shavings and Harry Mike at the village of Mekoryuk, Nunivak Island, circa 1949.

Courtesy of Hilma Shavings

Only the storekeeper, Paul Ivanoff, had a frame building, not a sod one. He was a Native trader from up north in charge of the reindeer on Nunivak. At Christmas, before we had a church or a school, Ivanoff honored even us. At that time, there was a distinction between a trader and the villagers. We didn't have a Christmas tree but we gathered driftwood, and we put it up together to look like a tree.

In 1910, before I was born, Ludvig Ost sailed from Sweden to Alaska as a Swedish Evangelical Mission Covenant missionary to Nome. In 1914, he established Elim Mission Roadhouse, a Covenant mission, orphanage, and school.

In 1936, Jacob Kenick, a Native missionary from Unalakleet, came to Nunivak to build a small church. Our parents didn't know about Christianity. They had their own gods to carry around to protect them. My dad gave me a kinda funny, kinda scary-looking ivory object to protect me. When we were growing up, the Swedish Covenant missionaries invited us to Sunday school where they gave us candy and taught us Bible verses as well as some choruses, so a seed was planted.

As a teenager, I worked in the Bristol Bay fish canneries. In the early 1940s, wages were bad: a month's work only paid two hundred dollars, but everything else was cheap too. Once when I left Bethel for the cannery, I had only four dollars. I was hungry and I bought some Oh, Henry! candy bars for five cents each.

Henry Shavings, motorboat to skiff, Mekoryuk Bay, circa 1957.
Courtesy of Hilma Shavings.

I saved my money from working at the Naknek cannery, and I got my own boat, the *Sea Messenger*. I began fishing off the Alaska Peninsula in Naknek and Egegik bays.

One beautiful day, I flew from Mekoryuk, Nunivak, with a stop at Tununak, Nelson Island, en route back to the cannery. There was no wind, but the airstrip was very short. The pilot kept cramming stuff into the two-engine Widgeon, and then behind, he squeezed the passengers in. I noticed that the pilot and co-pilot didn't test the motors as usual, but they just took off. After fifty feet, one engine quit; we dropped, hit the runway real hard, and then with the last engine running, we bounced back up. But the front of the airplane was going down; I could see the dirty ice and rocks of spring breakup coming closer and closer. Then, I heard, "Boom, boom!" followed by, "Is anybody hurt? Anyone alive?" We'd landed in the five-foot-deep river. One pilot's face was bleeding badly. The plane was upside down in the water with one wing torn off. The door was open and all the freight was washing down the current—mail sack, my suitcase, all was going down river. The pilot broke the window and began getting us out, one by one. I was pretty weak and I couldn't see very well. There was a lot of blood on top of my head. We were standing up to our waist in the current with snow and floating ice going by. We were taken to the local school until another plane could take us to the Bethel hospital. I was cut up, had smashed-up ribs, and I was pretty weak. Because I couldn't sleep—for some time—I went back and forth between the hospital; I was spitting up blood, and I was getting weaker all the time. I wasn't serving Christ then, but I knew I sure didn't want to go to hell. One day on the beach, I knelt down and prayed, "Lord, if you're up there, if you'll forgive all my mistakes, if you'll heal my body, I'll believe You." I prayed from the bottom of my heart, "I will serve You all the rest of my life." After that, I felt better, lighter, even though my body was still weak. Next time the doctor X-rayed me, he said, "You're okay." They sent me home; I was getting stronger. I ran to Jesus, and I started reading the Bible a lot.

At that time, I liked a girl, but she had poor morals. One day, I saw sixteen-year-old Hilma playing outdoors. She was good looking, and she had

Hilma Shavings, Fairbanks, 2007.
Judy Ferguson photo.

good parents. I asked her mom and daddy, "Let us marry?" Hilma only raised her eyebrows, and in our culture, that means, "Yes." A year later, when I was twenty-six, Hilma and I married.

Hilma began sharing her life and how her father came to Christ:

> *When my father came into town for supplies, the pastor explained to him about salvation. My father thought, "This is something strange, but it's better than what we got." At that time, our people had no hope, only fear. My father said, "This God they're talking about sets us free from fear." My dad loved tobacco but the pastor said it wasn't good for him, so he quit. Mom saw that this was a higher power and that it was something to pay attention to. She thought, "I've never seen him like this; he's got all this. Am I going to be left behind?" When the pastor visited the villages, he taught them how to sing. The first song my parents ever learned was, "Savior, You're More Than Life to Me."*
>
> *When I was sixteen, my dad had been trying to get me married, but I didn't like any of the men who asked me. Because of his conversion, Henry was different.*

Henry picked up the story:

For three years in the early 1950s, I went to Unalakleet Bible School where I learned English better, church history, counseling, health, guitar and banjo. Many wonderful things they taught me.

We were baptized in water, and one of the elders, a man of God, said "Henry, wherever you go now, nobody can stop you in your ministry." Every time I go somewhere, I go with that promise of permission, and the doors open. Once at the airport, there was a big gathering of senators returning home. One said, "Henry, sing for us!" I started singing, "Home, home, sweet home." They really liked it.

For five years, we volunteered as Covenant pastors in Scammon Bay and at Mekoryuk. After that, we started singing and began recording; a music ministry.

When our children were small, we moved to Anchorage where I began singing to patients in the Native hospital, going from room to room. Because the patients liked it so much, Hilma and our sons started joining me. But the crowd got so big—eighty to hundred people— that the fire marshals were concerned so we moved. Now we meet weekly with patients and visitors at the new Alaska Native Hospital's conference room, year-round.

Every morning wherever I am, I read my Bible; it really helps. I still fish in Egegik Bay. I make Eskimo wooden tools and sell them along with our music CDs at the state fairs. People know me as the "Singing Fisherman."

Henry Shavings, the Singing Fisherman.
Postcard courtesy of Henry Shavings.

Timeline:

1821: Russian discovery of Nuniwar by Captain Mikhail S. Vasilev, the first Westerner to contact the Nuniwarmiut.

1880: United States Revenue Steamer Corwin. Capt. C. L. Hooper went ashore. (Same cutter who shelled Angoon two years later.)

1897: Kuskokwim River Moravian missionary John H. Kilbuck visited, noting that the Nuniwarmiut were "a different tribe," with a "slightly different dialect."

1920: A limited U.S. Census recorded six settlements, total 189 people. Government introduced reindeer.

1928: Establishment of Nunivak Island (wildlife) Reservation.

1934: Musk oxen introduced.

∞

Chapter Fifteen

Precarious Home of Margaret Mary Ughitkuna Toshavik: King Island

When I first came to Alaska in 1965, I arrived in Nome for Thanksgiving break to visit my fiancé, an Alaska Airline employee. He took me to the south end of Nome's beach, site of the 1898—1899 gold rush. That November day, a King Island Iñupiaq man was dragging a seal from his beached boat to his home. "That's the chief," Michael said. "Let's go say 'Hi.'" That winter, the King Island school was closing permanently; families were relocating to Nome. Over the next few days as we visited, I saw seal skinning and ivory carving, a far cry from my life as a UCLA student. I was privileged to witness that unique interim time.

Forty-one years later while I was selling at an Anchorage Christmas bazaar, the daughter of King Islander Margaret Toshavik, Patricia, introduced herself and asked if I might interview her mother. Again, it was my privilege to hear Margaret tell her story.

Margaret Toshavik's father the chief of the King Islanders John Charles Olaranna, 1950.

Courtesy of Margaret Toshavik.

King Island, one mile wide, northwest of Nome, forty miles from Wales. Once home to 150-200 Inupiaq Aseuluk. Large white building at bottom is the former Bureau of Indian Affairs school.

1978 by Budd Christman, NOAA's America's Coastlines.

King Island is a steep island in the Bering Sea. One hundred fifty Iñupiaq (Ugiuvangmiut Eskimo) once lived there in forty houses on a twenty-foot-wide rock slide with an eighty-five-degree pitch to the ocean below. Our people used to paddle their skin boats (*umiaks*)

to Unalakleet and even up to Point Barrow to trade.

Thousands of birds land on our two-and-a-half-square-mile island, which is also covered with plants and berries. The sea is open July to October. We have big crabs, fish, walrus, and from their stomachs, we get a lot of clams, already cooked!

In 1778, Capt. Cook "discovered" our island and renamed it for one of his party, Lt. James King. Before 1850, we lived in half-underground homes with rock-tunnel entrances. Then, on driftwood pads, the people built double-walled homes of walrus hides, insulated with dried grass. One old house of walrus skin was still there through the early 1930s.

Margaret Toshavik's mother, Madeleine Asenna Olaranna, 1914.
Courtesy of Margaret Toshavik.

Ten years before I was born, our people built a church just above our houses. In the 1920s, the Bureau of Education wanted us to move to St. Lawrence Island, but my father firmly resisted.

I was born in 1925 on Ukivok, King Island, eighty-five miles northwest of Nome, to John Charles Olaranna and Madeleine Asenna Olaranna. In the 1930s, my dad built us a lumber house. We got our water from a creek in the summer.

Clinging to near-vertical cliffs of King Island is the village of Ugiuvak, built on driftwood stilts, The eighteenth century huts had walls of walrus skin until milled lumber became available.
1927, Library of Congress Curtis (Edward S.) Collection

135

My father, born around 1883, hunted seal, walrus, polar bear, birds, swans, and sometimes black whales. When the birds fly north, they always come to King Island. Kids went up the hills hunting those auklets and puffins. My father used to tie a rope around my waist, give me a bag, and then let me down the cliff to gather those small but good eggs. When I filled the bag, I pulled on the rope. I tried to pick a nest area with a nearby ravine where I could help push because when they pulled me up, it stung and ached. That was scary.

Men always went hunting and women always picked berries and greens for winter. Way up the other side of the hill, we get blackberries and lots of salmonberries. There are three greens we like. We sour one and preserve all three in seal oil. Wintertime, we make Eskimo ice cream using berries for sweetener.

A quarter of a mile from the village, we had a huge, double-chambered ice cave with steps spiraling up many levels. My sister and I used to take a gas lamp and take meat wrapped in skins to store in that cave. In wintertime or when it was storming, we would swing inside and play in the cave.

My mom used to dry peat moss to burn for fuel and also to make a soft wick for light. When she made seal oil, she washed three or four pieces of seal blubber and then put them in a barrel. With a po-

Chief Olaranna with Father Bernard Hubbard the glacier priest as his nephew Ken Chisholm paints "Agfa" on the chief's skin boat to make a trip to Point Barrow, 1938, Nome.

Photographer: Ray B. Dame,Ickes Coll, AMRC-b75-175-371, Anchorage Museum. Courtesy of Margaret Toshavik.

lar bear jawbone, she beat the seal blubber down, making it soft. When some came up, she put it in another pot and cooked it over a seal oil lamp. Later we used a little German kerosene stove and finally, a gas stove.

The men had a community house. They burned driftwood in the middle and piled up rocks, bathed, and told stories. My father was a good dancer, and he was funny too. But one scary story they told was about seeing Eyes. An old lady had been gathering greens when she fell down a cliff. Afterward, when people were out on the sea crabbing, they heard hollering from the sea and saw her eyes. One time when Dad was crabbing, he saw that lady. Water was filling up his hold; he was sinking. He said to the old lady, "Let's go home!"

Chief Olaranna dancing.
Fred Machetanz painting.
Courtesy of
Margaret Toshavik.

And he went home, back to King Island. But in 1937, after Father (Bernard R.) Hubbard brought the picture of Christ the King to us, we never saw those eyes or heard those voices again.

During the winter, my mother taught me how to cleat bearded seal (*oogruk*) hide into rounded soles for mukluks with my teeth. I also made sinew thread for my father's skin boat. Before stretching a new walrus hide over the boat frame, we treated the wood with seal oil to prevent rot. My father taught me to drill ivory with the mouth drill, and I made little ulu earrings and puffin and polar bear miniatures also.

My father used to go to Point Hope; Father Hubbard asked him to take missionaries there in his skin boat. So when I was twelve, we all went by skin boat from Nome to Point Hope. That was the first time the King Islanders went there.

Every summer, as soon as walrus hunting and greens-gathering were finished, we left for Nome in my father's four-family-size skin boat. (Those old people knew when the weather was going to be fair and when the sea would be calm.) During our three- to four-month summer absence, our sled dogs would take care of themselves. They fed on the birds and their eggs. It took us about thirteen hours to get to Nome in our large walrus-skin boat.

My father bought a Quonset hut house on Nome's east end for us. There, we carved ivory to sell to get food for winter. My dad worked as a longshoreman. If the dock needed handlers, they'd wake Dad early, asking for King Island people.

My father helped anyone who needed it; he was like a doctor. We used stinkweed, *sukuluk*, to heal every-

General Eisenhower with Chief Olaranna, 1941, Nome.
Courtesy of Margaret Toshavik.

137

Women and children on rocky King Island in 1952. Margaret is at left, packing her daughter Carmelita.

Courtesy of Margaret Toshavik.

thing, and it grew all over the island. My father delivered babies as well as being a hunter.

During the early war years, about 1939 to 1943, we weren't allowed to go to Nome and we had to stay on King Island. After the Indian Reorganization Act of 1934, which required Native people to form village councils and elect chiefs,

Margaret Toshavik holding photos of her parents with her daughter Patricia and husband Carl Toshavik, 2006, Anchorage.

Judy Ferguson photo.

my father was made chief from 1939 to 1946. He was also a part of the Eskimo Scouts organized by "Muktuk" Marston. When General Eisenhower visited us, my father met with him. Those war years made a big impact on the Iñupiaq.

I was in school until eighth grade. (It was hard to get teachers on King Island.) After I married, my husband worked at the school, so our house had two rooms, a good oil stove, and a couple of double mattresses.

In 1959 by the time I had four of my nine children, I left

King Island. In 1965–1966, the Bureau of Indian Affairs decided to close our school.

Today my husband, Carl, and I have a tent house twenty-three miles by boat from Nome, where I still pick my greens and berries. Every year, my son returns to King Island to walrus hunt, but I have not seen my house since 1959. Back in the 1940s, Father Hubbard used to worry that the rocks would fall and crush our houses. But after all these years, those big rocks are still there. Must be an angel is holding them up!

Margaret Toshavik on her mother's back, 1925, King Island.

Courtesy of Margaret Toshavik.

Bernard Rosecrans Hubbard, S.J. (1888-1962), legendary explorer, photographer, lecturer, and priest who led annual expeditions to Alaska from 1927 until shortly before his death, Hubbard became known to a national audience as "The Glacier Priest."

As an explorer, Father Hubbard used Santa Clara University, his alma mater and professional home for nearly forty years, as his base camp and the territory of Alaska as his destination. In 1931, Literary Digest *described Father Hubbard's work in this way: "Half the year the highest-paid lecturer in the world, the other half a wanderer among treacherous craters and glaciers."*

He spent part of 1937 and 1938, one year, on King Island studying the Arctic Iñupiaq. He wrote several books and compiled an Eskimo dictionary that included the story of Christ, a catechism, and prayers of the Catholic Church.

Timeline:

1778: Capt. Cook "discovered" King Island

1898–99: Nome gold rush.

1965-1966: Bureau of Indian Affairs closed the King Island school.

Circa 1970: King Island abandoned when the last villagers moved to the mainland.

∞

Chapter Sixteen

Black River Trapper Fred Thomas, Fort Yukon

In the fall of 2005, I flew with Janet Curtiss and Chief David Salmon to Fort Yukon for the installation of the newly elected chief, Fred Thomas' nephew Bruce Thomas. My hostess, Fred's sister-in-law Grace Thomas, introduced me to Fred, a respected elder and a lifelong trapper. During the 1920s and 1930s, Fred and his brother John grew up on the Black River, upstream from Fort Yukon. One afternoon at home, Fred shared his family's story.

Fred Thomas' nephew Chief Bruce Thomas and Chief David Salmon, Fort Yukon, 2005.
Judy Ferguson photo.

The oldest of Jacob Thomas and Margaret Schaeffer's nine boys, I was born in 1919 on the Porcupine River.

In 1898, as soon as my father, Jacob Thomas, was free from service in the Spanish-American War, he headed north to the Klondike. With a history as a riverboat pilot on the Mississippi River, he was able to get a crewing job on a steamboat to Alaska. When he arrived in Dawson, it was too late to get a good claim, so he decided to try trapping. At Fort Yukon, he found a partner, Paul Henry. In the fall, they lined a boat of supplies up the Black River. It took them a month to arrive at what became our home.

In 1902, my mother, Margaret, was born to a Gwich'in from Old Crow and a trapper from Alberta, Albert Schaeffer.

In those days, there were a lot of people in the woods. Every twenty miles or so, on a lake or a crick, there was a cabin and a family. A few prospectors settled in our area. When one developed scurvy, he crawled into his boat and died at what is now called Deadman's Riffle.

I grew up on the Black River about twenty miles below the mouth of the Grayling River.

At first, my family didn't do a garden but after awhile, we put in a pretty good one.

140

A couple of times, we got as much as five hundred to six hundred pounds of spuds. Every fall, Mother layered cranberries and sugar in a seven-gallon barrel. That's one thing; we had a lot of sugar. Sometimes, we made cranberry jam. Dad got a winter grubstake of rice, sugar, tobacco, and tea, which we supplemented with fish, game, and berries. We had no salmon, but we had pike and whitefish. Year-round, we netted fish with a gill net and dried the fish whole. From

Fred Thomas' father's partner Paul Henry and Fred Thomas' mother Margaret, 1930s, Fort Yukon.
Courtesy of Harry and Grace Thomas.

the middle fin to the head, we could eat suckers, but their tails are full of tiny bones. The belief was that, years ago, animals were once human. It was said that the man who became a sucker used to steal everything. One of the things he picked up was a bag of porcupine quills. Hence when he became a sucker, his bag of quills became a tail full of bones!

Sometimes Mother went to Fort Yukon to have her babies, but other times she had them in the woods. However, her only girl, my two-month-old sister, died after a German measles outbreak.

I understand Gwich'in pretty good. As a child, everyone around here kinda spoke Gwich'in but Mother spoke English to us all the time. My dad did not speak Gwich'in but they had a good, thirty-six-year marriage anyway.

When I was very young, my folks boarded me and two of my brothers at the St. Stephen's mission in Fort Yukon, where I finished third grade. After that, we learned to read and write at home from our father. There was no time for school; we had to trap or starve.

On our trapline we had a couple cabins, but my father used mostly tents. (Before chainsaws, it was easier to use tents than to build a cabin.) One of his lines had six campsites—it took nine days to check the sets—and we also had a couple of other lines as well. From the lakes, we followed a range of hills down to the village of Chalkyitsik. After we hit the river, we continued upstream and then returned through the lakes.

We sold our furs at the three stores in Fort Yukon: the Northern Commercial Co., Carter's store, and Jimmy Carroll's. Every winter a Jewish fur buyer, John Swagler—"Johnny Muskrat"—flew in from Fairbanks.

In the summers we came to Fort Yukon, where my father would sometimes work odd jobs. The first moving pictures that came to Fort Yukon were westerns. We used to play cowboy all the time. We brothers, me, Billy, Johnny, Harry, Emil, Charley, and Albert were known as the "Black River cowboys"! We made chaps out of green window shades and had a couple of hats too. We used willow branches to defend ourselves against "the bad guys," the "bees"

On left, Fred Thomas and partner with wolverine, fox, beaver, wolf, 1944, Black River.
Courtesy of Fred Thomas.

(yellowjackets) that we found in cans. Someone always got stung. Once it was so bad, I couldn't see out of my eye.

When I was old enough, I began setting number one traps for weasels. I began trapping with the old man. However, after a long day, when we stopped for the night—even though we were exhausted—we'd have to pitch a tent. I'd think to myself, "If I ever trap, I'm going to build cabins," and I did.

All winter, my six surviving brothers and I trapped. In 1943, I built a home up the north fork of the Grayling River. Whenever possible, I built trap cabins near rivers.

Before freeze-up, I'd head up the river, pull my boat out, and there I'd be for the winter. I traveled twelve to fifteen miles a day with seven to eight dogs. I had six cabins on my line; it took nine days to check the sets. In May, my brothers and I put our furs on the barge and returned to Fort Yukon to buy food and supplies for the winter. We got paid about $70 each for a "lynk,"

[lynx] sometimes $78. But in 1955, the price dropped. For a hundred lynk, we only got $4.21 each!

In the 1950s, my father had to go to the Hudson Stuck hospital in Fort Yukon for tuberculosis. At his request, I took him back home up the Black River where he died that fall.

With the exception of two years spent in a Tucson tuberculosis sanatorium, I trapped every year. Not long after I returned, I married Charlotte Williams and we began our family of six children. When our oldest child, Shirley, was school age, we had to move to Fort Yukon. But I trapped all my life, even when

Fred Thomas and daughter Shirley (holding ermine skins) with an enormous amount of fur: lynx, wolverine, fox, wolf, and marten pelts in 1955, when the bottom fell out of the fur market.

Courtesy of Fred Thomas.

I worked eighteen years for the 709th AC&W [Aircraft Control and Warning] base with the DEW Line.

When my job on base was over, I went back up the Black River. My brother, Alfred, had a cabin there. Instead of competing, I said, "Why don't we become partners?" So for four years, we were. The first year, we got eighty-three lynk. There had been a big fire; the rabbits were coming back good, plus nobody had been trapping there. The next year, we got 135 lynk, then 215, followed the third year by 315!

The fourth year, one day while I was off my sled, checking a set, my dogs scented a moose and took off. When they disappeared over a hill, I knew it was pointless so I walked all the way home. Later I found out that the day before a friend on a neighboring trapline had seen a wolf. When he spotted a couple of my runaway dogs, he thought he had a couple of wolves and he

but it was derailed by pressing national matters. The control of Alaska's natural resources wasn't considered "critical."

Salmon canneries in the Pacific Northwest using large fish traps had caused the near-destruction of Alaska's salmon runs. What amounted to the canneries' exclusive "right of fishery" with little taxation typified Alaska's colonial frustrations.

A fisherman and merchant, Frank Peratrovich, a six-foot two-inch Tlingit-Croat from Prince of Wales Island, knew firsthand the issues both of racial discrimination and the Outside canneries' monopoly. Peratrovich was the son of a Tlingit mother, Mary Skan, and a Croatian-born cannery manager, John Peratrovich. He was born in 1895 in Klawock, before Indians were even considered citizens. Peratrovich became a part of the Alaska Native Brotherhood (ANB), where he learned parliamentary procedure. He was educated at Chemawa Indian School in Oregon then Haskell Institute in Kansas. After serving as the grand president of ANB, he referred to a popular perception: "I wasn't singly responsible for the Natives' right to vote but I certainly supported it."

As a leader of the Southeast Seineboat Owners and Operators Association, Peratrovich fought against the monopoly of the Washington-Oregon canneries. In 1944, the seiners backed Peratrovich for election to the territorial House of Representatives.

When he wasn't fighting the monopolies, Peratrovich, his brother, Roy, and his sister-in-law, Elizabeth Peratrovich, worked to end discrimination in housing and public places. In 1945 they saw Governor Gruening sign into law their equal rights legislation, preceding the nation's by nineteen years.

By 1947 Peratrovich was a senator, and the following year he introduced the Fish Trap Referendum bill, calling for a popular vote. The ballot result was 19,712 against fish traps and only 2,624 in favor, sending a strong signal for self government and telling the national lobbies that their control was due for a change.

During the critical 1949 special session, Peratrovich was senate president when tax legislation was enacted on all businesses that derived their income from Alaska, including the transportation and fishing industries. This taxation helped support the territory and nationally demonstrated Alaska's ability to govern itself. In the following regular session, Peratrovich and Victor C.

Alaska Senate President Frank Peratrovich, Representative Jack Coghill, and unknown, circa 1954, Juneau.

Courtesy of Frank Jr. and Nettie Peratrovich.

Rivers proposed a bill forming the Alaska Statehood Committee, consisting of eleven members including Peratrovich. Frustrated over inadequate roads, poor airfields, meager tuberculosis hospitals, undependable and expensive shipping, and lack of national defense and security, Alaskans pushed to have two senators and a representative each with a vote in Washington, D.C.

In that effort, Anchorage lawyer Wendell P. Kay in 1953 introduced a bill calling for a constitutional convention, which failed.

In his State of the Union address, President Eisenhower in 1954 favored statehood for (Republican) Hawaii but not for (Democratic) Alaska. When asked, Eisenhower denied that partisan politics might be the motive. With nothing to lose, Alaskans formed Operation Statehood with Victor Fischer, Thomas B. Stewart, Niilo Koponen, and Territorial Senator John Butrovich to organize and begin research on constitution writing.

"Not many people in Alaska," Stewart said, "understood about how to write a constitution." On his own, Stewart left his job and traveled Outside to interview political scientists and experts in government regarding writing a constitution. Learning of the National Municipal League's Model Constitution, rooted in Eisenhower's State Constitutional Reform Movement, he became familiar with methods of routing power back to the state level. He established connections with the Public Administrative Service (PAS), which later provided the convention with constitutional studies and reference guides. In his research, Stewart was advised that Alaska should host its constitutional convention away from Juneau lobbyists and cloister in a university equipped with a library immersed in an academic atmosphere. He returned home, intimately informed on hosting a constitutional convention.

Wanting delegates representative of all Alaska, the legislature devised a special apportionment plan to elect delegates to ensure territory-wide representation.

Constitutional committee. Center, middle row: convention vice president Frank Peratrovich to the left of convention president Egan. Below photo, signatures of each member. University of Alaska, Fairbanks, 1956.

Courtesy of Jack Coghill.

November 8, 1955, fifty-five delegates gathered at the University of Alaska Fairbanks. Delayed three days by bad weather, traveling one thousand miles from Klawock to Fairbanks, Frank Peratrovich, the only Native delegate, arrived. Even while absent, Peratrovich was elected the convention's first vice president.

Jack Coghill and Frank Peratrovich studying considerations, Constitutional Convention, 1955–56, Fairbanks.

Courtesy of Jack Coghill

Convention president William Egan, a master politician and organizer, called upon former Territorial Gov. Ernest Gruening, who began, "Its greatest importance . . . [is] that [this] . . . is the first occasion which is wholly of, for, and most important, *by* the people of Alaska."

Congressional delegate Bartlett pointed out, "fifty years from now . . . people . . . may very well judge the product of this convention by the decision taken upon the vital issue of resources policy. . . . Only a minute fraction of the land area is owned by private persons or corporations. . . . Never before . . . has there been so great an opportunity to establish a resources policy geared to the growth of a magnificent economy and the welfare of a people."

For the next seventy-five days and through fifty-below temperatures, the gathering of merchants, lawyers, fishermen, housewives, homesteaders, and miners, representing two hundred thousand Alaskans, became statesmen, writing a document more appropriate to its time and place than any other state constitution.

Potential dilemmas facing the delegates were whether to have a unicameral versus bicameral legislature, the apportionment of the legislators from the Bush and urban areas, whether to have a strong executive, how to select judges, voting age, the complexity of local government, voting qualification, and the relatively new topic of indigenous land claims and their selection.

In debating about whether a voter should be required to be able to read, write, and speak English, Peratrovich, a member of the Suffrage, Elections, and Apportionment committee, wanted to limit suffrage requirements to "read or speak" only. He added that in his area some "can write their name . . . but . . . not letters." He reminded the committee, "These people are citizens entitled by the 1924 congressional act . . . and vote under that provision and should continue to do so."

Regarding indigenous land claims, Marvin R. "Muktuk" Marston, organizer and leader of the Eskimo Scouts, said, "Justice demands that something be done to help the Native people" (forty percent of the population) with their land rights. "The proposed Marston amendment," George McLaughlin re-

148

Marvin R. "Muktuk" Marston, organizer and leader of the Eskimo Scouts, said, "Justice demands that something be done to help the Native people" (forty percent of the population) with their land rights," and submitted "The proposed Marston amendment."

Constitutional Convention Delegate Photographs, UAF-1983-185-27

sponded, "would create a completely new set of property rights" that would cast a cloud over "every title in the Territory." After much discussion, the amendment was dropped. (This lack has been called the greatest failure of the constitution.) The legitimacy of land claims was, however, mentioned in the General Provisions article, deferring resolution of indigenous land claims to the federal government.

On the sixty-fifth day, Peratrovich pointed out that delegates with mining interests had protected Alaska's minerals from exploitation. After a debate on the correctness of including the question of fish traps in the constitution, Burke Riley, Eldor Lee, Seaborn Buckalew, W. O. "Bo" Smith, and Frank Peratrovich decided to include it rather in a separate ordinance on the statehood ballot. "It was a marvelous idea," chief clerk Katherine Alexander Hurley observed. Peratrovich summed up later, "It proved to be the linchpin in getting the Southeast vote out for statehood."

Although Hawaii had a constitution, it had not achieved statehood. Knowing more was needed, delegates listened to George Lehleitner, a New Orleans advocate for Hawaiian statehood, who advocated including the Tennessee Plan on Alaska's statehood ballot. Sidestepping an enabling act from Congress, the vote would elect provisional delegates to approach Congress, following the example of six previously successful states in their statehood bids, including Tennessee. On February 5, 1956, William Egan signed the Alaska constitution in the University of Alaska gymnasium.

For three years, disappointment dogged the delegates. With some concern about impending civil rights legislation, a national coalition of Republicans and "Dixiecrats" kept blocking the passage of an Alaska statehood bill. Delegate Bob Bartlett, the Tennessee Plan delegation, newly elected Senator William Egan, Senator Ernest Gruening, and Representative Ralph Rivers lobbied Congress vigorously. Finally, with the national coalition weakening, Congress passed the statehood bill on June 30, 1958. President Eisenhower signed the official proclamation making Alaska the forty-ninth state on January 3, 1959.

Fifty years later, former Republican delegate Jack B. Coghill reflected, "The form of government we set up in 1955 has worked well, serving both urban and rural Alaskans."

University of Alaska professor of political science and author Dr. Gerald McBeath added, "Our founding framers constructed principles of effective government, observable by all. Patterning our constitution after the American constitution, they created a basic foundational document for state governance, guiding the state legislature's development. They did not lock up areas of concern in tight language for all time."

Judge Andrew Kleinfeld of the United States Court of Appeals for the Ninth Circuit (selected federally, not under the Alaska Constitution) observed, "Alaska's constitution and system of selecting judges works better than that of other states. Our system of using a judicial council, bar poll, and gubernatorial appointment of judges attracts a higher quality of judicial aspirants and shields our judges from excessive politicization. Also, the practice of law in our Department of Law is less political, compared to states where the attorney general's office may be a political stepping stone to other statewide elective office.

"Since the Alaska Constitution has worked (in these areas I know best)," the judge concluded, "it should probably be left alone."

Agreeing with Kleinfeld, Dr. McBeath observed, "Needs, passions, and events of the people change from day to day. Those majority issues should be brought before and sifted by the legislature rather than expressed in constitutional amendments. Indeed, the constitution should go beyond majority passions and not react to perceived 'emergency issues' of the day."

Jack Coghill concurred: "The document's strength was its simplicity and flexibility. Other state constitutions," he pointed out, "direct government. We, Alaska citizens, gave power to the local government, to the people, rather than to a centralized government.

"Due to our lessons learned from the fish trap issue, no industry," he emphasized, "has ever been able to over-harvest us."

"Today on our fiftieth anniversary," [in 2009] Jack Coghill concluded, "only four of the convention delegates are living: Seaborn J. Buckalew, George W. Sundborg, Victor Fischer, and me." Adding, "In 1984, a day before Alaska's twenty-fifth statehood anniversary, Frank Peratrovich died on January 4."

Fifty years ago, Democrat and Republican, Peratrovich and Coghill, among the eight delegates born in Alaska, worked with the other fifty-three delegates for home rule, to prevent the exploitation of Alaska that she might forever retain her freedom and rugged beauty for the ages yet to come.

"Alaska State Constitutional Convention" *was first published in the state's only official statehood anniversary publication,* Alaska 50: Celebrating Alaska's 50th Anniversary of Statehood 1959–2009.

Frank Peratrovich Sr. (1895-1984), Ketchikan.
Ketchikan Daily News, January 7, 1984. Courtesy of Frank Jr. and Nettie Peratrovich.

Chapter Eighteen

God on the air, Gen and Don Nelson, KJNP

In the late 1960s through 1980s, while we were raising our children on our remote homestead, every night we listened to Trapline Chatter on KJNP, when it broadcast one-way messages to those living in the Bush.

In 1997, Don Nelson,

Gen and Don Nelson, founders of KJNP, North Pole, circa 1980.

Courtesy of Gen Nelson.

the founder of KJNP, passed away. A year later, when I was interviewing Alice Carroll in Circle, she mentioned how sad she was that since Don had died no one flew in to see them anymore. Moments later as KJNP's Village Voice came on, she put her hand on the radio and stopped the interview for an hour to listen to the singing and testimonials.

Nine years later, in their 170-by-140-foot log cabin radio station, Don's wife, Genevieve Lorraine Thompson Nelson, known as Gen, shared with me the story of KJNP and of her life with Don Nelson.

Don and I were both born in 1923 in Minneapolis. I knew Don all of my life. Our parents were close friends and non-Christians. In 1942, after Don graduated as an auto and airplane mechanic, he got a job working on the Alaska Highway. He was stationed at old Fort Nelson, Yukon Territory, but it was so cold there that he quit, saying it was "not fit for dogs." However, quitting made him vulnerable to the draft.

Don Nelson and a young Stevens Village man play guitars in the Nelson home, circa 1956.

Courtesy of Gen Nelson.

After we married, Don joined the army. He was assigned as a ball turret gunner in the belly of a B-17, shuttle-bombing across Europe. On his twenty-fourth mission, he was

Stevens Village dog team, 1957.
Courtesy of Gen Nelson.

shot down over Berlin. As a prisoner of war, he was marched for eighty-two days back and forth across Germany. He became a gaunt shadow, weighing only seventy-eight pounds. After the Allies liberated Germany, Don and other prisoners plunged into a petty thieving and drinking spree. Later, badly damaged from his plane's explosion, sick with hepatitis, deprivation, and exposure, Don was hospitalized in the states. Nevertheless, he continued drinking.

In 1946, our daughter, Judy, was born. During the following years, Don drank heavily and lived an erratic lifestyle. I made plans to divorce him.

One day, close friends invited us to Soul's Harbor Church in Minneapolis to hear Pastor Gordon K. Petersen. At the end of the service, Don, convicted by the Holy Spirit, went forward to the altar. I knew then that my plans for divorce had just been derailed. A few days

Man reading the Bible to young girl in Stevens Village, circa 1956.
Courtesy of Gen Nelson.

later, I got down on my knees and said to the Lord, "If you can change Don, then you can do that for me too. We could raise our daughter together."

After we were both saved and as Don waited on the Lord, he felt we were called to go north to minister, not to old Fort Nelson but somewhere similar, to work with the Indians. At first he resisted, but eventually he softened. After we got our ministerial papers from the Evangelistic Missionary Fellowship, we drove up the AlCan Highway. In 1956, we moved to the Gwich'in Indian commu-

Man in regalia coming out of snowy, dark building, ca. 1956, Stevens Village.
Courtesy of Gen Nelson.

152

Christmas play in a Jamesway hut, lighted by generator-run, single bulb in the portable military building, circa 1957, Stevens Village.
Courtesy of Gen Nelson.

nity of Stevens Village, which you can only reach by airplane or boat.

In the community of eighty people and three hundred dogs, we were accepted warmly. One summer in the nearby village of Venetie, our daughter, Judy, taught Sunday school. In her class, she had a cute little Gwich'in boy, Gary Simple, who spoke no English. Judy asked one of the grandmas to translate for Gary, not knowing that one day Gary would become an evangelist.

We lived in Stevens for seven years, hosting vacation Bible schools in the nearby villages. Don flew his plane and networked across the North. One Christmas, when weather prohibited him from flying, he transmitted his message to the people through a Fairbanks radio station. He began to realize that a radio station would reach more villages than he could through flying.

A Christian who had homesteaded and also subdivided seven hundred acres of prime land in the North Pole area, David Ainley, felt he should give some of his land between Fort Wainwright and Eielson Air Force Base to the church. The following summer, David and his pastor met us at a camp meeting in Fort Yukon. Together,

Don Nelson with his airplane, circa 1970.
Courtesy of Gen Nelson.

David, Don, and I went over his map of his subdivision, discussed and came to a decision where to build.

I was also praying for a bookkeeper. A young missionary, Bonnie Carriker, came to us. She had lost her husband in the 1964 Good Friday earthquake. She took a refresher course in bookkeeping and moved in with her two children. For every void, God sent us qualified men and women.

David Ainley was the first to move into the men's log dormitory. He answered phones. He passed the Federal Communications Commission tests and learned to become a board operator.

For training, Don and I toured a radio station in San Jose, California, and took notes. The head of a Cleveland electronics school walked us through our initial setup. Billy Graham's business manager helped us learn programming. Our growing staff studied and got their broadcasting licenses. Today, qualifying would be much more rigorous.

In 1966, Dick and Bev Olson joined us and helped us build cabins for staff. I fed our growing "family" in my home.

Initially, we wanted to go on the air with 50,000 watts, but we weren't allowed. On October 11, 1967, we began broadcasting during the day with 10,000 watts and 5,000 at night.

Don and Gen Nelson transmitting over new radio station, circa 1973.

Courtesy of Gen Nelson.

Over the years, Don made 150 trips down the AlCan to raise funds and to bring back needed equipment. David Ainley accompanied him on several of his trips. Frequently on Saturdays while

traveling the AlCan, Don would broadcast his progress in a special program, "Over the Coffee Cup."

We wanted to transmit at 50,000 watts. In 1970 we were required to go directional, but we had to put up a second tower. But before we could go on the air, someone cut the second tower's guy wires.

Don and Gen Nelson at KJNP radio station cabin after Don completed hundred trips down the AlCan, hauling supplies for KJNP.

Courtesy of Gen Nelson.

The man planned for the second tower to hit the first tower so both would fall on the sod roof of our log station. However, the tower spun and came back, careening toward the man. He ran so hard that his palm prints smashed into the dirt as the tower fell to the side of him.

KJNP is an interdenominational station and has always specialized in country gospel, a sound Alaska Natives love. When townspeople complained about

154

Don Nelson transmitting, circa 1990.
Courtesy of Gen Nelson.

the genre, we said, "Okay, we'll go FM and play mainstream Christian music, but you have to support it." So in 1977 we went FM. Four years later, we developed our television station.

Since we are now required to go digital with our AM, FM, TV, and outstations, we must now raise more funds, $1.5 million.

Once while in the Fort Yukon airport, Don overheard some Native men slandering whites. Don walked up and said, "You know, I'm a white man." They said, "Whoa, you may be white, Don Nelson, but you got an Indian heart." That summed it up. Don had a love and a burden for them, and they knew it.

Another time during a New Year's Eve all-night broadcast, a child was reported missing in Kotzebue. Immediately both a search and intercession began. In the morning, the child was miraculously found alive, face down in a light jacket under the snow on the frozen beach.

When we first arrived in Alaska, people asked us how long we might stay. I would say, "Oh, one or two years." It's now been forty-nine years.

In 2009, eighty-five-year-old Gen Nelson went to be with the Lord. In her online obituary written by Jeff Richardson of the Fairbanks Daily News-Miner, he described the Nelsons' initial move to Stevens Village: "The family immediately made an impression with the grit and perseverance that became their trademark. They spent more than seven

Don Nelson in boat during spring flood in Fort Yukon, 1982.

Courtesy of Gen Nelson.

155

years in the isolated village, minister-
ing in an area where some residents
didn't speak English."

The article continued, "Ann Goessel
remembered the Nelsons arriving in
Stevens Village when she was about
ten years old, and said, 'It has always
been amazing to me that these people
gave up their city-slicker life to go to an
all-Native village. They lived just like
we did—no electricity, no running
water. I thank God that they came to
minister to our people. They really changed our lives."

Don Nelson and the head of the Alaskan
Independence Party Joe Vogler, KJNP lobby,
circa 1989.

Courtesy of Gen Nelson.

Richardson went on, "Because so much of the state is rural, and with Don and
Gen living in Stevens Village, they realized there was a huge need and hunger for
Christian programs. They started working on the paperwork to establish KJNP as
a licensed radio station."

He quoted, "Goessel remembered the family operating a 'baby radio station' out
of their home. It offered just enough of a weak signal to bathe the tiny village in
Christian songs and stories, along with an assortment of homespun local greetings.
Goessel, who referred to Gen as 'Grandma Gen,' said her legacy will live on in the
many people she influenced with her Christian message. And added, 'The power of
those crackly static-ridden radio messages made an impression.'"

Richardson continued, "State Sen. Gene Therriault, who grew up in North
Pole, remembered, 'They built the first radio sta-
tion in, at the time, what really was the woods. The
community of course grew up around the station.'"

The obituary concluded, "Julie Beaver, a KJNP
employee since 1981, said of Gen Nelson, 'I've
never seen anyone more dedicated. The ministry at
KJNP was her life.'"

Gen Nelson remembering their
years ministering in Alaska,
KJNP, 2006.

Judy Ferguson photo.

156

Chapter Nineteen

Utopian moves: Niilo Koponen

Niilo Koponen's civic involve-ment and institutional memory began in territorial days, but his schooling reached further back, with graduate work at the London School of Economics and a Ph.D. from Harvard.

I first met Niilo and Joan Koponen in Fairbanks in 1968, but in 2006, their names again came up as I interviewed DeLois Ketzler Burggraf. She explained that her father, Charlie Purvis, an early activist, had worked with Niilo Koponen under the

Niilo and Joan Koponen at their cabin on the Chena Ridge homestead near Fairbanks in the 1980s.
Courtesy of Niilo Koponen.

umbrella of the Alaska Native Rights Association and then as the Alaska Party. I wanted to hear Niilo's story, so I arranged to meet with the seventy-eight-year-old in his home. His wife, Joan, had suffered a debilitating car accident and was play-ing cards in the next room. Niilo Koponen sat quietly in their long-time home and shared his story.

My parents were of eastern Finnish descent and met each other at Finn Hall in Harlem in New York City. At the high point of the economic boom, I was born in the Bronx in March 1928. My father worked at Bell Laboratories, where employees were not pro-tected from harmful radiation, which caused my father to develop cataracts. After the stock market crashed, he was laid off. For a decade, he struggled with poor vision and trying to find work.

I grew up in a five-story cooperative apartment filled with Finnish- and Yiddish-speaking neighbors. Together, we worked in a communal garden and bought at a local co-op. We socialized at Finn Hall, where my mother was an actress (but during the Depression, she worked for real money as a domestic). My dad was a stage manager, but they were only paid with meal tickets.

When I was five, my grandmother took me to the John Rockefeller Jr. fam-ily, for whom she worked as a domestic in Tarrytown. In the Rockefeller mansion, I had once seen an elevated toy train for the younger Rockefellers; it ran on an eighteen–inch-high elevated track. I was searching for it, going from room to room, when I ran into John D. Rockefeller Sr., sitting in a chair. He was in his nineties and looked like Pharaoh's mummy. He asked, "Whose little boy is this?" I got the heck out of there; I didn't wait for the dime I later heard he gave to kids.

I attended a public school, PS 82. In those days, the teachers had to pass an elocution exam, proving they could speak standard BBC English. In kindergarten, I imitated them, saying "eye-thur," rather than "eether." I had an awakening when the kids from the Bronx exclaimed, "Wat's a' mattuh wit yous? You tryin' to be snotty or sumpin?"

One week, after winning a Sunday school contest, a multicultural street gang of us began visiting churches, making the rounds, discussing issues. Because I was a good student, I qualified for one of New York City's progressive and multiracial high schools, which offered fine arts opportunities to low-income kids. During the World War II era, we got one of our Negro buddies elected as school body president.

Most people I knew were either New Deal Democrats or Norman Thomas socialists. Even the Republicans were progressives, like New York Mayor Fiorello "The Little Flower" LaGuardia.

After I graduated, I got a job at the Eastern Co-op Wholesale Warehouse on 145th. I met my first Quaker there, an older handicapped woman who was also my boss. Her views on nonviolence interested me. She told me that early stands for integration began during the Civil War with the Quakers, who fought not only slavery but also for women's rights.

During World War II, the Soviet Union bombed and seized my parents' ancestral home, Finnish Karelia. Not waiting to see what Stalin had in mind, thousands moved into central Finland, where they were allowed to homestead on church-owned land.

At the end of the war, I crystallized into a pacifist when the United States dropped the atomic bomb on Hiroshima and Nagasaki, killing more than one hundred thousand civilians. I applied for conscien-

"I bought this car for twenty-five dollars. I was taking it apart when Joan rode up on a bike and asked if she could help. I said, 'Scrape the gunk off the engine block' and she did. I was overwhelmed by that," Niilo Koponen remembered. Circa 1948.

Courtesy of Niilo Koponen.

Niilo Koponen with the American Friends Service Committee helping the Karelians in central Finland, circa 1946.

Courtesy Niilo Koponen.

tious objector status with the draft board and left three years later with the American Friends Service Committee to do my alternative service. I asked to help the refugees of my parents' ancestry, the Karelians in central Finland. Having spent my life in New York City, the north, the open air, the homesteading, the land of Finland—all that appealed to me.

When I returned, I wanted to attend Antioch College in Ohio, but I didn't have the six hundred dollars tuition, so I began university at nearby Central State College, Wilberforce, a black school, where I became the first white graduate.

At an Antioch square dance, I met Joan Forbes, the daughter of a psychologist and the graduate of a Quaker school. Joan and I married December 1951 at the Friends' Meeting in Cambridge.

I bought a second-hand, two-year-old Dodge Power Wagon. Remembering the Karelian Finn homesteading, I packed the Dodge for us to drive up the AlCan Highway to homestead. I had done electrical work on ships for Bethlehem Steel. I figured I could do the same thing on the gold dredges for the Fairbanks Exploration Company [F.E. Co.]. I had the name of an Antioch College graduate, Griffith, who lived at Olnes,

on the Elliott Highway today, in the Chatanika Flats, north of Fairbanks. At that time, most of the inhabitants were old timers who had struck F.E. Co. in 1908 to get a six-day, eight-hour-a-day workweek. When the strike broke, they filed on their own mining claims. Their claims filled up the valley from Dome City all the way to the Chatanika Flats. The mining companies could not persuade any of them to sell their claims. They just stayed there, working their claims, doing a little farming and hunting. One farmer, Herman Mackey, had

Tom Brice and Niilo Koponen in The Emperor Jones *at Central State College, Wilberforce, Ohio, circa 1948.*

Courtesy of Niilo Koponen.

a sauna where everyone went to socialize. On the weekends, we drove to Livengood. Good times. Great community. That winter, we moved into town. But in the spring, we moved to Chena Ridge where the town of Chena had once been in the early 1900s, at the junction of the Tanana and Chena rivers. Ted Kegler and his Quaker wife, Mary Ann Kegler, homesteaded on Chena Ridge first, followed by us. With Mary Ann, we began the Chena Ridge Friends meeting, but as our group grew, we rotated our meetings to various homes.

Kay Hitchcock at Tanana Chiefs Conference, 1962.
Photographer Theodore Hetzel.
Courtesy of Alfred "Bear" Ketzler Jr.

With a young teacher, we started an experimental high school; it was so successful that the territory drew up a high school program for other similarly isolated communities. Our Chena Ridge group began to grow. January 1954, Larry Brayton, fresh out of the navy, homesteaded next to us. Joan and I donated five acres to be used later for our neighborhood fire station.

That spring our family went to Nenana to watch spring breakup, the annual moving of the tripod. At the Ice Pool Dance, Charlie Purvis' daughter, fifteen-year-old DeLois Purvis, asked if she could babysit our son while Joan and I danced. We thanked her and whirled about the dance floor. Afterwards, DeLois introduced us to her father, Charlie Purvis. The following year, DeLois married Alfred Ketzler Sr.

At our Friends meetings at Chena Ridge, we talked about making a wilderness Quaker community. We envisioned a cooperative community where people worked together, got to know each other, didn't cheat, didn't get mad, looked out for and supported each other—a utopian atmosphere. I had experienced it growing up in our cooperative house and at Finn Hall house in New York. Homesteaders everywhere lived that way. We considered an abandoned area at Suslotna, near the Tok Cutoff and Nabesna roads, for our community, but since it was up in the mountains, it was not only isolated but it was hungry country. Also, Joan was

Charlie Purvis at Tanana Chiefs Conference, 1962.
Photographer Theodore Hetzel.
Courtesy of Alfred "Bear" Ketzler Jr.

Larry Brayton, after discharge from navy, 1946.
Courtesy of Larry Brayton.

not looking for community at the level that I was.

During the late 1950s, when the village of Holikachuk, on an Innoko River cutbank, was threatened, we contacted the Friends Service Committee. At the proposed new village site of Grayling on the Yukon River [procured through the Native Townsite Act of 1926], we set up a work camp to help make a new town. I was only free to organize and train people in the culture and language, but we sent a couple of people there. Two of the local men worked for wages, helping move the cabins.

Our Chena Ridge community was very interested in local issues like hiring Fairbanks union workers. A lot of Alaskans were very unhappy with Outside contractors bringing up their own work crews as they didn't hire local union workers. To address this and other issues, Larry Brayton, a journalist and videographer, decided to begin the Alaska Non Partisan League. Under this umbrella, we made suggestions to both the Democratic and Republican Parties. We were successful in getting both parties to adopt the homestead exemption, alleviating homesteaders from a portion of property taxes on their homes.

Through a letter to the Friends Intelligencer and after their inquiry to us about our

Howard Rock and Dr. Henry Forbes, circa 1962-1963.
Photographer Theodore Hetzel.
Courtesy of Alfred "Bear" Ketzler Jr.

correspondence education program, we met some new friends, Ben and Kay Hitchcock of Caribou Creek on the Glenn Highway. During the 1930s, Ben had come to Alaska with the Civilian Conservation Corps. He also helped organize the carpenters union in Anchorage. Kay had been a reporter for the Seattle Times, however in 1939, after her union lost their strike for better wages, she left Seattle and traveled to Anchorage with her son, Jim, where she met Ben. About the time the Glenn Highway was built, they moved to Caribou Creek near Sheep Mountain and Ben began building cabins. They were Quakers, anti-war folks, and we found we had many common interests.

Together, we began forming Friends meetings in Fairbanks, MatSu, and Anchorage.

Through our Nonpartisan League that Larry had begun, we advocated a constitutional convention to consider statehood issues. Ben Hitchcock and I ran for seats as delegates but we both lost. I spent the grand total of forty-two dollars on my campaign. However at the time, my job working for F.E. [Fairbanks Exploration] Company had terminated. As the union's grievance person, I had been too successful handling grievances and my job was liquidated.

Although I did not become a delegate, I was made the chairman of Dr. Ryan's Bill of Rights committee for the November 1955 Constitutional Convention. I testified for provisions in the constitution for a strong

Al Ketzler Sr, circa 1964, Fairbanks.
Tundra Times. Courtesy of Al "Bear" Ketzler Jr.

initiative, referendum, and recall to prevent abuse of power—as well as for a unicameral legislature.

At the end of the convention, some of us were dissatisfied with the results. Consequently we changed our Nonpartisan League to the Alaska Party. While the league had focused on labor issues, our new political party would concern itself with Alaska issues. We planned a convention for the Alaska Party in Palmer during the coming winter of 1956.

In the spring, Charlie Purvis moved to Fairbanks and joined our meetings.

LaVerne Madigan, Tanana, 1962.
Photographer Theodore Hetzel.
Courtesy of Alfred "Bear" Ketzler Jr.

He told us about his work with Alfred Starr in which he encouraged Natives in Nenana to get their Native land allotments under the Bureau of Indian Affairs. He said that in 1915, Judge James Wickersham had urged Alaska Natives to apply for Native land allotments or to consider reservations but they felt that there was no need for them to live on such small parcels when they had the whole of the Interior. [The Native Allotment Act of 1906 provided for conveyance of hundred sixty acres of public domain to adult Natives. Any single tract could be selected as long as the ground did not include mineral deposits. A few allotments were issued

in southeastern Alaska, but most Natives did not even know that such allotments could be obtained.] Native allotments for individual families could not
be sold or traded but remained as land held in trust. This provided stability for
families as their claim remained on maps whether or not they used it. However
during the interruption of World War I, the process for approving Native land
allotments had stalled. In 1952, the Bureau of Land Management office in the
Lathrop Building was still full of unapproved Native land allotment applications sitting on shelves gathering dust.

After talking with Charlie Purvis, our party adopted a plank supporting
Native land claims and we formed the Alaska Native Rights Association.
Working with Al Ketzler Sr., Charlie Purvis, and Alfred Starr, our aim was to
broaden and increase the movement toward a Native land claims settlement.
The Alaska Party began publishing a newspaper, *The Alaskan*, which set forth
the party's principles. Our goal was to raise the issue of Native land claims be-
fore statehood. Several of us—Ben Hitchcock, Charlie Purvis, Markle Ewan,
and I—ran for the territorial legislature. We networked with the Quaker
Friends meetings in Anchorage, MatSu, and Fairbanks. Eventually, the Alaska
Party would evolve into the Alaska Native land claims movement.

The winter of 1956 when we arrived in Palmer for our Alaska Party convention, Ben Hitchcock had just died of pneumonia. We made his coffin out
of a wooden crate in which a coffin had been shipped. We chipped away at
the frozen ground until it was deep enough to bury him (however today, his
gravesite cannot be found.) Before getting sick, Ben had filed as a candidate
for the territorial legislature. Kay, who later became our secretary in the Native
land claims movement, ran on the ballot in her husband's place.

At our Alaska Party convention, Ahtna leaders Walter Charlie, Oscar Craig,
and Markle Ewan, members of the Copper River Alaska Native Brotherhood,
attended. They said they had allowed the army to use their land at Lake Louise
for rest and relaxation but could not get it back. They were looking for help for
the return of their property. (Later, Markle Ewan ran for the legislature and
although he did well, he did not win.)

From the beginning, Kay Hitchcock was deeply involved in Alaska Native
land claims. After Ben died, she had to earn a living for her and her sons. She
returned to college; for her undergraduate thesis at the University of Alaska
Fairbanks, she wrote the "Natives' Land Rights in the State of Alaska," published in *Science in Alaska*, 1960, in Anchorage.

Through my contacts with the American Friends Service Committee,
I made contact with Ted Hetzel of Haverford College and chairman of the
Indian Rights Association, originally organized by Quakers during the 1880s.
Ted Hetzel came to Alaska and suggested that we contact the Association on
American Indian Affairs (AAIA), which we did. After contacting AAIA, we

discovered that Joan's uncle, Dr. Henry Forbes and his wife, Hildegarde, were on the Association on American Indian Affairs (AAIA) Alaska committee. Dr. Forbes had been a classmate of Alaska Territorial Governor Ernest Gruening at Harvard Medical School. Uncle Henry "Harry" Forbes was very supportive of our efforts. He came to Alaska where he met Howard Rock who was interested in starting a weekly newspaper, *Tundra Times,* that would champion Native issues including land claims, news that would not be covered in the mainstream media. For several years he covered most of its costs. *Fairbanks Daily News-Miner* reporter Tom Snapp agreed to teach Howard for a year how to publish a newspaper. (Later, Tanana Chiefs Conference presented me with a citation thanking me for my support.)

Through Uncle Harry, we met LaVerne Madigan of the AAIA staff. She flew to Alaska with Uncle Harry. After they met with Iñupiat Paitot at Point Barrow, they visited us and gave Al Ketzler a copy of the Iñupiaq land concerns. She helped support and attended the first Tanana Chiefs Conference in 1962, where a resolution for land claims was called. She committed AAIA funds to a second TCC conference in 1963.

To enhance communication, AAIA paid an amateur radio operator to set up a network of radios in hubs throughout rural Alaska.

Eben Hopson became the voice of Iñupiat Paitot. We contacted the Tlingits in Southeast but they weren't interested in a statewide land claims movement because they had their own land claims lawsuit pending for seven million dollars. However through our network, contacts were established in Point Hope, Nome, Barrow, and in the Copper River area.

Our role in Alaska Native land claims was not to lead but to become a support and encouragement to the Native leaders, to bring land claims to the attention of the U.S. Congress, and to concerned Americans in the Lower Forty-eight.

Uncle Harry invited Al Ketzler and me to testify on the need for a Native land claims settlement before the Committee on Interior and Insular Affairs where Representative Morris "Mo" Udall was a member. Our testimony resulted in an early bill for land claims. Although it did not pass, it provided a basis for the land claims bill that ultimately became ANCSA.

After statehood, the mainstream political parties passed a law making it impossible to run as an independent. The Alaska Party was ruled off the ballot. I wrote *amicus curiae* with which the judge agreed and forced the state to change the law.

With others, I also organized the first Alaska Civil Liberties Union.

Education dominated my next twenty years. In the mid-1950s, I earned a second bachelor's degree. I helped found the National Education Association-Alaska, the state's largest teachers' union. With only thirty-six dollars, several of us began a credit union to help new teachers establish in Alaska. It attained national credit union status, and the institution today is worth millions.

In 1962 at Harvard, I helped develop racial-integration busing plans for school districts in Boston and Hartford. I graduated in 1966 with a Ph.D. in education. In Fairbanks, as an innovator as well as a developer of team teaching, I became principal at Barnette and then at University Park Elementary. Stressing the critical window of time of a young child, I once said, "Criminals don't come out the woodwork but out of the second grade."

After working one year as district director of research, planning, and federal programs, I began developing Head Start programs in villages and establishing interracial community groups, as well as food banks. At the University of Alaska Fairbanks, I lectured in anthropology and northern people as well as sociology and Alaska history.

In 1982, I began the first of my five terms in the state House as a strong proponent of environmentalism and labor. In the middle of my fifth term in 2003, Joan was involved in a critical car accident. Before I retired to be at home with her, one of my final bills was to promote a state income tax, a renewable budget resource.

Today our Chena Ridge neighborhood hubs around our co-operative fire station. Homesteading was one step closer to my original utopian community ideal. My approach in life has been to first assess a problem and then discover how to solve it: a can-do attitude, looking for the answer that is there.

At the time of Niilo's documentation of the 1950s land claims movement, he listed the following surviving activists: Constance Griffith of Haines, Jim Hitchcock of Seward, Nels Hitchcock of Caribou Creek, Al Ketzler Sr. of Fairbanks, Ron Labe of Santa Fe, New Mexico, Georgianna Lincoln of Rampart and Anchorage, Ben Hitchcock's cousin Vivian Spurgin and Arlene Spurgin, both of Fairbanks, Dietrich Strohmaier of Fairbanks, and DeLois Purvis Burggraf of Fairbanks. Niilo also included those with "some involvement in the land claims process:" Ben C. Zeller of the Alaska Party, living in Raton, New Mexico, Ralph Perdue, Art Buswell, Barry Jackson, Jack Williams, H.O. and Jane Williams, Ginny Hill Wood, Terri Vierick, Lane and Dorothy Thompson, Christie and Lar Rowinski, Colleen Redman, Fred Brown—all of Fairbanks, and Walt Parker of Anchorage.

Niilo also included Kornelia Grabinska's History of Events Leading to the Passage of the Alaska Native Claims Settlement Act available at: www.alaskool. org/projects/ancsa/tcc2/TananaChiefs_Apnd.html

Koponen family, l-r: Alex, Heather, Karjala, Joan, Niilo, Chena and her husband Gary, early 1980s, Chena Ridge, Fairbanks.

Courtesy of Niilo Koponen.

In 1991, Representative Koponen with state senators memorialized Charlie Purvis' contributions to the rights of independent political parties and to Alaska Native land claims.

Courtesy of DeLois Burggraf.

In Memoriam

＊ CHARLES R. "CHARLIE" PURVIS ＊

Charles F. Purvis was born April 1, 1917, in Missouri. He met and married Dorothea M. Humphrey in 1938. During World War II, he served in the U.S. Army, Navy and Merchant Marine. In 1951, the couple moved their four children from Kansas to Nenana, where Charlie helped build the city dock. Later, he worked with the Alaska Railroad, on the construction of Ladd Field, now Fort Wainwright, at several DEW line sites, and as a millwright and finish carpenter with Carpenters Local 1243.

With his craggy, laughing face and rangy build, Charlie resembled an early Wyeth painting of the archetype frontiersman. A progressive midwestern agrarian populist, he was a member of the Alaska Party, a Territorial days alliance of homesteaders, union workers and Alaska Natives. At their 1956 convention, the party endorsed Copper Valley delegates' efforts to resolve Native land claims by broadening their proposal to include all Alaska. They ran no candidate for Governor in the pre-statehood election; when new rules assigned ballot rights only to parties receiving significant votes for Governor, the Alaska Party could not appear on the ballot. Charlie filed for the Legislature and filed suit. The major parties prevailed, until the Vogler decision. Barred from the ballot, Charlie and the party nevertheless played a major role in the aboriginal land rights struggle. The Alaska Native Claims Settlement Act of 1971 made him most proud.

During the mid-1970's, Charlie served as a union steward on the trans-Alaska pipeline. In the '80s and '90s, he worked his mining claims at Ester Dome and was active in preserving citizens' constitutional rights. He advocated both independence for Alaska and the Henry George theory of land taxation. Charlie was also a student of the teachings of Mary Baker Eddy, which gave him much strength and comfort through his life. He always had a smile and a positive word of encouragement for others. His infectious sense of humor never failed to lighten the load of those around him. Charlie died last week at age 73. His friends will miss him.

SPEAKER OF THE HOUSE   PRESIDENT OF THE SENATE

Date: April 3, 1991

Requested by: Representatives Koponen, Moyer, Boyer,
Bruckman, C.Davis, Foster and Lincoln; Senators Fahrenkamp, Menard, Halford and Frank.

Chapter Twenty

The Land Speaks, Forty Years After ANCSA; Fifty Years After the Reorganized Tanana Chiefs Conference; Where It Began: Alfred Ketzler Sr.

Al Ketzler awarded an honorary doctor of laws degree from the University of Alaska Fairbanks, 2004.

Courtesy of Ak Ketzler.

In 2005, when I was writing my monthly column for the Fairbanks Daily News-Miner, *Alfred Ketzler Sr.'s oldest son, Alfred Ketzler Jr. (known to everyone as Bear), called me. He said his younger brother, Alex Ketzler, had just finished research into their little-known maternal great-grandfather Nagita, from the Cantwell area. Alex discovered that Nagita had been murdered in 1910 around today's Denali Park and had been buried in Fairbanks. The Ketzler family had grown up in Nenana, but their ancestor had migrated from Dena'ina country to Ahtna territory in Cantwell. Bear said that he and his five siblings also wanted the larger picture documented of their parents' groundbreaking achievements with the reorganization of Tanana Chiefs Conference and the Ketzlers' critical part in Alaska Native land claims.*

I called Bear's mother, Al's former wife, DeLois Purvis Ketzler Burggraf, who now lives in Fairbanks. She was inclined to direct me to other people to interview, but she agreed to help me lay the groundwork. As we sat on her sofa, she began, "The Alaska Native Claims Settlement Act [ANCSA] was birthed by the life-blood, money, connections, and the time of those who carried it to passage. The land claims settlement was the culmination of a long human chain, people whom God put where they should be at the right time. ANCSA was a matter of aboriginal rights, not of race. The process was difficult to coordinate and to give life to a vision with little resources and much opposition while trying to feed a family of six children. By the end of the sixties, we were exhausted."

I met with Al Ketzler Sr. in his Fairbanks home. Through him is best under-stood the story of Tanana Chiefs Conference, the forerunner of Alaska Federation of Natives, and its resulting Alaska Native Claims Settlement Act. A large, mild-mannered man, he began Tanana Chiefs Conference whose Athabascan name is Dena' Nena' Henash or "The Land Speaks." Al Ketzler first called on interior Natives to organize and he was the first president of the Tanana Chiefs Conference. He began, "In 1961, the state already had received patent for Alaska's corridors: roads, railroad, and rivers. We [as Natives] were way behind the eight-ball on land claims and selections."

Over a period of several years, I met with Al Sr., DeLois, Niilo Koponen, Emil Notti, Don Wright, Frank and Nettie Peratrovich, Larry Brayton, Guy Martin (legislative assistant to the late U.S. Congressman Nick Begich), and Bill Byler, former executive director of the Association on American Indian Affairs. I met with those whose beliefs and fire in the belly had led to the reorganization of Tanana Chiefs Conference (TCC), the formation of Alaska Federation of Natives, and ul-timately to the Alaska Native Claims Settlement Act.

After the late 1960s and through the time of the Alaska National Interest Lands Conservation Act (ANILCA) in 1980, Alaska experienced great change. To under-stand this evolution, we must hear the voices of those who lived it.

Charlie Purvis, a rare man of vision, was born in 1917 in Missouri, a student by nature, a farmer, and a carpenter. His name, Purvis, meant *gatekeeper*, which was prophetic of his later role in Alaska Native land claims. He was a man of unusual sensitivity, the fourteenth of sixteen children, and had only five years of schooling. "Charlie had his own language," remembered his daughter DeLois Purvis Ketzler Burggraf. "He taught me and I learned it well." As a soldier when World War II ended, Charlie Purvis was stationed in the Philippines. There he saw, first hand, the poor treatment of the indigenous popu-lation. A sincere people, they'd first worked

Charlie Purvis, Texas, 1945.
Courtesy of DeLois Burggraf.

hard for the Spanish plantation owners and then they fought the Japanese shoulder to shoulder with the Allies, but always, the Filipinos were treated as tenants and not as owners on their own lands.

Charlie was disenchanted by the time he returned to the United States. With some friends, he traveled to Alaska, looking for something better. He returned home, sold his Kansas farm, packed up his family, and moved away from the America he had known. The winter of 1949–1950, he moved the family to Nenana in Alaska territory, in the time of transition from traditional Native subsistence to modern life.

There he met sixteen-year-old Al Ketzler Sr. whose parents were German-born Richard Ketzler and Bonita "Minnie" Ketzler of Nenana. Al Ketzler told Charlie Purvis that his father had been born in 1884 in Brandenburg. With war looming on the horizon, his grandfather had sent his son Richard first to Africa, then to San Francisco, where he heard about the Nome gold rush in

DeLois, Roseann, Charlie, Marietta, and Dorthea Purvis, Kansas City, Missouri, 1946.
Courtesy of DeLois Burggraf.

the early 1900s. Following the gold strikes, he arrived on the banks of the Chena River, where he met Minnie John, a sister-in-law of Chief Thomas of the original Tanana Chiefs Conference; the chief was the Interior's respected authority. Richard and Minnie married about 1922 in Nenana.

Al grew up trapping with his brothers. Although he loved hunting and trapping, he also enjoyed reading; he completed eight grades in seven years. When he met Charlie Purvis, Al had been trapping alone out of a remote cabin. That spring, he began working on the railroad, packing and pounding 115-pound rails as a gandy dancer from Seward to Fairbanks. Two years later when he was eighteen, he got work as a fireman on the steamboat *Alice*, which he later helped to destroy when the steamboat era came to an end.

In the early 1950s, another new family came to Nenana: the Alfred Starr family from Kantishna. Born in 1898 in Tanana, Alfred Starr had attended school in Tanana only for a few years. He had an inquiring mind. A teacher

encouraged him to contact William Paul, a Tlingit member of the Alaska Native Brotherhood (ANB) in Southeast and the first Native territorial congressman in 1925. Through their evolving correspondence, Alfred Starr learned that William Paul, a lawyer, was fighting for compensation for Southeast indigenous land. Wishing to know more, Alfred Starr traveled to the Pacific Northwest where he observed the reservation system around Puget Sound. In 1937, he returned to Alaska and began writing letters to officials. In 1938, William

Alfred Starr, circa 1980s.
Courtesy of DeLois Burggraf.

169

Paul came to Nenana, but he could not find anyone besides Alfred Starr interested in owning the land. For years, Starr carried William Paul's letters around in his leather suitcase. When he was at a potlatch, he made speeches: "We must secure our land!" But the people would say, "Ah, sit down, Al! Don't make trouble!" During the 1950s the pressure was to blend, for everyone to be an homogenized American. However, the Kansas farmer Charlie Purvis and Al Starr met often, discussing indigenous land claims. One day, Charlie Purvis concluded, "If

William Paul, Alaska Native Brotherhood, and Al Ketzler, Tanana Chiefs Conference, discussing land claim strategy, 1963.
Tundra Times.
Courtesy of Emil Notti.

what Al Starr says is true, the economic picture is upside down: the Natives are the wealthy ones and the rest of us are tenants." Charlie promised to help Al Starr in any way he could.

Through Charlie Purvis, Al Starr met another pioneer in Native land claims, Nick Gray, who was half Jewish and half Iñupiaq and called himself a "Jewskimo," and was a carpenter friend of Charlie's and worked in Fairbanks.

Nick Gray, ca. 1966.
Steve Smirnoff photo.
Courtesy of Emil Notti.

He'd listen to Charlie's ideas of indigenous land claims and then a lively conversation would ensue. The topic was so interesting to Nick Gray that he would travel to Nenana to talk with Al Starr and with Charlie. The conversation bore fruit; in 1964, Nick Gray founded Cook Inlet Native Association in Anchorage.

As a farmer, Charlie Purvis understood that the land is a man's source and security. He encouraged several local Native families to file for homesteads. The federal government required that homesteads had to be improved. To teach the concept, Charlie suggested that the people see it as "working for shares." Not realizing his idea was prophetic, Charlie reasoned with them, "A tribe is like a corporation." He felt the people could shape their homesteads into a creature that would not only sustain them but also create an ongoing sustenance for all.

In the mid-1950s, Al Ketzler was a tall, strong, young man and was packing freight for Yutana Barge Line on the docks of Nenana. At twenty-two, he married Charlie's daughter, sixteen-year-old DeLois Purvis, in 1955. An avid reader always looking to expand his mind, he took a correspondence course and got

Al and DeLois Ketzler, Tanana Chiefs Conference, 1962.
Photographer Theodore Hetzel. Courtesy of Alfred "Bear" Ketzler Jr.

a job in Yutana's office. Over the next several years, as his family grew, Al was only paid when he was on the clock; however, he was always expected to be on call. If that weren't enough, he had to endure the deprecating remarks of careless white colleagues, which contributed to a gastric ulcer. For three long hard years, he organized dockworkers in the International Longshoremen's Association AFL-CIO union, which helped prepare him to be a leader in the Alaska Native land rights movement.

Al Ketzler enjoyed talking with Charlie Purvis his father-in-law. Al remembered, "At a time when Natives had little financial or political leverage, Charlie worked to empower them. Gradually, he became a catalyst for Alaska Native land claims. He was a Ralph Nader sort of a guy." The Ketzlers and Charlie Purvis began to grow into a force for indigenous land claims.

In 1956, before statehood, Charlie Purvis moved his remaining family from Nenana to Fairbanks. Both Al Starr and Charlie were working for the railroad. Even though Charlie lived in Fairbanks, they continued their indigenous land issue discussions by walking the rail bed, meeting each other halfway between Fairbanks and Nenana. Charlie was a farmer who had no farm and only infrequent seasonal employment; he was funneling his erudition and passion into righting what was wrong with indigenous land claims.

Since the purchase of the Russian interest in Alaska, aboriginal land title had never been defined. DeLois explained, "It was only possible to define and award indigenous title within western jurisprudence. The law of the land as defined in the 1297 Magna Carta—described as 'the greatest constitutional document of all times ... the foundation of the freedom of the individual against the arbitrary authority of the despot'—stated that no freeman shall be divested of his goods or customs 'but by lawful judgment of his Peers, or by the Law of the Land.'" She added, "This was the foundation for British Common Law and served as a model for the American constitution." The United States was the first jurisdiction to acknowledge the common law doctrine of aboriginal title (also known as "original Indian title" or "Indian right of occupancy").

However in the 1950s, the villages had no TV, no telephones, no newspapers, and air travel was expensive. When there was intrusion on indigenous lands, there was no forum, no way to realize the mutual problems affecting all of the Native cultures. Before the construction of the Trans-Alaska Pipeline, many people told the Natives that their land had no value and called it "moose pasture." DeLois said, "They also said that if aboriginal claims had not been filed before 1951 that indigenous title was extinguished." [Possibly referring to the United States Supreme Court case Tee-Hit-Ton v. United States, 1955.] Alfred Starr and Charlie Purvis were two of the few who realized that Natives must obtain land title. (William Paul was also most aware of indigenous land rights, but he was seeking remuneration rather than land title.)

The topic of indigenous land rights became a focus for the newly organized Alaska Native Rights Association (ANRA), which included Sandy Jensen and Grant Newman, a young man who later became an IRS employee, as well as the Quaker members Niilo Koponen and Charlie and Kay Hitchcock. Kay and her husband were homesteaders. However, when Charlie Hitchcock died suddenly, Kay had to support herself and their two children. She returned to school to become a UAF English professor. (Later, reputedly, Willie Hensley was one of her students.)

Because Charlie Purvis had introduced Kay Hitchcock to the ANRA discussions regarding aboriginal title, she decided to use Native land rights for her master's thesis. In 1956, she wrote, "Natives' Land Rights in the State of Alaska" later published in *Science in Alaska*, 1960, Anchorage, stating that all title in the territory was clouded by unresolved indigenous land claims. [Possibly Kay was referring to Alaska constitutional delegate George McLaughlin, whose response to "Muktuk" Marston's proposal to address Native land rights in the new constitution was, "The Marston amendment would create a completely new set of property rights that would cast a cloud over "every title in the Territory."] With Alaska's statehood in 1959, the delegates included a clause in the constitution that referred to but did not define the status of indigenous claims but they left

Mayor Charles Ryan of Annette Island, Charlie Purvis, Oscar Craig of Alaska Native Brotherhood and Copper Center, Kay Hitchcock, photographer Theodore Hetzel, and Howard Rock, 1962, Tanana Chiefs Conference, Tanana.

Photographer Theodore Hetzel. Courtesy of Alfred "Bear" Ketzler Jr.

Howard Rock, LaVerne Madigan and her fourteen-year-old son Fergus, 1962, Tanana Chiefs Conference at Tanana.

Photographer Theodore Hetzel. Courtesy of Alfred "Bear" Ketzler Jr.

it to Congress to resolve. LaVerne Madigan of the Association on American Indian Affairs (AAIA) had lobbied for this clause with the conviction that only Congress could adequately define indigenous land claims.

As ANRA's correspondent, Kay Hitchcock then wrote to Congress regarding the unsettled Native land title. Congress replied that its position was that it would not consider a per-capita settlement because it was deleterious to the tribal unit, nor would it consider reservations, because their results were seen as a failure, characterized as "pockets of poverty."

ANRA wondered then what they could use as a solution. Charlie Purvis suggested the vehicle of corporations, a flexible instrument that was limited only by the designer's imagination and by the integrity of its members. Creating corporations was also an appealing idea to Congress as well as to many of the young indigenous leaders who did not want to rely on the old tribal mechanism.

One day when Kay drove Edwin Simon of Huslia to the Fairbanks airport to return home, she asked him his view on indigenous land claims. He slapped his leg and exclaimed, "This is the first time in my sixty-eight years that anyone has ever asked me what I think." (DeLois said, "That was the purpose of Charlie Purvis creating forums of dialogue like the Alaska Native Rights Association: for the empowerment of the indigenous people.")

Howard Rock, an artist from Point Hope, was also a friend of Charlie Purvis'. Howard sent his work to show and to sell in New York, to the Association on American Indian Affairs. When he learned about Project Chariot, the government's plan to use nuclear bombs for shovels to make a harbor that nobody wanted, he contacted AAIA to notify them. In July 1961, LaVerne Madigan, AAIA's executive director, came to Point Hope to meet with the village. She urged them to write to the secretary of the interior. The following November, she returned north to Point Barrow, where she organized Iñupiat Paitot, an

Iñupiaq council for indigenous land concerns. Both Howard Rock and Charlie Purvis were at the meeting. LaVerne gave everyone instructions on how to make a blanket land claim. Howard put his information in his pocket, but later he found that it was missing. It seemed that a high-profile Athabascan leader who was opposed to land claims had taken the instructions for filing a blanket land claim and sent it to the *Fairbanks Daily News-Miner* to publish. The result was not his intended exposé, but rather he had just given the public instructions on how to file a blanket land claim. DeLois explained, "In those days, we were not only fighting whites that were narrow-minded but also some Natives in high positions."

With statehood in 1959, the state received twenty-eight percent of Alaska's 365,039,104 acres from the federal government. The state could begin filing on land; however, statehood provisions only referred to, but did not define, right to title of land and resources "which may be held by any Indians, Eskimos, or Aleuts." Despite that indigenous land title had not been addressed, the state had received patent for rights-of-way for roads, railroad, and rivers. As if that were not enough, in the fall of 1961, the state began filing on 4.16 million acres near the villages of Minto, Tanacross, and Northway.

Over a twenty-five-year period, the state was authorized to file on one million acres of public-domain land. Roscoe Bell, director of the Division of Lands, promised the villages that they would not select on Native lands. However, in 1961, a small notice in the *Fairbanks Daily News-Miner* classified section advertised a state land filing. Sandy Jensen realized it was Minto, and she notified Charlie Purvis. Only one more day remained before it would become final. Charlie and his wife, Dorothea, drove to Nenana to tell Al and DeLois, who happened to know that the barge was in Minto. Al and DeLois took off, flying over sixty miles of dusty gravel, caught the ferry, and with only minutes to spare, they found Minto chief Richard Frank, a Yutana employee, on the dock. (Another signature besides the chief's was required. Robert Charlie may have been there as well.) Chief Frank signed the protest, blocked the claim, and jumped back on the Yutana barge to continue downstream. Had they not done so, the state would have owned Minto.

For a neutral banner under which to hold meetings, Al founded a chapter of the Alaska Native Brotherhood (ANB) in Nenana. With the understanding that they

Richard Frank, TCC convention, ca. 1972-1973. Elder Richard Frank passed away September 20, 2012.

Courtesy of Al "Bear" Ketzler Jr.

Tom Snapp of the Fairbanks Daily News-Miner, *1962.*
Photographer Theodore Hetzel. Courtesy of Alfred "Bear" Ketzler Jr.

were convening under ANB, the chief of Nenana allowed a meeting in George Hall.

In January 1962, Al called the meeting, inviting Kay Hitchcock to read her thesis on cloudy title. As she spoke, Robert Charlie of Minto and Lawrence David of Tetlin saw the light on in the tribal hall and stopped in. After her talk, Kay asked Robert Charlie if Minto might be interested in indigenous land claims, and he assured her that they were.

At a second meeting in February, along with people from Minto, the Ketzler- ANRA group were able to get both the press and the justice system in attendance: Tom Snapp of the *Fairbanks Daily News-Miner* as well as Justice Mary Alice Miller. After hearing Kay Hitchcock's thesis and the input from the villages, Kay asked, "What do you think?" Justice Miller nodded and said, "I think you have a case." The Ketzlers were a little amazed. DeLois remembered, "We had no credentials and many of us did not even have a high school education. When Justice Miller confirmed that we were on the right track, a light bulb went on in our heads." When he returned to work, Tom Snapp looked in the *Fairbanks Daily News-Miner* archives and found articles indicating that for some time, the state had been trying to quash the idea of Native land claims, which solidified his resolve to support it.

When Justice Miller signaled that ANRA had a case, Niilo Koponen, former head of the Alaska Party, the predecessor to ANRA, directed Kay Hitchcock to contact LaVerne Madigan.

When informed of the state's trespass on village land, Madigan was indeed interested and flew to

Al Ketzler, chairman of Tanana Chiefs Conference and Clarabelle Charlie, secretary, 1962.

Alaska Native Organizations collection. ASL-P33-38.

Alaska to meet the Ketzlers. She gave Al a record of Iñupiaq aboriginal issues recorded at Point Barrow, and she agreed to help him.

When Nenana still hosted dog races in March, Al Ketzler called a meeting of ten villages: Minto, Tanana, Tanacross, Beaver, Gulkana, Delta, Dot Lake,

Northway, Tetlin, and Copper Center. Before the races began, Al called on them to defend the land.

He explained the purpose of his invitation:

> *I have a copy of the Eskimo Iñupiat Paitot recommendations and policies. We have many problems, which are shared with the Eskimos. We have a statement in which they ask the government to define aboriginal rights. Nobody can say just what aboriginal rights are until Congress*

Tanana Chiefs Conference, 1915, Fairbanks, Alaska: (l to r, seated): Chief Alexander-Tolovana; Chief Thomas-Nenana; Chief Evan-Koschakat; Chief Alexander William-Tanana. Standing: Chief William-Tanana; Paul Williams-Tanana; Chief Charlie-Minto.
Albert Johnson Collection, UAF-1989-166-371.

> *defines them for us. . . . We should send a resolution to Congress asking for clarification of our aboriginal rights, as the Eskimos have. . . . We must urge Congress to define our rights as the problem will grow worse as time goes on. A lot of whites will be against it and they will have their lobbies in Washington put pressure on our legislators. That is why we have to speak up.*

During the course of the meeting, they took the name Dena' Nena' Henash—the land speaks—later called Tanana Chiefs Conference (TCC.) They discussed the land problems with the villages, saying that they agreed with the Iñupiat Paitot on their common indigenous land issues. The delegates passed a resolution in favor of the priority of their land claims and agreed that each village would send a representative to the traditional meeting site for in-

Al Ketzler addressing first newly reorganized Tanana Chiefs Conference. Left, fifth row, three in: Charlie Purvis. Left, third row: Alfred Starr. Right side, third row: DeLois Ketzler; second row: Mayor Ryan, Madigan's son Fergus, Howard Rock, LaVerne Madigan, Kay Hitchcock.

Photographer Theodore Hetzel. Courtesy of Alfred "Bear" Ketzler Jr.

terior tribes—Nuchalawoya, or Tanana, that summer. They all agreed that Al would handle the logistics.

For the first time since Judge Wickersham had addressed the Tanana chiefs about land issues in 1915, there was an historic gathering in Tanana in June 1962: the beginning of the reorganization of the Tanana Chiefs Conference. Al Ketzler was elected chairman.

Senator Gruening and the Bureau of Indian Affairs head, James Hawkins, attended the meeting in Tanana, as did people from thirty villages. To house and feed all the out-of-town guests, the Episcopalian priest, Father Cleveland, let people sleep in his house while a women's auxiliary group fed everyone.

Not every village had land issues. For some western intrusion meant that the hunting season didn't coincide with the local waterfowl migrations. Up the Koyukuk River, when it was finally time to legally shoot ducks and geese, upon which the people heavily depended, the birds had already flown south. If a man shot a bird out of season, he went to jail, depriving him of feeding his family.

Before closing, a second TCC meeting was planned for the following year in June.

However, in August 1962, LaVerne Madigan died in a horseback riding accident. She was replaced by William (Bill) Byler, a Yale graduate and a former congressional aide. This was a serendipitous replacement, because Bill Byler's manner was better suited to helping empower Alaska Natives. He was a quiet, respectful, and subtle man who sought first and foremost to present the will and voice of the Native people. Bill later described his friend, Al Ketzler, as not

Tanana Chiefs Conference recess, 1962: in profile to right is Alfred Starr. Right foreground: Mrs. Grant Sr.

Photographer Theodore Hetzel. Courtesy of Alfred "Bear" Ketzler Jr.

being an "ego-tripper"; and neither was Bill. By the telephone that fall, Bill suggested that Al write the villages asking them to map the lands that they used.

DeLois remembered, "That winter, Al sent out petitions to all the interior Athabascan as well as several Eskimo villages to recommend to the secretary of the interior to stop all land selections in Alaska pending settlement of Alaska Native land claims. He sent maps to the villages and had them outline their traditional-use lands. By spring, twenty-two villages had responded with a thousand signatures. In 1962, he sent those maps and land use records to President Kennedy, who gave them to Secretary of the Interior Stewart Udall.

However, that winter, the head of the Alaska Division of Lands, Roscoe Bell, flew to Minto where, DeLois remembered, "he tried to pressure the people into forgetting indigenous land claims." With a straight face, he said, "Let the state claim your land, then we will get title and sell the land back to you." When the Purvis-Ketzlers heard about it, they chartered a plane to Minto, where Charlie Purvis suggested to Bell, "Lean on Congress, not on Minto."

In April 1963, Al Ketzler flew to Washington, D.C., along with representatives of many other national Native interest groups, to meet with Secretary of the Interior Udall. Al remembered, "Coming from life in Nenana to being tossed into the Washington, D.C., scene was a real culture shock." He remembered, "Bill Byler of AAIA met me. At the group meeting, I asked Udall to freeze state land selections until the Native land claims in Alaska could be settled. Bill Byler committed $3,000 of AAIA funds to the 1963 TCC meeting in Tanana, and he agreed to meet us there."

In June, a second Dena' Nena' Henash meeting was held at Tanana. William Keeler, chief of the Cherokee Nation, arrived at the Tanana meeting with a Department of Interior task force under President Kennedy to take testimony assessing Alaska's indigenous situation. Bill Byler as well as the Corps of Engineers also attended.

Turok Newman of Beaver spoke up, "I am against Rampart Dam." After he spoke, DeLois recalled, "You could hear a pin drop. Then people from Fort Yukon and other potentially affected villages chimed in, 'Me, too,' 'I agree.'" As a unit, they protested the Rampart Dam project unless due compensation were

Tanana Chiefs Conference, 1963: Back row, l-r: Robert Charlie, Minto; Charlie David, Tetlin; unknown; Clarabelle Charlie, Nenana; Al and DeLois Ketzler, Nenana; may be either David Salmon of Chalkyitsik or Percy Herbert, Fort Yukon. Front row: Al "Bear" Ketzler Jr, Nenana; Jonathan David, Minto; David Paul, Tanacross; Benedict Jones, Koyukuk; Stanley Jonas, Canyon Village.
For a complete list of attendees, see Bill Byler chapter. Courtesy of Al Ketzler Sr.

made to the villages in question. [The Rampart Dam was a project proposed in 1954 by the U.S. Army Corps of Engineers to dam the Yukon River in Alaska for hydroelectric power. The project was planned for Rampart Canyon, 31 miles southwest of the village of Rampart, Alaska. Alaska Natives in the area protested the threatened loss of nine villages that would be flooded by the dam. Conservation groups abhorred the threatened flooding of the Yukon Flats, a large area of wetlands that provides a critical breeding ground for millions of waterfowl.]

William Paul of ANB talked with Al Ketzler, wanting to represent TCC in court. However, he wanted to settle it in court, which at best would mean only getting financial reimbursement for the land, and a trial could also mean losing everything. At that point, wanting foremost to protect their land, TCC parted ways with William Paul. Only Congress could define aboriginal land rights, so TCC chose the congressional venue over the court system. However, money was in short supply in early Alaska. Trips to Washington, D.C., for the lobbying effort would cost thousands of dollars. William Paul could not see how Alaska Native Brotherhood or TCC could find the way or the means to lobby Congress. AAIA proved to be a great help.

TCC continued to meet annually at Tanana until they moved their conference to Fairbanks sometime in the mid-1960s.

Continuation of photo from previous page: Tanana Chiefs Conference, 1963: back row, l-r: Ruth Charles, Dot Lake; Kenny Albert, Northway; Markle Ewan, Gulkana; Fred John Sr., Mentasta; front row: Matthew Titus, Minto; Oscar Craig, Copper Center; Mayor Ryan, Metlakatla; Howard Rock, Point Hope and Fairbanks.

Courtesy of Al Ketzler Sr.

After the second Tanana Chiefs meeting, Bill Byler traveled with Al to see Nenana and Minto. He went on to visit the Yukon and Koyukuk river villages by catching an airplane ride with pilot and Jesuit priest Rev. Jules Convert, who worked in the villages of St. Marys, Holy Cross, Kaltag, and Unalakleet.

Al remembered, "In those early years, AAIA dedicated most of their annual budget to land claims. They paid for the printing of our meeting minutes, boat gas, airfare, and later, my meager salary." He added, "Bill was with the association (AAIA) for seventeen years. They spent a huge amount of money on land claims."

When TCC needed to do press releases, Larry Brayton at KFRB and KTVF-TV would let Al know when was the best time. For fun, Al began wearing a Navajo hat (long before the appearance of "Native Pride" caps) to send a positive message that being Native was all right. "People liked my hat so much that they kept stealing it, so I had to keep a lot of hats on hand." He grinned.

In July 1963, as a result of Al's documentation protesting state land selections, Assistant Secretary of the Interior John A. Carver Jr. sent an in-house memo to deny land claims on Native protest land.

However overcoming centuries of mistrust among Native cultures was also a major obstacle.

(Back, l-r:) Department of interior task force Hugh Wade, the Alaska secretary of state (equivalent to lieutenant governor); associate commissioner of Indian affairs James Officer; chief of the Cherokees William Keeler speaking. Seated at table: unknown, Oscar Craig, Copper Center; Al Ketzler, Clarabelle Charlie, 1962, Tanana.

Photographer Theodore Hetzel. Courtesy of Alfred "Bear" Ketzler Jr.

From *Alaska Native Land Claims* by Robert D. Arnold, courtesy of Don Wright:

> *In 1964 two new organizations of Natives were established: Gwitchya Gwitchin Ginkhye (Yukon Flats People Speak), [made up of] the Yukon Flats villages, as well as the Cook Inlet Native Association in Anchorage.*
>
> *A conference to unify Native organizations was planned by Howard Rock; Al Ketzler; Ralph Perdue, the president of the Fairbanks Native Association; and Mardow Solomon, the president of the newly founded Gwitchya Gwitchin Ginkhye. The focus of the conference was for more political activity among Natives and the need for cooperative action. . . .*
>
> *Those who supported the idea of one statewide organization tried to persuade others, but they were unable to overcome a deeply rooted mistrust . . . of people outside of their own geographic regions. The task of overcoming mistrust became easier . . . in part through the Tundra Times, [as they realized] that they were facing a common threat of land loss. Communication . . . also increased as they gathered together in government-sponsored advisory committees dealing with housing, health, or education programs.*

After Al got involved with RurAlCAP, the Ketzlers went on RurAlCAP business to Bethel. For the first time, DeLois met Emil Notti. She asked him, "So, are you a land or a money Indian?" He replied, "I think Alaska is big enough for both." She knew then that they could back him for president of the Alaska Federation of Natives (AFN.)

In October 1966, TCC met in Anchorage with other statewide Native leaders and formed AFN, with Emil Notti as president. Al remembered, "AFN then began having meetings all over the state, but most of them were in Anchorage. We were trying to decide which way to go with the land. There was no statewide frame of mind but rather a very contentious atmosphere. Many started lawyering up. I said, 'Anyone who wants war can be the first one on the front lines.'"

Al added, "Later in my fourth year as TCC president in 1969, I hired a lawyer, Barry Jackson. That year at AFN, it became clear that the lawyers tended to be counter-productive, negotiating for a compromise in the amount of acreage. There was so much arguing that we asked all the attorneys to leave. We didn't want a lawyer telling us why we couldn't accomplish our intended goal. They were trained in negotiation; compromise with the land was not our intention."

As the years continued, the Ketzlers not only had to fight for land claims, but they were also hit with a barrage from the government. Senator Bob Bartlett sent his Iñupiaq aide to them to say that the Natives were being spoon fed by AAIA. A couple of years later, Bartlett sent a Yup'ik friend of their family's to try to talk them out of land claims. The Ketzlers pushed forward, hoping it would not get as bad as it was for Dr. Martin Luther King. DeLois remembered, "It was a very dicey time." They also had to combat the negative beliefs regarding Natives in that era. DeLois' message was, "Don't tell me what my kids can't do." The Ketzlers were also frequently told that all indig-

Emil Notti, Alaska Federation of Natives president, 1968.
Alaska Native Land Claims *textbook.*
Courtesy of Emil Notti.

enous land claims had been extinguished in a 1950s Court of Claims decision which, had it been true, was not legal. DeLois inserted, "Only Congress can extinguish indigenous claims." The Native position was also mixed. Some were opposed to land claims, asking if they "now had to move into the village and become Indians," while those in favor were divided between the urbanites who wanted a financial settlement and those, generally from the village, who wanted protection of the land.

Whenever they hit a brick wall, DeLois would say to her father Charlie Purvis, "This is the end!" But he'd find a relevant principle and say, "If this is so, then that is so . . ." and with that clearly reasoned path, they would fly over the new blockade. His clarity would inspire his daughter to write a letter to the editor. DeLois remembered, "He could discern points, use logic, and could express a lot in one letter."

Based on the maps and documentation that Al sent to Washington, D.C., in 1962, Secretary of Interior Udall issued a preliminary injunction halting further land conveyances from the federal government to the state in 1966. This indispensable land freeze got the attention of the state. Congress was being pushed to address Native land claims.

Until 1968, the land battle centered around preventing the state from usurping Native land. But after the oil lease sales and the historic 1968 bonanza oil discovery, pressure greatly increased as the state became nervous due to the high stakes of big oil.

In February 1968 when DeLois' brother-in-law was working up north, he heard someone on the CB radio say in an amazed and confidential tone, "Keep that core sample intact, get it securely on a plane and take it directly to the assay office. Don't say anything to anyone." That's when he knew it was a big discovery.

On July 18, 1968, Atlantic-Richfield (later renamed Arco) announced that they had discovered a five- to ten-billion-barrel oil field, the largest pool in North America.

The Alaska Department of Natural Resources had already held a competitive oil lease sale in 1964 followed by two more in 1967. However, the landmark sale was the year after the 1968 oil discovery. Oil companies paid over $900 million to the state of Alaska in 1969. That sale showed that if the state could sell leases on small tracts of land for so much money, Natives were not asking for too much in seeking a similar amount of money for the surrender of millions of acres.

Secretary of State Stewart Udall issued a preliminary injunction halting land conveyance from the feds to the state in 1966 which coalesced into a formal land freeze in 1968.
Tundra Times. Alaska Native Land Claims.
Courtesy of Emil Notti.

To get this oil to market, the pipeline would have to cross hundreds of miles of federal land, but due to the land freeze, BLM had stopped approving applications for right-of-way permits.

In January 1969, President Nixon appointed Wally Hickel to be secretary of the interior. Believing that the land freeze was driving Alaska into bankruptcy, Hickel quipped to a reporter in Seattle, "What Udall can do with a stroke of a pen, I can undo."

Trying to get right-of-way from indigenous landholders, Atlantic-Richfield attorney Thomas diZerega held a meeting with five key villages—Allakaket, Bettles, Minto, Rampart, and Stevens Village—urging them, "Let us go through your land." The villages responded, "You give us contracts for gravel or for building the road, give us jobs, and we'll give you the waiver of our right-of-way." DiZerega gave his word, but the promise was never put into writing.

Throughout 1969-1970, Al and Tim Wallis of the business arm of TCC Dena' Nena' Henash (DNH), its development corporation, met periodically with the Trans-Alaska Pipeline [TAPS] representative.

Trying to free up the pipeline right-of-way corridor, Hickel asked the Senate and House Committees on Interior and Insular Affairs for authorization to modify the land order that imposed the super freeze to exempt federal land inside the right-of-way. Scoop Jackson and Wayne Aspinall approved the request in December, and in January 1970, Secretary of the Interior Hickel signed an order that made the modification.

It began to become apparent that TAPS was not going to honor its agreement of giving contracts and jobs to the five villages offering right-of-way; worse, it began setting up camps to proceed with the pipeline construction. DeLois said to Al, "Okay, we're going to have to file an injunction to exempt federal land inside the pipeline's proposed right-of-way." They opened a telephone directory and tried to find a lawyer in Fairbanks or Anchorage who might consider it. "But in those days," DeLois said, "oil was like the three-letter word, 'god.'" They couldn't see a lawyer's name in the directory who would dare to file an injunction against the pipeline. Al said, "What about Legal Services?" It was an entity that had just started up, Alaska Legal Services Corporation. [The Economic Opportunity Act–funded antipoverty law firm that the Alaska Community Action Program had started three years earlier.] DeLois laughed and said, "Well, what have we got to lose? So the next day, we met Dave Wolf in his little hole-in-the-wall office on a side street in town. We asked if he would consider doing some work on behalf of Tanana Chiefs. He answered, 'Most of our case load is poor whites and poor blacks.' He admitted that the indigenous people were not getting the benefit of their services, and he asked, 'What do you want me to do?' We replied, 'File an injunction against the pipeline's attempts at right-of-way.' He replied, 'Okayyy. . . .'"

As a result of their request, the injunction was sought by TCC's DNH. On April 1, 1970, Judge George Luzerne Hart Jr. of the United States District Court for the District of Columbia ordered the Interior Department to not issue a construction permit for a section that crossed one of the Native claims. He issued an injunction against the project, preventing the Interior Department from giving a construction permit and halting the entire project in its tracks.

Protesters carrying signs outside Sydney Laurence Auditorium during twenty-third oil and gas lease sale in Anchorage. Signs read: "$2,000,000,000 Native land robbery." Sept. 10, 1969.
Photographer: Ward W. Wells.
Anchorage Museum at Rasmuson Center-wws-4794-15. Ward Wells Collection.

Ruby Tansy at an Ahtna business meeting.
Courtesy of Ahtna Cultural Center.

DeLois said, "It really hit the fan then. But we didn't want to file the injunction. The oil companies should have honored their agreement. After the injunction was in place, the contractors blamed the Natives. But if those contractors had joined in the suit, they would've been reimbursed for every dollar they lost because the oil companies had broken their agreements with the contractors."

After the injunction, the state came down hard on Stevens Village. They sent a representative to the village to say, "Look, we wanted to give you guys freezers and hire your kids but because you got this injunction, we can't do that now." The chief of Stevens Village, Gus Evan, relented. The next day's *Fairbanks Daily News-Miner* headlines read, "Stevens Village Doesn't Want the Injunction."

Al was flying back in from Washington, D.C., but DeLois was at home when Tim Wallis, Ruby Tansy, and others began calling her on the phone, upset. Larry Brayton, their press agent, was mad too because Al "hadn't told him anything."

That night after Al got home, the Ketzlers agreed, "Okay, Stevens is giving up but we're not. The other villages and us, we're standing. Our position was that we had an agreement with the oil companies, they broke it and—we're still standing."

The next morning, the Ketzlers met Larry Brayton for breakfast. He wanted to know what was going on. After they informed him, he said, "I tell you what! We'll go back into Stevens with our cameras and film them giving up! And we'll get all the other villages to go in too!" The Ketzlers began organizing. They called the village of Beaver: "We'll have a meeting with all the people, tell them what's going on and ask them, 'Is this what you really want?'" Sam Kito and Tim Wallis flew up the Koyukuk River to bring villagers into town. In Stevens Village, we told them, 'TAPS wants to give you freezers and jobs but to protect the land, you have to hold their feet to the fire. Do not give them right-of-way.'" After all was said, the Stevens Village people kicked everyone else out so they could talk in private. They voted to stay with the injunction. "That was very pivotal," DeLois pointed out.

"However," Al added, "on the way back from Stevens Village after dropping someone off at Beaver, the engine on our plane quit. Although no one was hurt, we had to spend the night on a mountain. Kito and Wallis flew over, saw our predicament, and dropped three sleeping bags out. However, there were four of us. Guess who was the one without a bag. It was colder than heck and I thought I might freeze to death!"

Al continued, "Sam Kito and Tim Wallis brought Bettles Chief Charlie Evans and the chief of Beaver in to meet with Chief Peter John of Minto, who was solid. There had to be a consensus among the villages to block the oil companies' right-of-way. They took a vote and together, they stood against TAPS getting venue."

Al Ketzler, Alaska Federation of Natives board meeting, 1968.
Alaska Native Land Claims.
Courtesy of Emil Notti.

After the injunction—particularly when the courts backed it up—things happened really fast. The delay was costing TAPS a lot of money, which caused pressure to accelerate the resolution of Alaska Native land claims.

Emil Notti, the president of AFN, and the vice president and the executive director, John Borbridge, and Willie Hensley, had to frequently be in Washington, D.C. While still president of TCC, Al Ketzler moved to Anchorage to also begin serving as the acting executive director for AFN.

With counsel from former Supreme Court Justice Arthur Goldberg and former Attorney General Ramsey Clark, AFN was considering only asking for ten million acres and a billion dollars. When Congress began pressuring Emil Notti to settle for those terms, not only did the decision have to be unanimous within AFN, but it had to be now.

Don Wright, a statewide businessman, had initially gone to Washington, D.C., with the Chamber of Commerce in the interest of pipeline tax dollars for Fairbanks. However, when the Native representatives clarified to him the critical strategy of the land freeze relevant to land claims, Don Wright switched sides. He moved to Anchorage to begin running Cook Inlet Native Association, begun originally by Nick Gray. DeLois remembered, "Don was fresh, not exhausted, not beaten down like the rest of us. He promised us that he would not settle for less than forty million acres if we backed him as president of AFN."

Henry "Scoop" Jackson, the chairman of the Senate Committee on Indian Affairs, began pushing his bill to give the Natives under ten million of Alaska's 375 million acres. AFN decided to ask for eighty million with the intention of negotiating for half. In an historic struggle in which Al Ketzler, DeLois Ketzler, and many other Alaska Natives lived in Washington, D.C., for weeks, Congress heard testimony. Al was on radio shows and testified in Washington before various committees. He was also on a five-person committee for nego-

*Representatives of the Alaska Federation of Natives discuss Native land claims legisla-
tion (or lack of) with Secretary of the Interior Wally Hickel. L-r: Tim Wallis, Charlie
Edwardsen, Eben Hopson, Emil Notti, Barbara Trigg, Willie Hensley, DeLois Ketzler, Al
Ketzler, George Miller, Larry Oskolkoff, Roy Levine, Harry Sorrelson, Ray Christiansen,
Frank Degnan, Gerry Grey. Standing: Barry Jackson, John Borbridge and Wally Hickel.*
U.S. Department of the Interior.

tiating land claims. He recalled, "At first, when we hit Washington, D.C., we
were told not to go see so–and–so but we said, 'We'll go see them anyway. Who
knows; maybe they will be interested.' We hit every congressman, every senator on the hill. Some Washington, D.C., person asked if we were lawyers. We
answered, 'We believe in what we are doing.' We attended all the meetings. We
were knowledgeable because we believed in what we wanted. We didn't take
other people's advice. We spent a lot of time lobbying and waiting. We learned
the system. It turned out really well. It was one of the most successful lobbying
efforts ever."

DeLois recalled, "Don Wright deserves the credit. He was smart; he got
elected, and he went to Washington, D.C. Because he didn't lean on a lawyer,
he had a much stronger position, shooting from the hip. When Congress got
snotty about his terms, the AFN board upped their demands to eighty million
acres. Congress was glad then to settle for forty million. (Forty million acres is
a hell of a lot more than the original ten million!)" Al added, "The process was
slow, but actually fast—passing in two years."

Al continued, "We got over forty-four million acres with the additional inclusion of cemeteries and town sites; very substantial. The lobbyists lived there
all the time. The labor lobbyists were helpful because the construction of the
pipeline was in their interest. Those pressures really helped. It was a real experience." Congress also authorized nearly one billion dollars (three dollars per acre
for ninety percent of lands lost) to Alaska Natives through a corporate structure. The Alaska Native Claims Settlement Act (ANCSA) of December 1971

Autographed to Al Ketzler from Senator Ted Stevens, Washington, D.C. meeting. (L-r, seated) George Miller, Joe Upicksoun, Nels Anderson, Al Ketzler, Frances Degnan, Donald Wright, Senator Ted Stevens, Adeline Katongan, Phillip Guy, Hank Eaton, and Al Naknek; (standing) John Katz, Max Gruenberg, Richard Frank, Brenda Itta, Fred Paul, Jim Wickwire, Charlie Edwardsen, Cliff Groh, Bob Willard, Iliodor Philemonof, and Frank Petersen.

Courtesy of Al "Bear" Ketzler Jr.

set up thirteen regional for-profit corporations for Alaska Natives—twelve in the state and one based in the Lower Forty-eight for Alaska Natives living in the continental United States. ANCSA also set up nearly two hundred village corporations.

Thirty-three years later, Al Ketzler explained:

> *When a bill is hashed out in committee, it is done behind closed doors. No one told us that they were calling in lawyers and setting up corporations to handle the corporate, regional, and village levels. The awarded money from the proposed settlement would ultimately come from the feds, so they made the corporation vehicle to manage the funding. That vehicle created a lot of problems for us. It wasn't what we wanted for our structure. I never thought it would really work.*
>
> *Nationally, the rate of corporate failure is very, very high. Coupled with putting corporations in the hands of a people who are not familiar*

with corporate structure at all, not surprisingly, many of the village corporations went into bankruptcy. Having no idea what to do, they sat on their money. The corporation is a foreign tool to us. Besides, in Indian way, the richest Native was the one who gave the most away. It's a different culture.

Additionally, regional corporations vote, but traditionally, Indians never voted. The chief made the decisions, and being chief was passed down from father to son.

Al Ketzler in his Fairbanks home, 2005.

Judy Ferguson photo.

I tend to think the idea of using corporations was always the long-range plan to get our land back into other hands. Possible bankruptcies would have to be paid off by selling our land, but Senator Ted Stevens helped that to not initially happen. During the first Native corporation bankruptcies in 1976–1978, under the IRS Net Operating Loss loophole, Ted Stevens made it possible for corporations to buy up our debt to lessen what they owed Uncle Sam. They paid pennies on our in-debt dollar, applying our loses against their gains.

What we did prefer over the corporation model was to own the land and to be nonprofit. Land that's undeveloped doesn't accrue debt, but risky developments can cause problems. I would have chosen to keep the land in a nonprofit status and to have left it in trust with the federal government. However, due to the help that Ted Stevens gave us at the outset in protecting the corporations, I have come to peace with the corporation model. Although for years I was upset about it, I am not anymore.

In 1975, the Indian Self Determination and Education Assistance Act was passed, which gave tribes the means to do their own contracting. That was a milestone. The law took the power away from the bureaucrats and gave the tribes the capacity to make and expand programs. TCC picked up some contracts.

After serving as Tanana Chiefs Conference president in 1962-1964, I returned as president from 1969 to 1971. I helped form the Dena' Nena' Henash development corporation, negotiating Native contracts with the Trans-Alaska Pipeline System for revegetation and erosion control. I *began serving as the AAIA field representative. I was also a member of the Bureau of Indian Affairs Tribal National Workgroup on Tribal Priority Allocations.*

When AFN could not afford to hire a director in 1971, I moved to Anchorage to work as the acting executive director, with half my salary paid by AAIA and the other half by AFN.

Between 1973 and 1974, I was back in Fairbanks running a grant-funded program at TCC. In 1978, I served my last term as president of TCC. At the end of my presidency, I moved to Anchorage to head up the RurALCAP federal Community Enterprise Development Corporation (CEDC) in 1978–1981. CEDC dedicated itself to raising the economic level of rural Natives.

In 1988, I served as TCC's director of natural resources.

In 1991, Will Mayo and I both ran for president of TCC. We agreed that whoever won, the other would go "upstairs" and work. So when he was elected president, I began serving as the CEO. For twelve years at TCC, I worked with first Will Mayo, then presidents Steve Ginnis and Buddy Brown. I retired in 2002.

In my years at TCC, by 1991, I had contracted twenty-eight million dollars, and by the time I left in 2002, TCC had a total of seventy-six million a year in contracts. I may be a lousy politician but I do pretty well in administration. I have a high standard and I fire as needed, calling it like it is. In all the years I have served and with all the people I have met, I have only been sued once. I imagine people realized that they needed firing when I did it. An employer has to trust his employees and to know they'll do their work. I never told my people how to do their job. If they couldn't do the work, I fired them. When I was there, TCC had a relaxed atmosphere. We served the villages, and their day began at 10 a.m. After I left, if employees didn't show up until 10 a.m., they got fired.

TCC serves forty-two villages; I had a thousand employees. We got our budgeting from Indian Health

Before Native Pride hats were available, Al enjoyed wearing Navajo hats but people kept taking them so he had to keep an inventory of hats on hand, 2011.
The Navajo are the largest federally recognized tribe in the United States. They and the Apache are considered southern Athabascans.
Betty Ketzler photo.

Service as well as from BIA, under whom we contracted fourteen programs; there were also a few state programs.

Everything in the village costs more than in the city. Half of Alaska's legislators are based out of Anchorage. They get elected and then they get more of their own kind elected. It's a vicious circle that cannot be fixed.

I spent twenty-two years working for TCC and other nonprofits. Today, I just go to meetings and listen.

In 2002, Doyon honored Al Ketzler with a citation framed with beaded moosehide, "to honor Al Ketzler Sr. for his tireless efforts on behalf of all Native people in Alaska, TCC is renaming the former Doyon building on First Avenue the Alfred Ketzler Sr. Building."

In 2004, as pictured on the cover of *Windows to the Land*, Al was awarded an honorary doctor of laws degree from the University of Alaska Fairbanks "for persons distinguished in general service to the state, to learning, and to humankind." Side by side with the former mayor of Nenana, territorial and state legislator, lieutenant governor of Alaska, and drafter of the state constitution Jack Coghill, Al was saluted as one of the initiators of the Alaska Native Claims Settlement Act, organizer and first president of the Tanana Chiefs Conference, and deputy director of Alaska Federation of Natives.

Every November, Al Ketzler goes to Washington, D.C., to see his lifelong friend, former executive director of AAIA Bill Byler, who is now in poor health. Neither man has ever sought the limelight. They are that rare breed of "ordinary" men, birthed out of the common life, who with integrity and alertness, despite their fatigue, discouragement, and loss, have done what needed to be done. These unsung heroes made epic changes in Alaska and in the world.

Today Tanana Chiefs Conference transacts about ninety million dollars a year in contracts.

In 1981, Morris Thompson went to work for Doyon, Limited, his ANCSA regional corporation. Originally hired as a vice president, he became Doyon's president and chief executive officer in 1985, when Doyon had an operating loss of $28 million. When he retired in 2000, Doyon was generating $70.9 million in annual revenues and had nine hundred employees and 14,000 shareholders. For fiscal 2010, Doyon reported a net income of $15.7 million on total revenue of $280.2 million. Doyon has 18,300 shareholders and is the largest private landowner in Alaska.

Al Ketzler Sr. and his children: (l-r) Craig, Robert, Stephanie, Al, Alex, Stuart, and Al "Bear" Jr., circa 2011, Fairbanks.

Courtesy of Al "Bear" Ketzler Jr.

Timeline

1297: Magna Carta.

1949: Purvis family moved to Nenana, Alaska.

Early 1950s: Alfred Starr family moved to Nenana.

1956: Kay Hitchcock's thesis on indigenous title and statehood.

1959: Statehood.

1961: State filed on Minto land.

1962, January: Al Ketzler called meeting in Nenana; Hitchcock read.

1962, February: Second meeting but with press and court judge. LaVerne Madigan of AAIA contacted.

1962, March: Meeting with ten villages at Nenana dog races.

1962, June: First re-organization of Tanana Chiefs Conference.

1962, August: LaVerne Madigan died, followed by Bill Byler at Association on American Indian Affairs (AAIA).

1962-1963, winter: Al Ketzler sent petitions to all Interior villages.

1963, April: Ketzler asked Secretary of State Udall for land freeze.

1963, June: Second Tanana Chiefs meeting at Tanana.

1964: Yukon Flats People Speak and Cook Inlet Native Association.

1966: Udall issued preliminary injunction against land selection. Alaska Federation of Natives begun.

1968: Bonanza oil discovery on North Slope.

1969, January: Wally Hickel became secretary of state.

1969, September: Landmark oil lease sales.

1970, April: Injunction against construction permit right-of-way.

1971, December: Alaska Native Claims Settlement Act signed.

1975: PL 93-638; Indian Self-Determination Act; could contract.

1976-1978: First Native corporation bankruptcies.

∽

Chapter Twenty-one

Windows to the Land, An Alaska Native Story: Emil Notti, First President of AFN

Emil Notti, Anchorage, 2005.

Judy Ferguson photo.

An aeronautical and electrical engineer, a man of vision, great restraint, and patience, Emil Notti was the gavel and the forum for the boiling cauldron of the embryonic Alaska Federation of Natives (AFN) at its inception in 1966. Five years later at his own personal and financial expense, he saw victory with the passage of the Alaska Native Claims Settlement Act (ANCSA) in 1971.

I first met Emil Notti in 1974 on the Yukon River. My husband and I were visiting Emmitt Peters' family at Melozi fish camp across from Ruby. Also on a river trip, Emil stopped to see his Aunt Mary Peters, Emmitt's mother. As a child, Mary had been adopted by Emil's mother's family, the Pitkas. Emil's mother, Madeline, and Mary Peters were sisters by adoption. Every July, Emil runs the river of his ancestors to visit his family.

Thirty-one years later in Anchorage, I asked Emil to do an interview. We met in the Ahtna, Inc., building where he worked. That evening, he began sharing the story of his life.

My maternal great-grandfather was Ivan Pavlof, the last official manager of the Russian American Trading Company post in Nulato. His name was given to Mount Pavlof, a volcano in the Aleutian Range of the Alaska Peninsula, and its nearby Pavlof Islands. In 1893, Ivan's son, Pitka Pavlof, and Sergei Cherosky discovered a large gold strike at Preacher Creek, a tributary of Birch Creek in interior Alaska. Because they were Natives, at the time defined as noncitizens, prospectors jumped their claims. (In 1924, Indians were made citizens.) For the rest of his

KOYUKON

life, my grandfather hunted Dall sheep and dried their meat in the mountains. As he hunted, he found gold nuggets. This time he told no one. He used the nuggets for the rest of his life for ammunition, tea, flour, bacon, and sugar: the basics to keep his trapline going.

My father, Joseph Notti, was a full-time prospector. He was an Italian immigrant and a friend of Felix Pedro, whose gold strike started Fairbanks. Dad went southwest to Ester Creek, where he discovered the richest gold mine in Alaska at the time. As was common, he was claim-jumped. After shooting one of the thieves in the leg, he was sent to the federal penitentiary on McNeil Island out of Seattle. He had been there a year when Judge Wickersham, on his way to Teddy Roosevelt's inauguration, stopped to see him. After hearing Dad's story, he asked Roosevelt to pardon my father. The former Rough Rider president gladly signed the release, saying, "If I had been he, I'd have killed the SOB."

Since this happened before Dad had a family, it's amazing that he returned to Alaska. With his partner, he headed for the Koyukuk River to prospect. There he met my mother, Madeline Pitka. They married and I, the youngest of four children, was born in 1933. After my parents separated, Dad and his partner continued up the Koyukuk River to prospect. How he found gold I don't know, but they found a spot and sunk holes all winter long, thawing the ground. They saved the dirt and then sluiced it in the spring. They kept finding gold but they couldn't find the vein. Eventually they abandoned the site without filing a claim. Twenty years later, a global concern, the United States Smelting, Refining, and Mining Company, went through my father's cabin floor with a rotary drill and hit the vein that my dad had been searching. That's the closest he ever came to a big strike.

I started first and second grades at the territorial school in Ruby, but I began alternating time between my parents. The fall I was seven, my brother, Dad, and I motored up the Koyukuk River, pushing a barge with a small boat and inboard. Below Hughes, at Dalby, we pulled the boat out. For the next eight months, the three of us trapped alone until the ice went out.

A countryman and friend of Joseph Notti, Felix Pedro, discoverer of gold in Fairbanks, 1902.

Historical Photograph Collection, UAF-65-20

That summer I went to Fairbanks for the first time to have my tonsils taken out.

SS Nenana at Beaver village in the 1950s.
http://www.newsminer.com/view/full_story/12285202/article-Elder-Robert-Charlie-to-share-stories-of-working-on-Alaska-steamboats-

Only seven, I remember coming up the river on the steamer *Nenana*, and then taking a two-car train from Nenana to Fairbanks. At that time, there were only 72,000 people in Alaska. We had unrestricted use of the land. We could move anywhere, cut down trees, build a cabin, and if the game was no good, we moved on. We could do anything as long as we didn't infringe on someone else's trapline.

However, when I was nine, I returned to Ruby and to school. I wouldn't admit I was only in third grade. I pretended that for the last two years I'd been in Koyukuk's BIA school. I acted like I was ready for fifth grade, the same as my friends. But it wasn't a problem because I was determined.

World War II brought lots of soldiers, followed by construction workers in the postwar boom, which greatly impacted Alaska's small population. A rough lot, these men drank, modeling a poor example of western culture to Natives while we transitioned into the modern era. All of us were affected.

My schooling took me from home and propelled me throughout Alaska. For sixth grade, I was sent to Old Eklutna boarding school near Palmer. The next year, in 1945, we boarding students were shipped to an old army camp at Seward for seventh and eighth grades. When the army camp closed, I began high school at Mount Edgecumbe in Sitka. During the summers until I graduated in 1951, I fished commercially in Klawock, Craig, and Hydaburg.

I joined the Navy during the Korean War. In boot camp, they ran us into the ground, running us all night and then during the day putting us on guard duty. However, after I took the normal standardized tests, an officer said to me, "Sometimes we get high scores back, but never 95 to 100." I was transferred to a navy electronics school, followed by security training and three years of duty in Washington, D.C. After I was discharged, using money from the navy and the GI Bill, I first attended Marshall University in West Virginia, followed by Northrop University in Inglewood, California, where I graduated with a dual degree in aeronautical and electrical engineering in 1961. I got a job working as an electronics engineer for the Autonetics Division of North American Aviation under contract to the Air Force Ballistic Missile Division, testing equipment for the guidance system on the Minute Man Missile in Los Angeles. After ten years in southern California, I got a job as an electronics engineer for the

Federal Aviation Administration in Anchorage. I was ready to return home. I began working as well for the state's Human Rights Commission because I was interested in the Natives' situation.

By the time I returned, Alaska was no longer a territory. During the battle for statehood, New York representatives opposed Alaska's admittance, saying they wouldn't support government in a land with no industry and low population with no way to pay for government. To help cover that expense, the federal government gave Alaska 103 million acres of federal land to select. In 1960 before the Prudhoe Bay discovery, Alaska supported government by the sale of its land. The freedom to use the land that I'd experienced growing up began to become restricted. It became increasingly necessary to get patents, title, and homesteads. As both individuals and the state began claiming land, they also began infringing on Natives' traditional use of the land. The state began selecting land at Minto, Dot Lake, and Tanacross, causing protests from the newly reorganized Tanana Chiefs Conference.

In 1963 in Anchorage, I met Nick Gray. He was half Jewish and half Eskimo, so he coined himself "a Jewskimo." Nick had been a valet for the pianist Ignacy Paderewski. He had traveled the world and he was very articulate. He had helped organize the Fairbanks Native Association. In Anchorage, he had begun buttonholing people on the street to fight for education, health, housing, and jobs; his efforts coalesced into the Cook Inlet Native Association. He fascinated me. He took me under his wing and invited me to go with him to newspaper and radio interviews where I loved listening to his use of language.

He explained that Native housing was extremely bad, that Native educational achievement was low. The statistics were terrible. The average age of death for Alaska Natives was thirty-four years old. Infant mortality was three times the national average. The worst tuberculosis epidemic ever recorded had occurred among the Natives. Very few people were working; jobs for Natives were very hard to come by. We began working on a host of social issues. Nick and Howard Rock became very prominently involved with indigenous land issues. In 1965, we raised enough to send Nick to Cordova, Bethel, and Kodiak to mobilize around the state. His vision was for a statewide Native

Emil Notti, president of Cook Inlet Native Association, circa 1966.

Tundra Times. Courtesy of Emil Notti.

196

Bob Bennett Alaska director of BIA with President Kennedy's task force to Alaska speaking as Al Ketzler Sr. takes notes, 1962, Tanana Chiefs Conference at Tanana.
Photographer Theodore Hetzel. Courtesy of Alfred "Bear" Ketzler Jr.

organization, but he contracted leukemia. When he was no longer able, I followed Nick as president of Cook Inlet Native Association.

In January 1966, Bob Bennett, a Minnesota Oneida Indian and nominee for commissioner of Indian Affairs, appeared for confirmation before the Senate Committee on Interior and Insular Affairs in Washington. Henry "Scoop" Jackson, a senator from Washington, asked Bennett, "You're an Indian. We've been dealing with the Indian problem in the United States for two hundred years. What would you do to solve the Indian problem?" As Bennett began to answer, Jackson interrupted, "Don't be extemporaneous. I want a ninety-day written report." Somehow in April 1966, I got a copy of that report. Bennett had devoted only a small section to Alaska, but he pointed out that BIA was about to draw up a final solution to the land selection problem in Alaska. I didn't know what to do. [According to DeLois Ketzler Burggraf, initially Emil had no support structure as Al Ketzler did with the Association of American Indian Affairs.] I thought about it, and in July I finally wrote a letter to fourteen people around the state. Some I knew by reputation but others, not at all. I suggested, "We should meet in Anchorage to discuss if we have any rights to the land. If we do, we should have something to say about the solution." Howard Rock got my letter and headlined it in the *Tundra Times*, saying, "Statewide meeting called for." From July to October every week, he ran a story relevant to the meeting.

When I wrote that letter, calling people to the statewide meeting, I envisioned fourteen people showing up, half of whom I wouldn't know. In October, instead of fourteen people showing up in Anchorage, there were three hundred people. It was exciting, but we didn't know each other. Traditionally we had been in conflict, so it was hard to get people to start trusting each other. That first statewide meeting in Anchorage in 1966 was the beginning of the Alaska Federation of Natives (AFN.) It was partly financed by the village of Tyonek, which had received $11 million in oil leases. We met in a building they owned on Fourth Avenue, where I chaired the meeting. We organized a committee to

Alaska Federation of Natives board, 1968: l-r: Don Wright, Frank Degnan, Willie Hensley, Emil Notti, Flore Lekanof, Al Ketzler, and Charles Franz.
Tundra Times. *Alaska Native Land Claims.* Courtesy of Emil Notti.

research land issues, headed by a very bright college kid, Willie Hensley. With everyone gathered, with a grease pencil, I sketched out the borders of each cultural region, to which all agreed.

We began having a lot of meetings. After I was elected president, I quit my job in 1967. Despite that AFN had only nine dollars in the bank and I had a young family, I began working for AFN full time. I got three months behind on our house and car payments. One week we lived on one pot of beans. Those who started AFN sacrificed financially and personally. They took time off from work and paid their own travel, hotel rooms, and meals. Harvey Samuelson [late president of Bristol Bay Native Corporation] once told me he had spent twenty to thirty thousand dollars attending AFN meetings. Cecil Barnes [Alutiiq founder of the Eyak Corporation] mortgaged his house. There are many people like them who never received recognition or thanks for their efforts. They did it because they thought it was the necessary thing to do.

Cecil Barnes, Alutiiq founder of the Eyak Corporation.
Alaska Native Land Claims. Courtesy of Emil Notti.

Harvey Samuelson, the late president of Bristol Bay Native Corporation.
Alaska Native Land Claims. Courtesy of Emil Notti.

As I presided over AFN, I had to bury myself, showing a calm demeanor while the clashing Native cultures wrestled it out. It was critical that they got everything on the table to render a land claims bill that was fair to everyone. I was careful to only interrupt when it was absolutely necessary, but the gavel became my best tool. Once when a particularly aggressive and obscene man was exploding, I struck the gavel hard once, abruptly. He stopped in his tracks. Issue by issue, we arrived at a position on the amount of land and the amount of money we sought. The land issue was complicated by there being two formulas, one based on population and the other based on area lost by the tribe. These matters were hammered out with great emotional conviction.

From the beginning, we insisted on being a part of the decision-making at the national level. The reservation system had a track record of two hundred years of failure. We considered the corporation model. Alaska was going to grow, and we wanted to grow with it. We didn't want the Bureau of Indian Affairs making our mistakes and our decisions, which is what they did. We wanted more to say about what happened in our lives, not be dictated to by a government that was distant from us. As owner of the land, we could make any kind of a deal with a willing buyer. Originally, we asked for two percent in perpetuity of any underground resources but they said, "We're not going to give you an open-ended check." We didn't have the political muscle or financial base to get what we asked, and in the end, we lost a lot.

AFN proposed one statewide corporation with only one set of economic advisers, lawyers, and planners but Congress broke up that single entity into villages.

In 1935, Tlingit-Haida were authorized by Congress to file a lawsuit regarding their indigenous land. In 1968, they received no land but a cash settlement. Although not members, they began coming to AFN, seeking membership with the hope of sharing in a possible land settlement. There was an intense discussion on whether their membership might weaken AFN's position, since they had already received a settlement. I decided, "We're going to decide this without lawyers." Protesting, the lawyers said that this was not possible. When they were out of the room, I put it to a vote. It gridlocked and I cast the tie-breaking vote. [Due to their becoming part of ANCSA, the Tlingit-Haida went from a $7 million dollar settlement to $170 million plus acreage, their share of land claims.]

Tyonek's attorney Stan McCutcheon of Anchorage, who helped organize the first statewide conference of Natives.
Anchorage Daily News. Alaska Native Land Claims. Courtesy of Emil Notti.

In 1966, Secretary of the Interior Stewart Udall issued a preliminary injunction to freeze all transfers of land, pending indigenous land claims.

To typify our new unity of cultures, I drew the AFN logo of three circles, which represent-

199

ed Aleut, Eskimo, and Indian. It had the title "Integrity, Pride in Heritage, Progress," which was our focus. With the help of Stanley McCutcheon and a Washington, D.C., attorney specializing in Indian law, Marvin Sinoski, AFN drew up documents regarding our position. I wrote the bylaws, and the newly created AFN adopted them in Anchorage in April 1967. We submitted our document to our congressional delegation. Our proposition was introduced as the first [statewide] land claims bill, Senate Bill 2020.

Alaska Federation of Natives logo designed by Emil Notti.
Courtesy of Emil Notti.

Governor Wally Hickel was sure the land freeze was going to drive Alaska into bankruptcy. He and the attorney general had filed a lawsuit. In January 1969, Hickel knew he was going to be appointed secretary of the interior when Nixon called him to Washington, D.C. When he landed in Seattle, a reporter asked him what he was going to do about the land freeze. After he made his infamous statement, "What Udall can do with a stroke of a pen, I can undo," the board voted unanimously to send me to Washington, D.C., to try to block his nomination. We agreed that we would endorse him only if he supported the land freeze or remained neutral. Eben Hopson, John Borbridge, Willie Hensley, and I went to Washington, D.C. for three days where we lobbied, saying we would only support his nomination if he promised to keep the land freeze. But on the last day when we walked into the hearing room, the first four rows for the Alaska delegation were reserved so we sat in the fifth row.

Hickel's new appointee who had just filled the late Bob Bartlett's senate seat, Ted Stevens, entered, escorting a jet-load of Alaska's top brass: the leading newspaper editors and the head of the Teamsters. Anybody who was somebody in Alaska marched in and sat in those four front rows in front of us. Ted Stevens began, "Before we start, I would like to introduce these outstanding Alaskans here in support of our governor. Would they stand?" But we remained seated. A guy turned around and growled,

Emil Notti and John Borbridge, president and vice president of AFN on Channel 29, Philadelphia, 1969.
Photographer Theodore Hetzel. Courtesy of Alfred "Bear" Ketzler Jr.

"What the heck is wrong with you guys?" We said, "We're doing what we have to do." After three days of grilling, Hickel finally agreed that he would not lift the freeze, which enabled us to endorse him as secretary of the interior.

While we fought with the whole world watching, some of the AFN board changed their position, coerced by Hickel's people. While I was making the rounds of Congress, representatives began telling us that members of the board, those who had sent me there to speak for them, had changed their position. They wired their support to the Interior Department for Wally Hickel as secretary of the interior. If I were asked, I'd say to members of Congress, "Oh, don't pay any attention." But after I returned home, I said to the AFN board, "Don't you ever do that to me again. When I am down there, doing what you asked me to do by your unanimous vote, when I am carrying your water for you, don't you ever undercut me like that again." But friends of theirs had gotten to them, warning, "You don't want to upset the governor because you will have to deal with him either as secretary of state or as governor." Feeling overwhelmed, they would not make a stand. It happens today; it's all about money.

Over four years, there were eight land claims bills. Everybody got into the act: the Senate Interior Committee, the Department of Interior, the State of Alaska, the Federal Field Committee, the House Committee on Interior and Insular Affairs, and AFN—eight bills in all. And there were others. Everybody had an idea how to solve the problem.

Laura Bergt of Fairbanks.
Tundra Times. Alaska Native Land
Claims. Courtesy of Emil Notti.

Two months before the Alaska Native Claims Settlement Act passed, knowing that it would and despite requests to remain, I didn't seek another term as president of Alaska Federation of Natives. I had run the distance.

I credit the final obtaining of the forty million acres of land to Don Wright and Laura Bergt. Through Don and Laura, what AFN was asking was clearly communicated to Vice President Spiro Agnew. Over dinner, Agnew agreed that AFN's terms were not unreasonable, and that then became the president's position. A lot of people were involved at the right time; they had the right words and they made the right phone calls to make it happen. Meantime, we were going around the country talking to as many support groups as we could. Willie Hensley was on *Good Morning, America*. Laura Bergt appeared on Johnny Carson's *Tonight* show. I went to Detroit to Cobo Hall and talked to the National Council of

Churches. Ten thousand ministers were in the audience; they passed a unanimous resolution backing our position on land claims. We also got the backing of the AFL-CIO. We had a hard time before the Senate and House because there were some skeptics who didn't quite agree with what we were doing. It was quite a feeling when we finally got some lawyers to support us. The first time I sat down before a Senate committee, we had Supreme Court Justice Arthur Goldberg on one side of us, and Attorney General for the United States Ramsey Clark on our other side; suddenly the whole atmosphere changed. All of a sudden they started taking us much more seriously. Everything came together step by step. When you look at it, it was a major accomplishment.

Willie Hensley, AFN president in 1972.
Photographer Theodore Hetzel.
Courtesy Alfred "Bear" Ketzler Jr.

When ANCSA finally passed in 1971, it was not a negotiated land settlement. Behind closed doors, Congress picked sections from the eight land bills and unilaterally handed out a bill.

ANCSA became law December 18, 1971. Thirteen regional corporations were formed, a social experiment in capitalism.

We hit a window of time when we were able to maximize on land and money. Ten years earlier we probably could have gotten more land. Later, after oil was discovered, land would have been much harder to get. After there was a lot of money coming in from oil, we could have gotten more money, but less land. I think we maximized on both. At the time it was the biggest land claim settlement the United States had ever made. Forty million acres is bigger than all the reservations in the United States put together.

But we had no illusions. We knew we had a lot of work to do, and the signing of ANCSA just meant that we needed to shift gears and look inward. How do you take a people from a subsistence lifestyle and jerk them into an economy imposed upon them? Forty years ago, how many of us knew about shares, annual reports, investments, and all the things that go into running a corporation? Few of us.

In 1973, I took over as president of the Alaska Native Foundation. The foundation with Bob Arnold and I wrote the book *Alaska Native Land Claims* whose preface I authored. Every region and village needed a land manager; our foundation trained them as well as the bookkeepers. We taught the managers to identify land, write leases, and do record keeping.

Emil Notti, president of Alaska Native Foundation, in a land claims training session, 1973.
Tundra Times.
Alaska Native Land Claims.
Courtesy of Emil Notti.

I am disappointed today with companies and their hiring policies. In 1966, Bill Egan was the last governor to talk with oil companies about local hire. Before the pipeline, the villages had eighty percent unemployment. Today it is still eighty percent, while Alaska has grown in wealth and population.

To air the subject, Governor Sheffield researched the issue of sovereignty, which is a misnomer. The state has the right to take a life and to conscript an army, but we cannot do that so we are not talking sovereignty. We're asking for limited self-government, to be able to make a few decisions about trapping, hunting, and fishing. Legally, we can control people hunting on our land but the state will not enforce it.

We came up with a social experiment: the corporations. It will take time to see if it will work. Had corporations not been formed, there would have been no protection of the land. If the land were developed and if it became a part of a borough or a city, the land could be taxed and could, conceivably, go back to the government. The only way to protect it— and that's not likely—would be if Congress put it in tribal status.

The U.S. Securities and Exchange Commission (SEC) laws are strict. The SEC governs what corporations can put in their annual reports, their rules, and what they can write off. Since we had no experience, we were afraid of getting involved with the SEC. We got a five-year exemption, saying that when we got some years behind us, we could consider what goes into those reports and try to start meeting SEC rules. Somewhere in that five-year period, the corporations became forever exempt. Senator Ted Stevens earmarked a sentence in a bill stating that the federal government would forthwith deal with the corporations as tribes. That federal exemption from the SEC also preempted the state from ever having any authority over the corporations. As a result, there's no accountability, no oversight of them. Congress was supposed to hold oversight hearings to see how the corporations were doing but to my knowledge, they have never happened. There are abuses in the corporations but since they don't report to the state banking and securities (which corporations come under) or to the SEC rules, there's no real accountability. Most of the corporations' annual reports look pretty good but they operate under different rules for what they have to report than do other corporations subject to the SEC. If we were

203

under SEC rules, there might be some problems. The very tool we worked to create has become a tool of self-indulgence and abuse.

ANCSA changed Native people, because Native people had to change. In 1940, Alaska had 72,000 people living in a very different economic structure. Today we have 710,231 of whom only 14.8 percent are Alaska Natives. As Alaska grows, we as a minority will only continue to shrink. Alaska Natives have been learning to participate not just as workers, but as managers. Owning their own corporations adds immeasurably to the Native people's confidence. Not only can they deal with bankers and accountants, but they are becoming the bankers, accountants, and lawyers. We have learned to function in the economy and we must continue to do so. We need to increase employment in the villages. Instead of hiring locally, outsiders come here and take our jobs, flying in and out of the state, two weeks on, two weeks off. Those jobs should go to the villagers. When that happens, when our unemployment rate approaches the averages of the rest of the state, we will have accomplished one of our major goals of land claims. Today, everyone has a chance to get involved. It's an educational experiment to get people participating in the economic system; we are already way ahead of the economic possibilities on the reservations.

Before ANCSA and ANILCA, when the initial land use studies were being done, BLM went out to the villages with big maps. They asked villagers to show where they trapped and how they got there. The people drew their trails on the maps. The state declared them as "old trails of commerce" and withdrew that land as "existing easements," RS-2477. With the existing right-of-way as a

Forty Years after ANCSA. L-r, front row: Al Ketzler Sr., Emil Notti, Mary Jane, and Bud Fate; back: Mike Bradner, moderator Willy Templeton, in front of Templeton the late Richard Frank, unknown, journalist Tim Bradner 2010, Fairbanks.

Photographer Rob Stapleton. http://ancsaat40.org/Our_Panel_Discussions.html Courtesy of Emil Notti.

precedent, the state used that as a basis for constructing roads. Such easements crisscrossed all over the Mat-Su Valley. In Mat-Su, there was such a roar over it that the legislature dropped the state's right to exercise the trails as an easement on the land. For the urban arena, the issue was nullified, setting a precedent for the Bush. The same should be done for Native-owned land.

DeLois Burggraf observed:

> *The paradigm of land ownership changed after the 1980 Alaska National Interest Lands Conservation Act, or ANILCA. Before the 1970s, the federal government did not own land; it held the land in trust through Native reserves, the military, homesteads, homesites, trade and manufacture sites, and mining claims. People had access to vast acreage. However, with ANCSA and ANILCA, there was a policy switch, a change of relationship between the people, the government, and the land. All federal land programs relating to homesteading, homesites, headquarter sites, and trade and manufacturing sites within Alaska expired in 1986 as a result of the Federal Land Policy and Management Act (FLPMA) of 1976. Today BLM has no land disposal program. Freedom and access to the land have become much more constricted.*

Emil Notti continued.

When I left AFN, I opened a shop in Sitka, working on boat radars, sonar, and transmitters. In 1972, the Alaska lobbyist Alex Miller came to Sitka. He said he ought to hire me as Governor Egan's deputy commissioner of Health and Social Services. I gave up my business and went back into government. In 1973, supported by Congressman Nick Begich's widow, Peggy Begich, I ran against Don Young for Begich's vacated U.S. House of Representatives seat. I lost by only 1,900 votes, the closest margin Young ever experienced. After serving three years as president of the Alaska Native Foundation, I served from 1976 to 1981 as senior vice president and then president of Doyon, Limited. I went into consulting 1981 to 1982. My big client was ARCO and Petroleum Equipment Suppliers Association. ARCO wanted a Native lobbyist, but I wound up helping them with a tax problem, saving them over a billion dollars in taxes. For a year

Peggy Begich, 1970.
Courtesy of Tom Begich.

under Governor Sheffield, I was first special assistant for legislation, and from 1984 to 1986, commissioner for the Division of Community and Regional Affairs. I spent the next seven years consulting for AT&T Alaska, followed by a consultant position for AHTNA regional corporation from 2004 to

2005. Until I retired in 2010, I served as commissioner of Commerce, Community and Economic Development for Governors Sarah Palin and Sean Parnell. For thirty years, I was on the board of the National Bank of Alaska. I hold an honorary doctorate degree from Alaska Methodist University.

Since my birth in the village of Koyukuk in 1933, I have been privileged to be a part of the shaping of our land. Indeed my life has been a window to the land, a story of the journey of Alaska Natives. We have made great strides, with many more likely to come.

Emil Notti, 2005.
Judy Ferguson photo.

Timeline:

1867: Russia sold its possessions in Alaska to the U.S.

1893: Pitka Pavlof and Sergei Cherosky find gold at Preacher Creek.

1906: Ester Creek gold strike.

1924: Alaska Natives became U.S. citizens.

1935: Congress authorized Tlingit-Haida to sue for land claims.

1942: World War II.

1960: State of Alaska began selecting land including Native land.

1961: Tyonek sold its oil leases.

1964: Cook Inlet Native Association.

1966: BIA Alaska head Bob Bennett reported on Alaska Native land.

1966: Emil Notti began Alaska Federation of Natives.

January 1969: Walter Hickel became Nixon's Secretary of State.

December 1971: Alaska Native Land Claims Settlement Act passed.

1976: Federal Land Policy and Management Act.

1980: Alaska National Interest Lands Conservation Act, or ANILCA

∽

Chapter Twenty-two

Bill Byler and the Association on American Indian Affairs (AAIA)

After I met Al Ketzler Sr. and DeLois Ketzler Burggraf in 2005, they referred me to Al's friend, William (Bill) Byler, former executive director for the Association on American Indian Affairs (AAIA.) After Al Ketzler and Bill Byler met in April 1963, they began working closely together to secure Alaska Native land claims.

In this day of Native corporations, it is difficult to grasp that there was a time, after statehood, before Congress had defined Native land rights and

William "Bill" Byler, executive director of the Association on American Indian Affairs. Courtesy of Bill Byler.

before modern communications and transportation had alerted and unified the indigenous people to their common land concerns, when the state was making critical land selections that usurped Native land. Due to the Natives' isolation and the lack of awareness of Alaska Native land rights, the state was able to select strategic lands from the federal land holdings, including Prudhoe Bay. Working in the background, Bill Byler's AAIA was a tremendous enabling force to empower the Alaska Natives. AAIA both bankrolled and educated the people. At the time, a support structure was critical.

In 2006 when I spoke with Bill Byler by telephone in his home in Silver Springs, Maryland, I asked him to sum up the impact he and AAIA had had in Alaska.

He responded, "I can say that AAIA has greatly made possible village life, but self advertising isn't something I or AAIA do. The point was to get the American public to support the Native people. It was the Natives who were raising this fight. We were the oilcan. We made the machinery work. AAIA loved the land, and that is everything."

I have used phone interviews with Bill Byler, Don Mitchell's Take My Land, Take My Life, *a website based on Byler's work, and a Mitchell*

interview with Byler, among other sources, to present his story and that of AAIA in Alaska.

A history of AAIA based on Bill Byler's Princeton files at website, http://findingaids.princeton.edu/:

AAIA was founded in 1922 in New York as the Eastern Association on Indian Affairs to assist a group of Pueblo people who were fighting efforts to dismantle their pueblos. Over the years, several leaders led AAIA through name changes, through amalgamations with other groups, and over the roller coaster of history.

In 1924, the Eastern Association on Indian Affairs, forerunner of AAIA, widened its focus in Indian affairs to education, industry, health, and sanitation, land tenure, irrigation, religion, and autonomy. The EAIA asserted that "the best education of our Indian wards would be achieved by developing instead of destroying their pride of race and by calling into active service, instead of suppressing, their group loyalties and communal responsibilities." Positions such as this marked a watershed change in non-Native thinking and led to the Indian Reorganization Act of 1934, the high point of a reformation in Indian affairs during the Roosevelt administration.

Oliver La Farge, president of AAIA, 1933.
http://todayinsci.com/8/8_02.htm

Notwithstanding its achievements, the EAIA was on the verge of collapse in 1933 when Oliver La Farge, a writer-anthropologist, became its president. Four years later, EAIA became today's Association on American Indian Affairs (AAIA). Its mission was "to promote the welfare of the American Indian in the United States by creating an enlightened public opinion, by assisting and protecting him against encroachment of his constitutional rights, and by promoting suitable legislation and enforcement of law; by aiding in the improvement of health and educational conditions and in preserving and fostering his arts and crafts; and in furtherance of this object it shall gather and disseminate facts bearing on the welfare of the Indians and shall assist in formulating and making effective a constructive national policy on Indian affairs." AAIA was one of the last in a line of turn-of-the-century great benefactor movements.

From Judy Ferguson's *Parallel Destinies*:

In 1938, Moris Burge was the first AAIA field representative to come to Alaska. Since 1915 in Alaska, John Hajdukovich had been the key trader serving the villages from the upper Tanana River to the Canadian border. He headquartered at Big Delta. After the Indian Reorganization Act of 1934, inexpensive loans were made available for Natives to run their own stores. As a result, John, who had a lot of Native debt on his books, was told in 1936 that he could no longer trade in Tetlin. He approached his wealthy friend Edward Mallinckrodt of St. Louis, one of the planners of the Tetlin Reserve, for help. Mallinckrodt wanted

Chief Peter Joe, Tetlin, circa 1936.

Tetlin Photo Collection. UAF-1987-0114-56. Courtesy of Larry Mark.

a second opinion. He paid an investigator, Moris Burge of the AAIA, to check into the situation. In 1938, Burge reconnoitered the upper Tanana with John and was impressed. Burge reported, "The Tetlin area in which John does his trading and offers his hospitality is somewhat a paradise under any conditions, with abundant game, fur, and fishing. In John Hajdukovich's business with the Indians, he has never let his personal interest stand in the way of decent humanity. He has made it his constant effort to keep sobriety and industry at the highest possible point among the Indian Alaskan patrons."

Burge continued, "Largely as a result of his insistent efforts, the Tetlin Indians have maintained a clean, straight thinking, and nobility of character that speaks well for the lives they live. Their genuine, wholesome way of living has given them a share of pride not often found among the more discouraged Alaskan Indians of other sections. John has helped keep the standards and has thereby brought real lasting wealth to the Territory. The Indians rely on him for matters of all importance, and had it not been for his influence, the picture would have been entirely different."

"But," Burge concluded, "one day, Hajdukovich will be gone and the Indians cannot rely on one man always." He suggested more governmental involvement in the area and pushed for a larger game reserve.

Continued, based on Bill Byler's Princeton AAIA files website:

During the 1950s, AAIA (the Association) President Oliver La Farge was most concerned with the federal government's policy of termination, a goal of ending its involvement in the lives of Native Americans by abruptly relinquishing its responsibilities towards both tribes and individuals. Termination drew the Association's fire, for, if fully implemented, it threatened to do incalculable harm to the material wellbeing and cultural identity of Indians throughout the United States. In 1956, the Association presented an alternative to these policies in an **American Indian Point IV Program** *aimed at developing the social and economic potential of Native American communities, eliminating the disparities between Natives and non-Natives, without destroying the indigenous culture. By 1955, Native Americans joined the AAIA staff.*

The same year, La Verne Madigan became AAIA's executive director. Although she was low-key, Madigan was a take-charge, self-confident individual with enormous persistence. Notably, the AAIA helped dissuade Congress from writing provisions into the Alaska Statehood Act that would have compromised Native land rights. She also pioneered Native land rights in Alaska. According to Don Mitchell's *Take My Land, Take My Life*, on a trip to Alaska in 1960, her goal was to "find out exactly what the areas of our ignorance are in order that we may know what we have to learn before we can form an Alaska policy" and "to find locals to organize a local AAIA branch." On a reference, she flew to Point Barrow to speak with Guy Okakok, an Iñupiaq who wrote a Barrow news col-

Guy Okakok, circa 1962.
Photographer Theodore Hetzel.
Courtesy Alfred "Bear" Ketzler

umn for the *Fairbanks Daily News-Miner.* She found that Guy and his friends thought that "land ownership could never become a problem . . . but any interference with their hunting and fishing would make them very angry." Madigan recommended to AAIA that they develop an Alaska Native policy "because no one has one now, and if an issue comes up, the Natives could lose important rights or property while we looked frantically for a set of principles on which to stand."

An artist from Point Hope, Howard Rock, sent his work to show and to sell in New York, to the Association on American Indian Affairs (AAIA). DeLois Ketzler Burggraf pointed out that he notified AAIA about Project Chariot. [This was a 1958 U.S. Atomic Energy Commission proposal to construct an artificial harbor at Cape Thompson in far northwestern Alaska by burying and detonating a string of nuclear devices.] LaFarge and Madigan suggested that Congress should address indigenous land claims before sending in the Atomic

LaVerne Madigan, 1961, discussing at Iñupiat Paitot meeting. Tundra Times.

Energy Commission to blow up a harbor at Cape Thompson. LaFarge and Madigan made the seminal decision to commit AAIA resources and time to the defense of Natives both at Point Hope and throughout Alaska.

LaVerne Madigan and AAIA Alaska Native committee head, Henry Forbes, flew to Alaska in 1961. BIA head James Hawkins told her that he thought that if Project Chariot went forward that the government would clear the people in a ten-mile radius, but he wondered about the effects on the caribou upon which the people depended.

To draw Iñupiaq attention to their land concerns, five months later, Madigan flew to Point Barrow and met with seventeen village representatives in what became Iñupiat Paitot. Without modern communication, the various villages had not realized that they all shared mutual land concerns. As a consequence, the statement of policy and recommendations from Iñupiat Paitot (IP) urged Congress "to settle . . . Alaska Native claims." Until that was done, IP demanded that the Department of the Interior, the overseer of both Bureau of Land Management (BLM) and the Bureau of Indian Affairs (BIA), protect Native land rights.

Don Mitchell's *Take My Land, Take My Life* says that after Madigan returned to New York, she reminded Secretary of the Interior Stewart Udall that the land surrounding Point Hope and Ogotoruk Creek was subject to unextinguished Iñupiaq aboriginal title that the Department of Interior had an obligation to protect.

According to Don Mitchell, three months later, Charlie Purvis, Niilo Koponen, and the Alaska Party, "a loose-knit group of Natives, homesteaders, labor dissidents, displaced left-wingers, populists, and old time Alaskans" were meeting, partly prompted by the political activity from the Alaska Constitutional Convention. With the burgeoning awareness of indigenous land rights, the Alaska Party gave rise to the Alaska Native Rights Association (ANRA) to address land selections the state filed on Native land. When the state began filing on land in Minto, Tanacross, and Northway, ANRA contacted Al Ketzler, who called ten Interior Native villages to a congress at Tanana, which resulted in the reorganization of Tanana Chiefs Conference. Niilo Koponen suggested that they contact AAIA's LaVerne Madigan; however, in the summer of 1962 she died unexpectedly in an accident. The following year, AAIA president Oliver LaFarge also passed away, but he was replaced by Roger Ernst, a former assistant secretary of the interior.

At Christmastime in 1962, the office of executive director was filled by soft-spoken Bill Byler, a Yale graduate and a former congressional aide. Bill was dedicated, adept at moving quietly, with his eye on the goal, and able to take a back seat while doing all he could to empower Alaska Natives.

As recorded in a 1989 interview by Don Mitchell, Bill Byler remembered the early opposition in Fairbanks: "Due to the people who were in the new Alaska Native Rights Association (ANRA), it was controversial, perceived to be left wing. However, the issue of Alaska Native land rights was neither left or right wing, but by definition, was nonpartisan."

He remembered, "To enable communication between the villages, Sandy Jenson of ANRA wanted to get trained radio operators in the villages. We at AAIA helped her with that." He continued, "The *Fairbanks Daily News-Miner* was rabidly opposed to land claims, including C. W. Snedden, so—there was an

ad hominem feeling against the Native leaders. It wasn't easy to have even small meetings of Native gatherings. We met in the kitchen of the Tiki Cove but not out in the open because there would be a bad reaction from the public. Individual Natives could eat there but not convene such a meeting. At that time, 'Good Natives' were accepted. But there was a lot of public drunkenness in Fairbanks and of course, that didn't help."

He added, "People didn't know what to make of me. I seemed exotic; folks were baffled by who I was. However, LaVerne Madigan had been perceived as being from a communist front organization or at least

Howard Rock, Editor, Tundra Times; *J.W. Bill Sneddon, Publisher* Fairbanks Daily News-Miner; *Laura Bergt,* Tundra Times *board member, circa 1964.*

Tundra Times, 01164.

left wing, even though Barry Goldwater had been on the AAIA board in the 1950s, I believe. On the other hand, sometimes in Alaska I was accused of being a right-winger. It was schizoid; it seemed to depend on the politics of the perceiver. Initially, Willie Hensley thought that AAIA was a conservation group. We were, but only as the environment was relevant to the Alaska Native."

When Bill Byler came on board, AAIA's income was small and its reserves were even less. AAIA was quite possibly facing extinction. It had a small, wealthy membership, which Bill felt was the wrong approach. He enlisted a solid, "little people," broad-based membership who would dedicate themselves both financially and to writing strategic letters.

From his tenure of 1962–1980, Bill Byler's work, not only with Alaska Native land claims but also with national Native affairs, resulted in AAIA being called "the house that Byler built." AAIA was a staff-driven organization, which gave him the freedom to guide it in the direction he felt most critical.

A wise and subtle man, Bill Byler began with AAIA financing of the second meeting of Dena' Nena' Henash (Tanana Chiefs Conference) in 1963 at the village of Tanana.

Through telephone interviews and e-mails in 2006, Bill explained his early life to me:

> *I was born in 1931 in Chicago where I grew up in a foster home as well as in a half orphanage. I returned home for a couple of years. Then I went to live on a farm where I was farmed out.*
>
> *I got a scholarship to Andover Phillips Academy but I ran away. After that, I was awarded a football scholarship from the alumnae to go to Yale. However when my knee got hurt, I couldn't play football anymore so they stopped my scholarship payment.*
>
> *About 1950, I had to face the draft so I joined the Air Force. After I got out of the Air Force, I put together some financing with the GI bill after a period of real, real starvation, living on one dollar a week for food. (Granted, food was much less expensive then but almost overnight, I lost thirty to forty pounds.) In 1955, I graduated with a B.A. in classical Greek and comparative literature, followed by a couple of years in graduate school.*
>
> *After graduating, I worked in public relations for two publishing companies, Yale University Press and Doubleday, followed by a stint as a congressional aide.*

Bill and Mary Lou Byler, circa 1974.

Courtesy of Bill Byler.

> *I had no prior experience with Natives or with Alaska. And I had no special interest in Native American culture or issues. I was interested in the role of poverty in foreign affairs.*
>
> *When LaVerne was killed in an accident, I was the aide to U.S. Rep. Frank Kowalski (D-CT). AAIA lawyer Art Lazarus, who was representing airline pilots and had needed votes on the House side, asked me whether I would be interested in LaVerne's old job.*
>
> *After some consideration, I told the AAIA board that I would take their offer for three years only. But once you get involved, it's hard to drop out in the middle of the process. When the AAIA announced my*

213

appointment, they said that I had worked with Indians. That was a bit of a stretch. I had told them that one summer I had dug ditches with some Chippewas in Wisconsin.

Right after I came on, AAIA's Alaska committee met for the first time. The Massachusetts Audubon Society and geographer Don Foote of Project Chariot were there. At that point, the government had still not released the land withdrawn for Project Chariot. Even though the

Harold Moats and Col. Kenneth Sawyer of the Corps of Engineers explaining the Rampart Dam to two unidentified men and to Fred John Sr. of Mentasta (standing and in glasses), circa 1962.
Photographer Theodore Hetzel.
Courtesy Alfred "Bear" Ketzler.

project was nullified, there was still concern that unless the government released that land, they might start messing around up there again. The meeting concerned various Alaska land uses. One of my first responsibilities was to deal with the Rampart Dam proposal. [The Rampart Dam was proposed in 1954 by the U.S. Army Corps of Engineers to dam the Yukon River in Alaska for hydroelectric power. The Development

Young Percy Herbert Sr., circa 1940, Fort Yukon, later a leader of Gwitchya Gwitchin Ginkhye (Yukon Flats People Speak) 1963, Tanana Chiefs Conference.
Titus Peter Collection, UAF-1988-96-11

and Resources Corporation released a report in April 1962, stating that the project was economically feasible and would attract new industries to Alaska.] There were powerful forces promoting it, including the state. I pondered what was the best way to beat Rampart. What was the compensable interest? I knew if the price of Rampart got high enough, it wouldn't be built. How could the cost be driven up? If the land claims issue weren't enough, what would the economic payoff for the Natives be? Give them a share of the power? At that time, the propaganda spouted that high energy users like aluminum factories would be interested.

I recruited Ted Stevens, a relatively obscure Alaska lawyer, to ask if he'd meet with the people of Rampart to inform them of the impact of the proposed dam and of their recourse. We paid him and he did it. Even though Stevens confided to me that he supported the dam, he gave the Yukon Flats delegations the key strategy. I have always credited him for that.

The BLM had no intention of holding hearings but AAIA leveraged them to hold the meetings. Percy Herbert, a leader of Gwitchya Gwitchin Ginkhye (Yukon Flats People Speak), came to Fairbanks to protest Rampart but he never appeared and his body was never found. There was conjecture that he had been murdered.

AAIA helped defeat Rampart by taking a leaf from the Project Chariot playbook. I wrote to all the U.S. aluminum companies to find out how much energy from the dam they would be in the market for. No one was interested! Not one!

In April 1963, I first met Al Ketzler, who had called for the reorganization of Tanana Chiefs Conference. He came to Washington, D.C., protesting state land selections and pushing for a land freeze until Alaska Native land claims could be decided. From the beginning, we had a

Diamond Jenness, Canada's first chief anthropologist.
http://www.civilization. ca/cmc/exhibitions/ archeo/hnpc/ npprefae.shtml

good connection. I found Al Ketzler to be a pragmatic man, rather retiring, not an ego-tripper, and someone with a following. Land claims were not his chief interest, but he took it on because he knew it needed to be done.

In those days, whites in Alaska frequently called the land "moose pasture." They also denigrated the concept of reservations, calling them "poverty pits," trying to brainwash the Natives from owning their own land. As a result of that influence, during the 1930s, village after village, including Minto, voted down having reservations. Establishment non-Natives didn't want those "racial enclaves." When we discussed the villages owning their own land, even Ramsey Clark, a former attorney general who represented AFN, railed at the notion: "What do you want to do, create ethnic zoos in Alaska?!" (And he was the legal counsel for the Natives.)

Masked in the guise of humanitarianism, "Die on the Vine" was a phrase used by Diamond Jenness, Canada's first chief anthropologist who published The People of the Twilight in 1928. He said the kindest thing to do in Canada was to let the villages die on the vine, which meant to not support the schools and deny help so that the people would abandon the land and move into the cities. That was the policy in Alaska and Canada. An example of that was King Island when BIA closed its

pro . . . pro . . . product of the BIA boarding schools, and I object." The BIA withdrew and the churches let it go. The task force never met again.

Father Convert flew me to Galena, Nulato, Kaltag, and Unalakleet, where I talked to the people about state land selections.

The Native blanket protest claims initiated by LaVerne Madigan were not having any effect in Washington, D.C.; they were not specific enough. We had to document exactly what land was being used and by whom. When I went to the villages, the Natives sketched out their specific areas with great precision. They could have made sweeping claims but they

Matthew Titus and Peter Jimmy with the Minto dancers, 1962.

Photographer Theodore Hetzel.
Courtesy Alfred "Bear" Ketzler.

were not greedy. They didn't draw a large circle but an arc with all kinds of squiggles, documenting where they were born, had fish camp, picked berries, trapped, where someone died. On the Yukon River, they were generally not aware of the threat to their land because their territory was not being selected, but Minto, which had been selected by the state, was on the firing line. I began trying to explain to a villager the concept of privately owned land and state land selections, but it meant nothing to him. I'd heard that in the Lower Forty-eight, whites had excused stealing land by saying that Indians did not understand the concept of private land ownership. However, they did understand territoriality, which was also true in Alaska. To find an analogy for them, I said, "If you own a boat and an outboard and you keep loaning it to someone, and then one day, he says that the law says you don't own it anymore, but that it is his." As the man understood, his eyes widened in horror. That was the difference between Anglo ownership and tribal territoriality, territory held in common by the village. Once, to test the concept of territoriality, which was central to establishing Native land claims, I asked Minto Chief Peter John how he greeted someone from a neighboring village who was hunting on land he considered Minto's? He replied, "I don't say nothing to them. I just kick 'em in the ass."

As the Natives described the land they used, it became clear that some of their previously used lands had been abandoned. Some land had been left involuntarily and some, voluntarily, as new trading posts and schools became hubs for villages. High-powered rifles also meant need-ing less hunting grounds. Since less Native land was being claimed, that gave room for both Native land and state selections of some magnitude. It seemed like everyone could come to an agreement. After I returned to New York, AAIA also began sending out our newsletters to the villages.

Possibly Point Barrow or Unalakleet. Iñupiaq church congregation, circa 1961.

Photographer Theodore Hetzel.
Courtesy Alfred "Bear" Ketzler.

When I was in Nenana with Al Ketzler, a woman pointed how un-easy she and her friends would feel if they ever ran into people from the Yukon Flats. She had been taught that they were frog people and that was creepy. [Similarly, former TCC First Traditional Chief David Salmon said that they were taught that people took on the nature of the area in which they lived, e.g., those from good duck hunting areas never looked anyone in the eye but kept their eyes skyward and those from beaver country always looked downward.] However, as people came together in the first Tundra Times *meeting in 1964 and subsequent land claims meetings, they found that they were just the same, that they weren't creepy, and that they had a lot in com-mon: the need to protect their land.*

In Unalakleet, which was heavily influenced by the Swedish Covenant church, a woman told me that she had previously tried talking about indigenous land rights but the local missionary had told her that such thoughts were ungodly and that she should be grateful to America for saving them from Russia. Chief Peter John of Minto asked me once, "You aren't a Christian, are you?" I wasn't but apparently, he figured that any white man who talked for Native land rights couldn't be a missionary. Apart from that, I knew that he didn't like the local Minto pastor, who was also the trader and the postmaster. When veterans of the Korean War got their checks, the pastor postmaster would cash their checks but in scrip, only redeemable at his store, making it impossible to do mail-order purchases. [It had long been common in rural Alaska for a trader to pay in bingles, *a trade currency, useable only at that trader's store.] In those days in the village, there was no cash money. AAIA broke that system, clarifying that holding the people hostage was not the role of the U.S. post office.*

Don Charles Foote, who had had a critical role in unmasking Project Chariot, began working for me. To quantify how many acres a subsistence hunter might need to sustain his way of life, I asked Don to figure how many calories subsistence hunters expended per how many acres to sustain their way of life in the Shungnak and Kobuk areas. Based on his work, I estimated that the Natives of Alaska were using eighty million acres of land, the only reasonably accurate guestimate available. In the original draft bill that Art Lazarus prepared, it was stated that the Native villages should receive title to an aggregate of eighty million acres. For the land they had to involuntarily abandon, they would be entitled to compensation. For lands voluntarily abandoned, they would receive nothing. This was the formula that had ruled in countless Indian land claims cases. The draft was village oriented. There was no thought of a corporate structure or of stock ownership.

The Interior Department had received the large blanket land filings that LaVerne had started but those were not stopping the state land selections. Al Ketzler said that during the winter of 1962–1963, Secretary of the Interior Stewart Udall promised to withdraw from selection any land claimed by villages. That was fine before a land selection was advertised, but once legal notice of selection had been advertised by BLM, notwithstanding village claims, that selection would rule unless formally protested. A critical misunderstanding could have resulted from Udall's counsel. When the state started selecting land from the feds in the early 1960s, BLM put ads in the newspapers advertising each selection, giving a window of time to protest the claim before it was finalized. However, those vast claims by the state were not blocked or protested. There

Possibly Pt. Barrow, circa 1961-1962.
Photographer Theodore Hetzel. Courtesy Alfred "Bear" Ketzler.

was no protection; the land freeze wasn't on, so I asked AAIA lawyer Arthur Lazarus, the guiding genius in this, what the technical way was to block the state's blanket claims. He said to watch for the ads and to help the villages file a protest. I began subscribing to the Fairbanks Daily News-Miner *and the* Anchorage Daily News *and Jensen's Weekly, maybe. I'd look for land selection notices. I had all the USGS quad sheet*

Man in middle, Tom Snapp of the Fairbanks Daily News-Miner, *agreed to teach* Tundra Times, *editor Howard Rock (on left) for a year how to publish a newspaper. To right, photographer Theodore Hetzel, circa 1961.*

Theodore Hetzel. Courtesy Alfred "Bear" Ketzler Jr.

maps. I'd find the selection and look to see if there was a village in a reasonable distance. Then I'd get on the phone and call Al, or someone, to verify if it was a selection that would impinge on land claims, and it usually did. [Usually the state] would file along the highway for timber access. They weren't looking for oil. They were trying to get a fast start [at financing the state.] They were even advertising wilderness estates at the World's Fair.

Al Ketzler [traveled around, notifying villages to protest] but it was beyond our means to keep abreast of all of it. Through Secretary of the Interior Udall, for whom Bob Bennett, the BIA Alaska area director, worked, we pressed the BIA to appoint realty officers. They appointed fewer officers than we wanted, but they did it. Frank Anderson was appointed to the Fairbanks office and he was very good, very committed; also, he had BIA resources, e.g., airplanes to fly. Having people watching the ads was very successful to begin blocking the state's selections from being processed.

It was agreed that each state land selection would be communicated from the BLM to the BIA, who would notify any affected village councils. If protests were disregarded and a land selection was sent to and signed off by Under Secretary of the Interior John Carver, the state got title. At the local level, the state's BLM office countered by appealing the Native protests and sending them to Udall's special assistant, Newt Edwards, in Washington, D.C., to pass on to John Carver. Before the land freeze, Edwards was sure that if he sent them to Carver to process, before indigenous title was defined, that the outcome for the Natives would not be good. Over the years, Edwards chose to do nothing but to let the BLM appeals stack up in his drawer.

A glaring case in which the Native protest wasn't made was the North Slope selection at Prudhoe Bay. I kept seeing the ad and I tried to reach Frank Anderson but he was on vacation. This was before Charlie Edwardsen started the Arctic Slope Native Association, and on the recommendation of Iñupiat Paitot I contacted Hugh Nichols, the Iñupiaq executive director of the North Slope Native Association. I told him to formally protest the land selection or they could lose it. He said, "No problem; I'll take care of it." I suggested that he telegram or use a seven-cent stamp to mail the protest, but be sure to protest. I suspected that he would not do it and he did not. Charlie Edwardsen maintained that Nichols was a CIA agent and a bogus Iñupiaq to boot. It would've been fascinating [how it played out] if those Native protests had been filed [on Prudhoe]. In 1964, the Alaska Department of Natural Resources held a competitive oil lease, including 610 Prudhoe Bay tracts.

As I got involved with Alaska Native land claims, it was never my idea to make one large land claim out of all Alaska's indigenous land claims. LaVerne had focused on the Arctic Slope. But now the state was seeking selections south of Eisenhower's Yukon–Porcupine (Y-P) line, forcing us to consider the southern section. As I shifted AAIA strategy from the Arctic to land south of the Y-P line, I was accused of trying to bankrupt the State of Alaska. [President Eisenhower had regarded Alaska as too large and sparsely populated to be economically self-sufficient as a state. He also saw statehood as an obstacle to effective defense of Alaska should the Soviet Union seek to invade it. He designated as the Y-P Line "the 320 miles through which the 141st meridian extends between the Yukon River and . . . may be designated as the Yukon-Porcupine section, and the northern one, . . . the boundary line, or about 225 miles above its confluence with the Yukon River" (Bulletin of the American Geographical Society, *vol. 44,* American Geographical Society of New York). *The area north of the Y-P line would be part of the new state, but the president would be granted emergency powers to establish special national defense withdrawals in those areas if deemed necessary.] The state was only allowed to build infrastructure like airports north of the Y-P line. The navy had the petroleum reserve up there, and the whole area was considered oil rich, but whether the military wanted to keep control of that petroleum, I don't know. There was concern that, lacking the land north of the Y-P Line, Alaska might not be able to make it, so it*

U.S. Senator Gruening (to left) pushing the federal government to improve Alaska's rural post offices, circa 1961.
Photographer Theodore Hetzel. Courtesy Alfred "Bear" Ketzler.

Sixty-two-year-old Peter John of Minto testifying at the state sponsored, Alaska Federation of Natives hosted Land Claims Task Force, Anchorage, 1967.
Alaska Native Land Claims. Courtesy of Emil Notti.

was decided that ten percent of subsurface royalties would go to the feds while ninety percent would go to the state.

To my surprise, in 1964 Howard Rock decided it was time to have a statewide Native land rights meeting, which Al also supported. I wasn't sure about the timing. The statewide move put AAIA in the role of responder, not as initiator. Howard and Al handled the logistics for the statewide meeting in Fairbanks. However, at that time, no one was able to focus on a statewide settlement with any fairness. The mindset was that of offering only small acreage around the villages with a small amount of money. (At that time, subsistence was the only means of survival for Natives.)

Like many, Udall felt the Natives' prosperity, like any other citizen's, should come through the success of the state. I pointed out that Nenana was in a perfect place to develop, because it was near both the highway and the railroad; however, half of the people were white while the other half, the Natives, were on welfare. (I was told that one Native woman in Nenana preferred to live on muskrats rather than take welfare because she felt it was, literally, a pernicious disease.) I pointed out to Udall that state development was not the answer for Natives because the vast majority of villages were not on the road system. Even in Nenana, which was in the ideal location, the Natives were not prospering.

Rather than consider a sweeping statewide indigenous land claim, AAIA decided to focus on a small area, Minto, to try to save its land. Minto was threatened not only by state land selection but also by white sports hunters. The village leadership and the Tundra Times *worked together to show the catastrophe facing Minto. I met with Peter John and the council and discussed trust title, including the formula that for land involuntarily abandoned, they would get compensation but for lands voluntarily abandoned, they would receive nothing. In 1965, Art Lazarus and I designed the Minto land bill as a template for awarding the Alaska Natives legal title to all federal land subject to aboriginal title, which was legally still owned by the federal government. Senator*

Gruening said he'd have Governor Egan set up a bill. The point of that early Minto bill was to get everyone, including the Natives, to focus.

To celebrate three years in business, the Tundra Times *hosted a banquet in December 1965 and AAIA paid for it. Howard charged a fee for those who could afford it. Because* Tundra Times *sponsored it, a lot of political leadership attended. I gave a speech at the meeting and someone from the audience threw a libel at me. Ralph Perdue was one of those against AAIA and was in close connection with BIA. Barry Jackson, a Fairbanks lawyer, supported Native rights, which surprised me. I asked around about him. He had a history of sticking his neck out to defend Natives. Afterward, I talked with Bartlett alone and suggested, "What about giving a use and occupancy trust title to village lands in exchange for the state selecting north of the Y-P line but without sacrificing the North Slope villages, who would also be given fee-simple title for their lands?" (Since the state would still get ninety percent of subsurface rights based on the initial deal from the feds, to open the land north of the Y-P to the state was actually double dipping, but I figured the state could justify itself by saying that they had had no idea the Native land claims would be so vast. The deal I of-fered Bartlett would reduce the competition between the state and Native villages.) He liter-ally leapt out of his chair with excitement. I set up a meeting to discuss the AAIA proposal with Senator Gruening. However, af-ter Bartlett found out Gruening was going to be involved, he was livid, apparently wanting sole credit for the idea; at first he refused to attend the meeting. However, he eventually did; it wasn't great, but Bartlett suggested we meet in Juneau at the governor's office with Senator Gruening, Chief Peter John, Governor Egan, Bartlett, and attorney Barry Jackson later that month.*

The BIA Alaska area head, Bob Bennett, was not happy or supportive about AAIA's proposal. I talk-

Oneida Indian, Alaska area head of BIA, Bob Bennett, 1962.
Photographer Theodore Hetzel. Courtesy Alfred "Bear" Ketzler.

Barry Jackson, at-torney for Al Ketzler Sr. and AAIA, 1970.
U.S. Department of the Interior.

ed to Secretary of the Interior Udall because his man, Bennett, needed to be in accord with BIA policy. With me there, Udall told Bennett that the department supported the concept of trust title based on land use, voluntary and involuntary abandonment of the land, so there would be no question that we were all on the same page.

In December at the first statewide meeting based on a Native proposal, Bennett and I met again in Juneau with congressmen, the attorney general, deputies, and others. We also paid Barry Jackson's fee and his transportation as well as bringing Chief Peter John to Juneau. We laid out the concept and there was discussion. To my amazement, Barry suggested that if there were compensation for Native land claims, that the vehicle of state-chartered business corporate structures should be used to manage the land. We had no thought of a corporate structure or of stock ownership. He hadn't discussed it with Peter John or AAIA, his employer. Further, it was an untraditional way of treating Native land. Also contrary to Udall's instructions, Bob Bennett poured cold water over the acreage notion, saying that it was too much land. He said, tepidly, that yes, there should be some kind of land settlement, but he talked more in tune with the governor and the congressional delegation. We left the issue on the table. The benefit was that it did make us focus on a finite point concerning state selection issues. They discussed the Minto bill and then, over time, it sort of petered out. We never had any real expectation for a Minto bill to pass, but it set a precedent. The Minto bill served its purpose but there were 217 "Mintos" with indigenous land to defend. Bartlett was okay to work with, but his view of indigenous land claims fell far short of Native expectations. Gruening was worse: old-fashioned and completely against the Indian Reorganization Act (IRA of 1934) reservations.

Another Native land issue erupted when oil was discovered in Tyonek, regarding whether it was a reserve or a reservation, which determined who profited, the village or the state. The outcome was fortuitous. The solictor's office in Washington, D.C. ransacked Tyonek records for the executive order or the paperwork behind it so the case wouldn't be blown down the tubes. Finally the secretary found the needed letter, the letter of transmittal to the president. It had the language that showed that the intent of Tyonek was to have a permanent claim there, determined to be a reservation. Tyonek could lease its land and receive its reward. From its good fortune, it contributed a bunch of money to the first Alaska Federation of Natives meeting in October of 1966.

State land selections had become statewide, intruding into Native property. Groups were forming. Questions were raised about the oil *company bids on the North Slope.*

Governor Hickel was enraged because Udall had not yet opened the bids on the North Slope. AFN sent Udall a telegram saying, "Don't open the bids," but that wasn't going to do it. I sent a telegram. Newt Edwards must've been involved with Udall in hanging it up, delaying the oil leases, which led to big pressure from the state. Edwards wasn't favorable to Natives, but he was intellectually conservative and professional in his land policies. He made a recommendation to Udall to either open the oil bids or to return them to the bidders.

Alaska Federation of Natives meeting, in center: Eben Hopson and Emil Notti, circa 1966.

Alaska Native Land Claims.
Courtesy of Emil Notti.

Udall returned the bids, which led to the land freeze in 1966, racheting up the situation for the state.

Until then, the Native claims had been blocking some land along the highway; now they were blocking the oil on the North Slope. Newt Edwards told Udall, "Do this in aid of legislation. The secretary has an obligation to make a decision here." Not giving the land leases was very appropriate, followed by the general land freeze against all land selections. Udall saw that a Native land claims settlement must occur. The oil made people ready to talk about large land settlements. After the oil discovery, everyone knew that under "moose pasture" there might be oil.

AAIA sent $5,000 seed money to start the statewide Alaska Federation of Natives (AFN). AAIA had almost no role in AFN because we were out of the organizational mode by then. Howard Rock, Willie Hensley, Byron Mallott, and Emil Notti wanted a statewide organization. The first AFN meeting was a result of the December 1965 Tundra Times banquet in Fairbanks. The AFN meeting in 1966 was a very large, very impressive meeting. When they went into executive session, they asked that all non-Natives leave. I went and talked to people in the coffee shop. Later I was asked, "Bill, where did you go?" I said, "Well, you said . . ." He replied, "That wasn't supposed to apply to you." I said, "Well, you

Barrow dancers, circa 1962.
Photographer Theodore Hetzel.
Courtesy Alfred "Bear" Ketzler Jr.

should've made that clear." They decided to have a statewide organization. The discussion at that first AFN meeting concerned which course they would follow: Charlie Edwardsen's [lawsuit pending of the Arctic North Slope Native Association] or the state's. It was a very intense discussion. If the bids were opened up and the leases were awarded, the economic constraints would be taken off the fight for land claims. There was also the aspect of the right-of-way for the pipeline corridor. Al Ketzler and AAIA coordinated the injunction against the right-of-way.

By 1966, a critical mass had been reached. Apart from those in Southeast who had their own particular history that set them apart, there were now enough Natives who were hip enough to run things, and the movement broadened to statewide. Native leaders who'd held back initially now joined in because it had become a respectable cause, not a quixotic thing by some people from the East Coast. People like Nick Gray and Ralph Perdue got involved. Although Southeast had had some kind of land settlement, they also joined ranks. This statewide evolution was not part of the AAIA grand scheme, but the Natives felt it was time. Howard Rock was the main catalyst for a statewide organization. We were a couple of steps behind, absorbed in trying to block the state land selections. At that point, AAIA was used for financing and for letter writing.

Some enjoyable moments at the convention involved the breaking of the ice between cultures that had historically been in conflict. For instance after the Minto Athabascans danced, the Eskimos good-naturedly mocked them with their own dance. Everyone caught on; it was great, joking [through an art form].

In 1967, soon after he took office, Governor Walter J. Hickel struck back at Secretary Udall, condemning Udall's failure to act on the state selections. He filed suit against the Secretary in Federal Court to force him to complete transfer of Native lands around the village of Nenana.

In a landmark case, argued by the attorneys for the AAIA and the village of Nenana, the U.S. Court of Appeals reaffirmed that tradition-al Native use and occupancy created legal land rights and that lands subject to Native use and occupancy are exempt by the Statehood Act from expropriation. The U.S. Supreme Court refused to hear the State's appeal.

That same year, Interior Secretary Udall appointed a three-person Alaska Task Force on Native Affairs with hearings held in Anchorage. The task force's report, issued in January 1968, urged the conveyance of 160-acre tracts to individuals for homes, fish camps, or hunting sites; the withdrawal of "small acreages" in and around villages; and the designation of areas for Native use (but not ownership) for traditional food-gathering activities. Natives, with the assistance of the AAIA, flatly opposed the task force's recommendations and successfully fought their implementation. I was very disappointed with the Task Force report because they chose the Senator Gruening approach, a relatively small amount of land around the villages with a little money and some eco-nomic development. A bill was circulating to codify that which would have been very damaging.

L-R: Taos Pueblo leaders meeting over Blue Lake: Tribal Council secretary Paul Bernal, Taos Pueblo Governor John Reyna, Mary Lou Payne Byler, Seferino Martinez, Senator Robert Kennedy, Bill Byler, Penn Station, 1968.

Courtesy of Bill Byler.

I began working on what Don Wright's later political consultant, Adrian Parmeter, felt became a precedent to Alaska Native land claims, the return of Blue Lake to the Taos Indians. [In 1906 when Carson National Forest was created, Taos Pueblo lost thousands of acres of land as well as Taos Lake, a sacred Pueblo shrine.] I laid out the successful strategy for Taos Pueblo. To get support, I recruited New York Senator Robert Kennedy to lead the charge.

Unknown to Congress, President Richard Nixon was sympathetic to Native Americans. While Congress was locked up trying to decide Alaska land claims, Nixon endorsed the pending Blue Lake legislation in 1970. After the measure passed the Senate, Blue Lake and the surrounding wilderness were returned to the people of Taos Pueblo. Seizing the decision, Don Wright, now president of AFN, and Adrian Parmeter [advisor and consultant to Wright] perceived that not only was the White House the lynchpin for support of Alaska Native claims but also, the return of Blue

Don Mitchell, lawyer and historian, author of Sold American *and* Take My Land, Take My Life, *1997, Anchorage.*

Photo by Jim Lavrakas, *Anchorage Daily News,* http://www.adn.com/adn/ features/indian_country/ 01a7.html

Lake served as a precedent. After a battle in Congress, Don Wright was able to carry Alaska Native land claims to passage.

Credit for leading the charge belongs to the Ketzlers and to Tanana Chiefs Conference. Going through the courts, as William Paul advocated, would have been a disaster. AAIA and TCC pushed for going through Congress. While TCC laid the foundation, AFN had a valuable role in pulling the Natives together. There were many conflicting cultures, including the rural and urban mindsets. The regional view subdivided into those who wanted the settlement based on the claimed acreage and those who wanted it based on population. I preferred the formula that when a baby was born into a village, he inherited the land. When that person died, he left nothing behind. The heirs always inherited the land. Having proven its use and occu-

pancy, the village owned its own land. But that concept got lost in the jockeying back and forth; everyone wanted their piece of the action. I would have chosen eighty million acres with subsurface rights based on village, not individual, entitlements. The idea of revenue sharing came

U.S. Senator Mike Gravel, Governor William A. Egan, U.S. Senator Ted Stevens, and U.S. Representative Nick Begich, circa 1970.
Tundra Times. Alaska Native Land Claims. Courtesy of Emil Notti.

> *later. So there were a lot of competing interests that forged this thing.*
> *But that's where I started out.*

Twenty-five years after the passage of ANCSA, Anchorage former attorney and vice president for AFN, author Don Mitchell interviewed Bill Byler in Washington, D.C. An invaluable transcription of the conversation follows, 1992, Washington, D.C.: AAIA and ANCSA from 1969 through 1971.

Don: Going forward to January 1969, Washington, D.C., the scene had changed. [Senator] Bartlett had died and Ted Stevens took his place. Senator Ernest Gruening [1959–1969], who'd been an impediment to the whole process, had been defeated by Senator Mike Gravel [1969–1981]. Nixon was president and had appointed Wally Hickel to replace Stewart Udall [as secretary of the interior]. In January, there was a whole new cast of players.

Bill: I had recommended that they get Goldberg. Charlie [Edwardsen] was in town with a lot of other Natives. We were getting to the point where there would be hearings, and we needed a dignified public figure. Who better to get than a former cabinet member of Kennedy's, a Supreme Court justice, an ambassador to the UN, Goldberg had it all. We didn't expect Goldberg to learn the history, all the details. (At that time, I didn't know that Goldberg had a son up in Alaska.) Up to that time, the Native cause had only the Natives for support and that was exceedingly important. [But] it had to have some elevation into the non-Native world. At the time, I had no idea that Ramsey Clark [former attorney general] would be asked by Goldberg to do most of the hands-on work. [Byler felt that it would also be important to have an Alaska Native speaker from the village. Andrew Isaac of Dot Lake had a good character and spoke well. Byler and Ketzler asked Isaac if he would consider going to Washington,

230

D.C. to speak on behalf of Alaska Natives and their connection to the land. Isaac said he'd never been Outside and that he had never made a speech. However he did go and he made a powerful impact. Isaac was the window for national legislators to meet the rural Alaska Native.]

Ramsey Clark, former attorney general and Alaska Federation of Natives representative.
http://en.wikipedia.org/wiki/Ramsey_Clark.

Bill: I never talked to Goldberg about the substance of his bill and the form it took. I believe Art Lazarus [AAIA lawyer] was at the hearing and that he testified. He had prepared a draft bill. He may've talked extensively with Goldberg.

Don: I ask because of what developed inside AFN regarding Goldberg. Fred Paul [Seattle lawyer and son of Tlingit lawyer William Paul, 1885–1977] was bitter about it. Goldberg's approach wasn't a land rights approach but [rather, his attitude was] "these poor Indians and Eskimos, you really should do something for them." The tone [he used] was wrong. The real issue was that the Natives had legally viable land rights issues. That was the beginning of the schism with Goldberg.

Bill: I never knew any of that. I assumed they'd be working on whatever the AFN position was. As events took a startling turn, casting the forty million acres aside (which Goldberg buried), I assumed that Goldberg could be persuaded and that he would persuade Clark and Jackson, who weren't enthralled about that amount of acreage, and they would go along with it. (There was a massive public relations effort going on with unions, church groups—a massive effort.) I wasn't aware until it was coming before the Senate how much the Native support had eroded.

Don: I could not find any AFN paper trail, in the minutes. . . . Barry Jackson told me that as of June 1969 that he'd quit as any kind of counsel for AFN general counsel, but he continued working for TCC. He said that Goldberg-Ramsey Clark had convinced the AFN steering committee, Notti and Borbridge [AFN president and vice president], that S-1830, Scoop Jackson's bill [one billion dollars and eight to ten million acres], was the best deal they would get and was the way to go. TCC was very adamantly against it. Attorney Barry Jackson was then divided and decided to go with TCC. His friend Clif Grohs, an attorney, had already quit over Wally Hickel [as secretary of the interior]. Barry Jackson continued for TCC.

Bill: When the bill was going to be presented on the floor, Ramsey Clark met with me in Washington, D.C., July 1970—over public relations and floor strategy. I asked the contents of the bill: one billion dollars and under ten million acres. I countered that the Native position was forty million acres. His response was startling. Clark said that amount of land in Native hands would retard the growth of Alaska, and he asked if I was proposing that Congress establish anthropological zoos? Clark added, "Natives get emotional about land. I have someone up there now whom I've counseled to hold the hands of AFN." That meeting didn't last much longer. I went to update Hackett [public relations firm hired by AAIA] who was doing some work on land claims about what was going on. He replied, "They're getting screwed." We went to see Ted Kennedy and he said he would help. Tom Sussman, a staffer whose job it would be to work with us, was in the room. We told them that the bill would soon be coming to the floor and that it was not the Native position. I called Al Ketzler and we agreed that the TCC position was forty million acres, and we said, "Yeah, let's go for it." I added, "Kennedy will want to know what AFN's position is." I found out that Emil Notti and John Borbridge were going to be in Washington, D.C., for Emil's birthday. I ran into them on the street then and said, "Kennedy will go for the forty million. Will you support it?" They seemed surprised and said, "Sure." That was that.

We were trying to get ready to meet with the Kennedy staff level for the floor fight, but even hours before the noon presentation, we, me and Fraser Barron [public relations employee for AAIA], and Tom Scanlon still weren't successful getting our counter-presentation ready. We despaired of getting the staff we needed. So I went over to the Senate and pulled Fred Harris [D-OK] off the floor to meet with me in the visitors' room of the senate side. I gave him a very hurried presentation and he said he would do it. I may've had an amendment with me but we started using scissors and paste and together, we put together the amendment we proposed. We didn't expect it to carry (it only got twelve to fourteen votes) but—that was important.

Kennedy said that when he presented the bill later (the following year) for sixty million acres, he could not have done that had he not voted against [S-1830] bill, based on our amendment. There was no other opposition to Jackson's bill on the floor, nothing from AFN or anyone else. There was no lobbying effort out in the hall, no effort to oppose Jackson's bill at all. Only whatever Kennedy and Harris could mobilize by reading the amendment we hastily put together. I never met Ramsey Clark since then.

Seventy-year-old Tanacross Chief Andrew Isaac testifying at the state sponsored, Alaska Federation of Natives hosted Land Claims Task Force, Anchorage, 1967.
Alaska Native Land Claims.
Courtesy of Emil Notti.

Don: In July 1969, you committed AAIA money to AFN to hire Hackett for public relations.

Bill: That was strictly our idea. There was a lot of land and there'd be opposition from the administration, from Jackson, and the Alaska delegation. The Natives had a position. We stayed away from the newspaper for a long time to give it a rest. People get bored with the story. But then it was time to get behind it, pushing what the Natives wanted, the land. The public wasn't going to be interested in how much cash and certainly not in the corporate aspect, which I was frankly appalled by.

We were also assisting AFN then. They needed an executive director and we provided for Al's [Ketzler's] salary. *Tundra Times* was in a dicey situation because [AAIA's Dr. Henry] Forbes cut back the money, so we paid half of Howard Rock's salary.

The problem was also that there was too much focused on land claims and not enough on Native culture and the environment. That represented a substantial shift away from the very early AAIA focus of setting aside the North Slope as a wildlife refuge. Some of these expenses were built into the budget but if it were some really extraordinary expense I'd go to the board.

I could not attend the board meeting because I was meeting with AFN. So I called a board member, Ben O'Sullivan, to offer the financial causes we needed for AFN. The first $25,000 was a grant, the next was a loan, and the final was another grant. The money came from the AAIA membership.

I had started a serious direct mail effort and we were receiving by that time probably a half million a year in income. It was from the little people. You can't have a handful of fat cats giving only because they were always changing where they gave and they weren't ones to write letters. The money came from those who write letters. We got money from even people on welfare, who said, "This is all we can give."

Regarding David Hackett and Associates: after Oliver LaFarge died, I had become involved in Blue Lake for AAIA. Bobby Kennedy was the senator from New York at that time and I'd recruited his interest in Taos/Blue Lake. When he decided to run for president, either Fraser Barron or Hackett called me, asking me to help in mainly Bob Kennedy's South Dakota presidential campaign, where Indian people had voted Democratic nine to one, and I also thought a lot of JFK. Bobby Kennedy had gone around the country because he'd taken over this [thrust for] Indian education.

After Bobby's death, we were at the point with AFN that we had to get ginned up. I thought Hackett was a big public relations operation. Not so! Wonderful man. He'd worked for Bobby in Justice, headed up

the Juvenile Justice System, and was very involved with the Kennedy prototype to the War on Poverty.

For PR stuff, like getting radio spots on, [we relied] on a woman
named Felice Mayor in New York who did the PR for Blue Lake. We had
an art center, the American Indian Art Center, and she did the PR for
that. We did our own coverage ourselves, ginning up letters to the editor,
typing them up for the various senators and congressman for each district
in each state, and sending them to AAIA members who'd sign them and
send them on to their newspapers in their state. It took many forms but
that was part of what we did. Hackett was mainly a Washington lobbyist
PR presence and distributed a brochure about land claims. Fraser Barron
talked to senators as opposed to getting interviews for the TV program
Today. I can't recollect if AFN paid for Hackett and Claude Desetelles.
Either AAIA paid for this or made grants to AFN and AFN paid for it.

Don: In the fall of 1969, AAIA gave AFN thirty thousand dollars, but pretty much all of that got chewed up. Jim Thomas opened a PR firm in
Anchorage and that went belly up by March. The money was gone. I have
heard AFN's minutes where Thomas is embittered saying, "This isn't my
fault. You guys used the money for Emil's salary and lots of other things."
[Byler and Mitchell agreed that Fraser Barron's salary and other expenses
were not coming out of AFN funds.]

Bill: The lobbying effort didn't go to shoeleather until it was discovered that
the bill was going to go to the floor with less than forty million acres. So
then that effort reverted to challenging the bill as repped by AFN's counsel, Clark. We kept our ear to the Interior committee and tried to counter
any resistance there.

Don: Goldberg-Ramsey Clark got geared up the spring of 1969 and you got
geared up the summer and fall of 1969 with Hackett. In December of
1969 is when, for the first time, the Senate Interior Committee sits down
and looks this thing over.

Don: We've talked about Jackson but did you know Ted Stevens and Mike
Gravel?

Bill: Oh, yes, my contact with Ted Stevens goes back to the time when I first
went to Alaska in the spring of 1963. Stevens had already done some valuable work for the Natives. I had a high regard for him but I never did get
to know him really well.

When Rampart Dam was an issue, I called Stevens. He said he supported Rampart but he could go up there to Fairbanks and talk with the
three Gs [Gwitchya Gwitch'in Ginkye, the Yukon Flats Native organiza-
tion] and give them advice on how to beat Rampart. And I thought that
was just terrific. This was long before he became a senator.

Don: Did you talk to him during the senate committee mark-up at all?

Bill: No, we felt that Goldberg-Clark, that was AFN, the Natives', representation [were taking care of it.] We, and our PR efforts, then became an auxiliary function.

The element that surprised me was using the corporate model, which I thought was a terrible mistake. I looked at it from the point of view of the Osage headrights. [A "headright" is the right to receive a quarterly distribution of funds derived from the Osage Mineral Estate.] The full-bloods have almost no control over their assets.

In doing early bill drafts with Arthur [Lazarus], we said to AFN, "If you use the corporate model, at least let the nonprofit corporations have fifty-one percent so they NEVER lose control." That was stripped out of the bill. Jackson didn't understand what these "shadow corporations" [nonprofits] were for. I explained the concept to him and he thought that was a pretty good idea, but the guarantee of that control got stripped.

We'd hired Don Foote to do two caloric studies in the Shungnak and Kobuk areas. How many calories are expended hunting and how much territory did they need to harvest those calories? I'd had Yukon River villagers draw maps where they hunted. They were absolutely guile-less, drawing the maps exactly where they were using ground. They left large areas vacant. Using those and my Foote studies, I figured the land they used and occupied ran to about 80 to 120 million acres. At that time, the non-Natives didn't care much about the land. So this was the Native package. At the same time, by blocking the oil companies, we had to keep that pressure on. The quickest route to the oil was through a very generous Native land claim settlement.

Interior Secretary Stewart Udall, center, with Chief Jack House of the Ute tribe of Colorado and Rep. Wayne Aspinall (D-Colo.) in 1966.
Washington Post. http://media.treehugger.com/assets/images/2011/10/stewart-udall-photo

Don: So going back to the process. The next thing that happens is you get Fred Harris to offer the thirty million acres and that bill gets destroyed.

In July of 1970, it passes the Senate and then this whole caravan immediately moves across the White House to the Interior Committee.

Bill: Before that, a crucial moment, Hackett called Richard Harwood, who was and still is with the *Washington Post*. He felt we needed to discredit the Senate action [to spotlight the Native position]. "How can we build an effort," we thought. Harwood sees Clark-Goldberg [AFN's noncredible counsel] in one seat and Kennedy in another. It's hard for Harwood to discredit Goldberg. He needs more than Byler-Hackett [to be sure of AFN's position, to warrant countering Goldberg.] So either we got Howard Rock or Ketzler on the phone or we gave Harwood the *Tundra Times* article [reflecting AFN's position.] Result: Harwood ran the *Washington Post* article. I called Ketzler to come town, "We've got to start on the House as soon as possible." He arrives. We go around the committee, vote by vote by vote. So now we have the *Tundra Times* article [affirming AFN's position], the Harwood article, and the Natives' opposition to the Jackson bill and to the Clark-Goldberg bill.

Don: Wayne Aspinall [Congressman, D-Co, chair for House Interior and Insular Affairs committee] refused to move the bill. And the whole thing died in Congress. It was a big effort to get him to move any bill. It was Haley's [chairman Rep. James Haley, D–Fl of Indian Affairs Subcommittee of the House Interior Committee] subcommittee, but he was a stooge for Wayne Aspinall. Did you think no bill was preferable to any bill by Aspinall?

Bill: Definitely. Wait and take next year with more mobilization and with a much better run at the thing, try to mobilize the Senate. The Natives were encouraged with the good vote count in the House; they had a majority in the committee. Why take less?

Besides Ketzler, Fraser Barron, and me meeting with senators, AAIA was running a grassroots letter-writing campaign into the various districts of the House, doing radio spots, and writing newspaper editorials. (I found somewhere stacks and stacks of editorials, letters to the editor.) It was targeted to the districts, a regular grassroots lobby. It was beyond really our means to do it. In the House, it's pretty hard to get a floor amendment. You have to do it in the committees, you know.

Don: While we were suffering consternation with the AFN lobbying, meantime, there were those in the Native community in Alaska, for lack of information, who thought that this whole thing stunk. The nearest I can figure out is that's sorta what led to Don Wright's ascendancy into being the president of AFN.

Bill: Yeah. Did you go to the AFN convention in October?

Don: Were you surprised when Don Wright became president?

Bill: No, nothing would've surprised me.

Don: He was only elected by a slim margin. He never was really supported by the AFN board. He and Ralph Perdue [president of Fairbanks Native Association] didn't know beans about Washington, D.C., but they felt like they were getting sold out. They didn't like Notti or Borbridge. They thought it was more of the same.

The first thing Don Wright did was to get hooked up with Adrian Parmeter [advisor and consultant to Wright]. Did you know him from the Kennedy committee at all?

Bill: I knew him some from the Kennedy era. I didn't assess his presence there. He was just there. He said to me, "I want to be a part of this." He identified it correctly as a great cause, and he wanted to be a part of it. He figured the Native goose was cooked unless you could change the odds in the administration. He figured out what was going on in the administration with Brad Patterson [assistant to Leonard Garment, domestic policy advisor to Nixon] and Bobbie Kilberg [served on Nixon's Domestic Policy Council]. He just was feeling it out but he didn't have as much information as it looked like. He was the right guy at the right time with his approach because of what was happening inside of the White House. He figured it out by a natural extrapolation, based on the Nixon Indian position in 1970.

So we have to go back to Nixon's earlier Indian policy to understand the current decisions. I know that at the beginning of Nixon's administration that Alvin with Parameter's help talked about a memo he had put into the White House. It's very mysterious because the memo just sank. Brad Patterson said no one in the White House ever heard about the memo or cared. Edgar Cahn was a friend of John Gardner who was a friend of Leonard Garment [Nixon's domestic policy adviser]. When Cahn put together that book, *Our Brother's Keeper*, Cahn asked Leonard Garment, "Could I get my people into the White House to give the song and dance to tell the sad state of Indian affairs to get everyone interested?" Garment brought them in.

Totally unrelated, John Ehrlichman [counsel and Assistant to Nixon for Domestic Affairs] had submitted a memo to the White House staff, "Do you have any suggestions for presidential initiatives next year?" It was all about timing. Patterson and Garment said, "Well, hey, we've just been dealing with Cahn about this Indian thing." Everyone said, "Yes," and they began having meetings. So that led to the president's statement on Indian policy July 1970.

Shortly after the announcement of Nixon's policy, July 8, 1970, shortly after you wrote Patterson a memo, trying to get him interested in Native land claims. It seems like they didn't take the bait then because they really don't get involved until that December when Adrian [Parmeter] makes the big push.

Bill: The timing was right for the memo [to Patterson]. Forrest Gerard [lobbyist for AAIA] was on Jackson's committee so he knew Patterson. At Forrest's suggestion, I went over to see Patterson. He was not excited, at all [about land claims].

Six months later, in December, I think that's when Adrian asked to accompany me [to see Brad Patterson]. [With him,] I took the approach of oil development and that the Natives were succeeding in blocking [access to the oil corridor] in courts. That we were opposed to [the right-of-way corridor issue] going through Congress and I told Patterson that the risk to the pipeline was not going to be permafrost but rather, Eskimos with bombs, unquote. He frowned; he did not like that. (I got a standing ovation when I said that to an audience at Columbia University a few months before that.) He wanted a memorandum right away. I went to Art Lazarus who worked up a long memo, the legal memorandum. I was off in another room writing up a short memo including Foote's caloric count and the village mapping of land use, all of which we fit into Art's memo and he signed it. We thought that was pretty important to get to Patterson.

Don: Interestingly, it was January 29, 1971. [The Alaska Native Claims Settlement Act (ANCSA) was signed into law by President Richard M. Nixon on December 23, 1971].

Bill: Without my prompting, Patterson, Adrian, all of them, thought that with Arthur's usual precision, it was very useful.

Whatever the timing was: after the floor fight, there was [first] the uninterested meeting with Patterson. Then, the interested but annoyed meeting with Patterson, and that same day, Arthur prepared the memo [for him]. That was the extent of my involvement at the White House.

Prior to that, the other thing was that we were looking for presidential contenders to co-sponsor the Native position, to make it clear that this was going to be a priority for the job.

Don: What clicked off a lot of people's imagination, at least Parmeter's, was a whole separate story, Taos/Blue Lake. It's worth reviewing. Blue Lake showed that Jackson and the committees could be beat on an Indian issue if you had a coalition of the Kennedy liberals combined with the White House.

Bill: that certainly wasn't my perception at the time. Forrest was brought onto Scoop Jackson's committee, not for Alaska Native land claims, but because Scoop Jackson didn't want another experience like Taos/Blue Lake again, and he wanted someone to give him good advice.

Don: The senate vote on Taos/Blue Lake was Dec 2, 1970. That's when Adrian Parmeter and Don Wright approached Bobbie Kilbrook in the gallery, watching the final vote on Taos/Blue Lake. That's when Scoop Jackson left the floor, furious that this had been done to him.

Bill: Separate and apart from Taos/Blue Lake, regardless if there were a precedent, Blue Lake wasn't the basis [of Alaska land claims] at all. Regardless if there were a precedent, you do all you can to win the Alaska Native position of forty million acres. Even though the committee chairman, the governor, the White House are opposed to you, you stick around and try to get those who aren't to support your cause, to win. You do all that you can with no certainty what that outcome was going to be. The job was to line up enough votes in the Senate such that Senators Jackson and Stevens thought it was plausible to bring this bill to the floor and get beaten as they had been beaten before on Blue Lake. They weren't going to pull their punches if they thought they had the votes. They thought they had the votes. Forrest told Bill Van Ness that I, Byler, thought they had enough votes to beat them on the floor. Fraser Barron went around, vote by vote by vote, and that's what has to be done.

Don: When Arthur Lazarus drew up an AFN bill in 1969, that's when the Senate mark-up began, that December. Gravel had introduced [the bill] and that Stevens had introduced as an amendment to S-1830. It was obviously never considered in the Senate process in 1970.

Then in 1971, when things started over again, Jackson held his first chairing February 17, 1971, and that's when Fred Harris, who was not on the Interior Committee, testified, putting everyone on notice that he had a sixty-million-acre bill with co-sponsors. That was another bill that Arthur had drafted.

Bill: AIAA was providing drafting services here. I assume that Arthur talked with the Ramsey Clark shop but I don't know that he did . . .

Don: In going vote by vote, office to office, were you coordinating with the new AFN lobby of Wright and Parmeter or were you doing it separately?

Bill: I guess separately. I wasn't aware that the latter were lining up votes. I think ninety-nine percent of the Senate votes Barron was lining up, using the strategy that Don Wright liked, "Get people that have presidential credentials," to have credibility, political dimension, not just moral persuasion, although that was what ultimately did it. Kennedy and Harris were for moral suasion. The political dimension was to focus the White House that something else is going on here.

Don: Well, also, Scoop Jackson was running for president.

Bill: Right. And the notion was that if you do all these things: you freeze everything on the floor and you're looking good in the House and you work with the oil companies, is that—if you want oil (I want to get to the oil companies and to Claude), if you want development in Alaska, the Natives have it all BLOCKED. On their own, the Natives may not be able to get their bill of forty million or sixty million, but they can without insulting him, potentially causing him to dump the whole thing, which he still could do as chairman. And that leads us to this whole thing with Claude Desetelles. The mysterious Claude. Whose idea was it to get him, why, and what was his purpose?

Bill: Well, again, you pick someone thinking they are one person and they turn out to be different. I asked Hackett who would be a good person to work the House, someone who really knew Aspinall well. He said, "Claude Desetelles." I asked him to talk to Desetelles. He'd been President Johnson's liaison to Congress. He was a former partner with Larry O'Brien and he was a lobbyist. When he was available, I told him what we needed. He was a wonderful man. He told me he was the godfather of Aspinall's kids. He said, "I'm over at Aspinalls in the summers for cookouts. We're extremely close friends. I never lobby Aspinall." He knew everybody and they all knew him. Of course, he was Johnson's man and he "never lobbied Aspinall." When I walked up to the hill with him, he stopped in at the minority staff side and he had a good clear idea of what was going on there and gave tactical advice. Like a good lobbyist, he never let on what he was doing. I think he was an important element in the success of the effort. There's no way of attributing any particular aspect to him. He was there and did what Claude did well.

Don: Was he technically paid by AFN on money AAIA passed through or was his client AAIA?

Bill: I think "pass through." We made certain grants to AFN to relieve them of expenditures and thereby they were able to afford Claude. He normally charged $8,000 but he'd do it for $4,000 to $5,000 per month. And that was it. He didn't say he'd work for one hour or hundred hours. He'd do what needed to be done and he didn't guarantee success.

And another important aspect involving Claude, whether he ever talked to the oil companies, I don't know, but he or Hackett told me who in the oil companies to talk to. I approached with, "The perception is that you are supporting Jackson or the administration's stance on this. Why do you care? If you continue to support a bill that in our view isn't going to go anywhere, you're not going to get oil out of Alaska faster. If you can't support the Natives, why don't you declare yourself neutral on the legislation?" That was one approach.

ARCO was part of the oil consortium. There was a New York Indian woman who worked for one of the principals of the firm. She would feed in stuff to ARCO about what was going on in the land bill that the oil companies weren't getting. So at the coalition meetings, the ARCO rep would get the inside land bill information from the principal, who worked with the American Indian woman, who was getting it from me about what was really going on. In late September to early October of

1971, Arctic Slope [Native Association] filed a lawsuit. She called me and asked, "What does this mean?"

Don: After the claims act, the lawsuit became *Edwardsen v. Morgan*. It originally started out to invalidate all the [state land holdings] lands of Prudhoe Bay, which they must have found highly amusing.

Bill: I may've called Arthur Lazarus to see what kind of vitality that suit would have. I passed that information on to the lady.

ARCO was terrified that morning when the market opened because stock was projected to go from $65 to $45, just based on that news. But it didn't. (It would've been great if Charlie had won.)

Congressman Lloyd Meeds.
http://m.spokesman.com/
stories/2005/aug/21/
cancer-claims-lloyd
-meeds-ex-congressman/

Don: Wickwire never expected it to go anywhere. It was just a lobbying effort that sort of spun out of control. These things do take on a life of their own.

Bill: They didn't know what the outcome would be, so it required a big financial institution to drop all of that ARCO stock.

Don: I asked you about Claude because of this whole play inside the House Interior Committee. On one hand, having put together this coalition led by Lloyd Meeds on basically doing what the Natives want but you couldn't push it too far because if you totally overloaded Aspinall, he had the ability, unilaterally, to kibosh it.

Bill: Unless the bill gets petitioned out and onto the floor. I can't remember if there was a petition underway and Aspinall knew he could lose it if he didn't let it go.

Don: One of the things about letting it go. After they put together what essentially became the House bill inside Haley's subcommittee, there was a meeting in Begich's office at which Ziegler came in and told everybody, "Aspinall won't move this bill unless you guys swear a blood oath that this is it." He's gone as far as he's going to go, unless you guys promise no amendments of substance in committee, on the house floor AND that you'll stay with this bill all the way through Congress, that we will not report the bill. It was basically blackmail. In a very constructive way, Don Wright sort of fudged the agreement. AFN held with that agreement all the way through the House, but it was a preposterous agreement with respect to the Senate.

Bill: I was not at that meeting. [It was] toward the end of the process while we were focused on forty million acres, in broad. However, AFN decided that that was going to be worked out, getting sponsors, support for that

Bill: Of course, there is also Ben Rifle from eastern South Dakota, but I don't know if he grew up on a reservation.

One of the most stunning political Indian victories was the referendum overturning state jurisdiction. The legislature had passed a law taking over formal and civil jurisdiction. People who'd never voted, old Indians arriving in buckboards came. It was really stunning. The tribes still have that right to their own jurisdiction.

In any event, when the vote was going on for the final time for ANCSA, AFN knew. I think that experience has been extremely important for the Native people of Alaska. They come in often to Washington, D.C. I wish they had a little more time in D.C. for some of the issues that arise. But they are very, very sophisticated. Became that, more than any tribal effort I've seen, doing it themselves. Usually you have a lot of D.C. lawyers doing the work. But in this case, there was an awful lot of opposition to it [lawyers carrying the ball].

In a phone call in 2008, Guy Martin, former legislative assistant to U.S. Congressman Nick Begich, said, "Wayne Aspinall [chairman of the house Committee on Interior and Insular Affairs] would never have passed the Alaska Native Claims Settlement Act bill had he known Alaska Natives would come back and claim tribal sovereignty. It was agreed that ANCSA extinguished sovereignty." In an interview for the Anchorage Daily News, *Don Mitchell, former vice president and legal counsel for Alaska Federation of Natives, said, "Alaska Natives chose corporations instead of tribes when they settled land claims in 1971. The tribal sovereignty movement is a horrible mistake."*

The AAIA took many steps to promote the self-sufficiency of Indian communities. Besides Alaska Native Claims Settlement Act, AAIA has played a critical role in landmark events that benefited Native people particularly in the Lower Forty-eight states.

After leaving AAIA, Bill continued advocating for the Native American community, first at Gerard, Byler, and Associates and later at William Byler Associates. Bill is now retired after spending a significant part of his life, at a pivotal time, quietly parting the waters for Alaska Natives.

With great thanks to Bill Byler, Al Ketzler, and Bear Ketzler. To Don Mitchell for the use of his two taped interviews with Bill Byler in 1989 and 1992, Washington, D.C.

Timeline

1922: AAIA is formed and helps Pueblos protect land and water rights.

1945: AAIA helps to establish National Congress of American Indians

1959: Alaska Statehood Act includes provision to not take lands of Native peoples.

1961: Alaska Natives organize to protest "Project Chariot" - a plan to use nuclear weapons to blast an artificial harbor into existence in Northwest Alaska.

1962: Reorganization of Tanana Chiefs Conference. The *Tundra Times* established.

1966: Alaska Federation of Natives formed in Anchorage, Alaska.

1968: AAIA works to protect Taos Blue Lake.

1971: Alaska Native Claims Settlement Act becomes law.

1972: The Marine Mammal Protection Act with the provision that Alaska Natives continue traditional use of marine mammals.

1978: Indian Child Welfare Act signed into law.

1980: The Alaska National Interest Lands Conservation Act created over eighty million acres of additional parks, preserves and monuments in Alaska. It also contained language supporting continued traditional and customary use on designated Federal lands.

1984: Tribal Government Tax Status Act became law.

1990: Native American Graves Protection and Repatriation Act enacted.

1991: Amendments to ANCSA took affect.

1994: Amendments to American Indian Religious Freedom Act approved.

2006: AAIA created Dakotah-language Scrabble game and hosts first tournament

2008: Tribal amendments to Title IV-E Foster Care and Adoption Assistance Act approved in Fostering Connections for Success and Increasing Adoptions Act.

Howard Rock painted this according to the description of his brother Allen Rock, the whaling captain, of getting the huge whale near Point Hope, Alaska.

AMRC-b85-27-2326

Chapter Twenty-three

Don Wright, the Winning of ANCSA

As I interviewed Frank and Nettie Peratrovich, DeLois Ketzler Burggraf, and Emil Notti, they mentioned Don Wright often with accolades as well as grins about his personal style. Don agreed to meet with me twice in his large natural log home on the banks of the Chena River in 2006. Like his ancestry and his life, his home was a museum, an excursion through Alaska history with his family's threads running throughout.

Don Wright airing up my tire at his home, Fairbanks, 2006.
Judy Ferguson photo.

On one interview, my twenty-two-year-old son, Benjamin, accompanied me. As we entered Don's house, Ben mentioned to me that our rear tire was low. At the end of the conversation with Don, he kindly agreed to air up the questionable tire. While inflating the tire, he grinned up at me and I thought, "This is pretty incredible." A couple of years later when Ben was studying Alaska history and Alaska Native Claims Settlement Act (ANCSA) in school, I said, "Ben, you remember the man who once aired up our tire? He was the man who won ANCSA."

As Don and I sat in his lodge home, he shared his family's story.

My grandfather Henry Wright, a prospector, came to Alaska in 1887 to the Fortymile River country. At Tanana/Nuklukayet, where there was a Northern Commercial trading post, he met my Gwich'in grandmother Annie Glass, originally of Old Crow. As was common with miners in those days, they took up with each other. Two years later, my father, Arthur Wright, was born to them. As a child, living with his mother in Tanana, my father spoke only Athabascan. When my grandfather decided to return to his native Montana, he didn't want his son to grow up Native, so he left him with Rev. Jules Prevost who had opened St. James, a new mission, in Tanana. After years of school and learning English, in his teenage years, he left for Carlisle Indian Industrial School in Pennsylvania. In 1908 when he was twenty, he returned to Alaska as an interpreter. During

GWICH' IN

the summers, he ran Archdeacon Hudson Stuck's boat, the *Godspeed*, up and down the river, establishing churches. In the winters, he helped run the archdeacon's dog teams, accompanying Stuck and Dr. Grafton Burke to the new mission at Allakaket and Alatna.

In 1910, the archdeacon sent my father to Mount Hermon School for Boys in Gill, Massachusetts. When he returned, he helped the archdeacon build the church in Nenana. In 1913, my dad and Johnnie Fredson mushed Stuck and Walter Harper to the ten thousand-foot level of Denali, where they maintained the base camp until the climbers returned after that first successful ascent of Denali. The archdeacon dedicated his book *Voyages on the Yukon and Its Tributaries* partly to my father.

Jules Louis Prevost (1863-1937) who with his wife Anna Louise served as a missionary in central Alaska from 1892-1906.
http://justus.anglican.org/ resources/bcp/ 1892/koyukon.html

Five years later, my mother, Myrtle Rose, and her sister, both missionary nurses, came to Alaska from Boise, Idaho. They walked and rode horses, resting in the villages and following the rail bed from Seward to Nenana. At the Nenana mission, Mother met my father. When the Spanish flu hit, only she and another nurse never got sick. Seventy-five percent of the village died. My dad got very sick, but Mother pulled him and many others through. After her two-year tour, she went home but apparently with a plan. She met Dad in Seattle, where they married in 1922.

Archdeacon Hudson Stuck and Don's father Arthur Wright, cross the Alaska-Yukon border in 1911. Two years later, Arthur maintained a base camp while Hudson Stuck led the first ascent of Denali.
Courtesy of Don Wright.

They returned to Nenana, where Dad was ordained an Episcopal deacon.

Bishop Peter Trimble Rowe wanted my dad to be the bishop of Alaska, but the church would not permit it; instead, Dad became "a marryin' and buryin' priest." He and Mom were stationed at St. Timothy's Mission at Tanana Crossing, where my brothers Arthur Eugene and Alfred were born. In 1923,

Governor Wally Hickel and Don Wright on the right with Igloo-Puk celebrating the Alaska Purchase centennial, Anchorage airport, 1967.

Courtesy of Don Wright.

Anchorage. That same year, I joined the Bartlett Democratic Club and the following year, I was a delegate to the Democratic convention, along with Gov. Egan and Sen. Bob Bartlett and attorney John Rader.

I got into Native issues because I thought it was needed. Sometimes I had money and other times, not. In Anchorage, I followed Nick Gray and Emil Notti as president of Cook Inlet Native Association, a parallel to Fairbanks Native Association, which was headed by my brother Jules. A Tlingit lawyer, William Paul Sr., who had known my mother and father before they married, usually carried a briefcase full of documented Native

258

Dog Race. During the resolution of Alaska Native land claims, my brother Jules served as chairman of the state senate.

In 1952, I met Congressman Richard Nixon when he and Bob Hope campaigned in Alaska for General Eisenhower's first run for the presidency.

During the 1960s, Wright Truck and Tractor incorporated and began competing with all the big boys. As a contractor, I drove Cats, hauling drilling mud and cement for Atlantic Richfield and Arco for the construction of the first camp in Prudhoe, before the Dalton Highway was built.

In 1967, to celebrate the centennial celebration of the purchase of Alaska, I was in charge of the construction and management of the Native cultural center, Igloo-Puk, near the International Airport in

Don Young, president of Cook Inlet Native Association, announces his candidacy for the U.S. House of Representatives at the Democratic convention in Sitka, 1968.

Anchorage Museum, B1990.14.5.Pol.01.53, Steve McCutcheon Collection.

land issues. He had no money and no place to stay. He moved into my house, where we talked night and day. We were a great help to each other.

In the Lower Forty-eight, I represented Alaska in the National Congress of American Indians. At the meetings, I met representatives from every tribe. I got on their boards and became an area president for fifteen years. But in that group, there were too many lawyers, non-Natives, and a concentration of big money; it was a platform for many non-Natives to get into Native business. I went

Jules Wright, Fairbanks, member of the Alaska House of Representatives, with Ralph Perdue, former president of the Fairbanks Native Association.
Tundra Times. Alaska Native Land Claims.
Courtesy of Emil Notti.

to every reservation in America then, about a hundred. No one else would take the time to do it. We formed the National Tribal Chairmen's Association, for which membership required being a tribal member. I got my education from the chiefs and from the national tribal chairman job. From the lessons of the Navajo, Mescalero Apache (a southern Athabascan tribe), Bob Jim at the Yakima Nation, Joe Dan Osceola (the chairman of the Seminole), and Tandy Wilbur Jr. of the Swinomish, I learned the value of our land, of our rights.

Alaska Federation of Natives board, 1968: l-r: Don Wright, Frank Degnan, Willie Hensley.
Tundra Times. Alaska Native Land Claims.
Courtesy of Emil Notti.

As president of Cook Inlet Native Association in 1967, I worked with Tyonek, a little village on Cook Inlet. The Beluga gas and coalfields, where electricity is generated for Anchorage, is adjacent to the Tyonek property. Initially, those villagers had no experience in energy production, but today they own their own gas and oil, timber, and they deal with big oil companies.

In 1966, a bunch of us—Emil Notti, Nick Gray, Willie Hensley, John Borbridge, later Byron Mallott, Frank Degnan of Unalakleet, and Eben Hobson of Point Barrow—organized the Alaska Federation of Natives (AFN). Emil was the first president. Tyonek put up $100,000 to haul representatives in from all over the state to meet in Anchorage. We also had bingo games

allowing us our own sovereignty. If each area had wanted to form its own corporations, that would be different, but this was a mandate from the federal government. I'm in favor of a corporation if it's controlled correctly. If I bought

As AFN president, Don Wright met President Nixon in Washington, D.C., in April 1971. Nixon signed the Alaska Native Claims Settlement Act into law on Dec. 18 that year.
Courtesy of Don Wright.

a corporation and it's mine, then okay, but not permeated and driven by big business interests.

The real point is that the federal government never "owned" Alaska. It has always belonged to the Natives; we were born sovereign. Venetie and Arctic Village chose not to be a corporation but to keep their former reservation land. There are only about three hundred to four hundred people there, and they have 1.8 million acres of sovereign land plus the use of another 3.5 million acres. People at the local level want to control their own lives and monies, not go through a large corporate entity. In Canada today, the Inuit have sovereignty in Nunavut. We Natives were born free and independent; the government has no right to define and leverage our sovereignty.

Once land claims were settled, I fought for construction of the pipeline. In 1978, Joe Vogler and I established the Alaska Independence Party. Ever since, I have run for governor every four years, pushing for the development of Alaska.

My father was a good man. He taught us to be Indians; he taught us the value of the land and that we owned the land. Because of my father, I felt I had a duty to do the Indians' business and I did.

Five of the seven Wright brothers: Don, Jules, Al, Gareth, and "Link" Lawrence, 1986, Fairbanks. {The youngest, Forest, and the oldest, Arthur Gene, were deceased).

Courtesy of Don Wright.

Myrtle Wright in the house Don made for her.

Courtesy of Don Wright.

Timeline

1892-1900: Tanana mission under Rev. Jules Prevost.

1898: Klondike gold rush.

1913: Archbishop Hudson Stuck and Walter Harper climb Denali.

1946: First North American Championships (NAC) sled dog derby.

1947: Ladd Field/Fort Wainwright at Fairbanks built.

1948: Alaska Dog Mushers Association founded.

1964: Cook Inlet Native Association begun.

Late 1960s: "Hickel Highway:" attempts at winter haul road.

1966: Alaska Federation of Natives begun. Etok bring suit.

1965, 1968: Udall's injunction followed by formal freeze in 1968.

1970: Don Wright elected president of Alaska Federation of Natives.

December 18, 1971: President Nixon signs ANCSA.

1974-1977: Alyeska Pipeline built.

1978: Alaska Independence Party formed.

❦

Chapter Twenty-four

Alaska Native Claims Settlement Act: Nick Begich Sr.

In 2007, Nick Begich Sr.'s second son Tom told me the story of his father's work on Alaska Native land claims as well as the subsequent loss of him at an early age.

left to right, with Congressman Nick Begich in the center, are Donald R. Wr dent Alaska Federation of Natives; Tim Wallis, 2nd Vice President; Phillip G ice President; Frank Degnan, Sergeant-at-Arms; Frances Degnan, Secretary; els Anderson, Treasurer.

U.S. Congressman Nick Begich with the Alaska Federation of Natives staff, 1971.
Courtesy of Tom Begich.

Until I was nearly twelve, I grew up with a man who was a legend, the son of Croatian immigrants, but who disappeared on October 16, 1972, into the clouds. No trace of him was ever found. My father, U.S. congressman Nick Begich, was critical in the 1971 passage of Alaska Native Claims Settlement Act.

The son of a Croatian immigrant, my dad, was born in 1932 and grew up in the Mesabi Iron Range in Eveleth, Minnesota, where his father, John Begich, spent his life working in the iron ore mines. Dad's older brothers worked in the mines, but my dad was destined for the books.

Eleven years after he was born, the mine, mill, and smelter workers were finally allowed to organize openly, and Dad was introduced to the world of politics and debate.

During World War II, my grandfather lost most of his relatives back home to Tito's partisans, causing him to hate communists and always support an independent Croatia. He was very active in the CFR, the Croatian Fraternal Union, as was his friend John Blatnick, an American-Croatian politician. Blatnick greatly influenced my father when he was only eight years old. Blatnick encouraged my dad to go to college and to consider politics.

In high school, my father excelled in everything from sports to academics. He accumulated a year of college credit and enrolled at the local teachers college in St. Cloud. He pushed so hard that he got his bachelor's degree in three years and graduated with a cum laude degree in history and political science. While teaching high school, he got his master's degree two years later, and he was working on his doctorate when he died. A member of the Farmer Labor Young Democrats, he supported Hubert Humphrey for his second term in the U.S. Senate.

As a teacher, Dad's plans for a Minnesota political life changed when he fell in love with a former student, Pegge Jendro. In 1956, Dad's mentor Hubert Humphrey got Dad a job in Anchorage, where he could jump-start his political career. He moved, and that winter he returned to Minnesota to marry the student, my mom.

Nick Begich campaigning for state senate, 1960.

Courtesy of Tom Begich.

In 1957 Dad and Mom drove up the highway to Anchorage, where my father pursued his career as a teacher and politician. He always believed that an educated population was critical to Alaska's success.

In 1960, as principal of the elementary school at Fort Richardson, Dad was elected president of the Alaska Principals Association. As he fought for teachers for the next two years, he was still naïve about public service. He believed people naturally served altruistically. He was aggressive about politics and didn't understand compromise.

In 1960 when I was born, Dad decided to run for the Alaska Senate. He went to union leaders for backing, but they used him to pressure other Democrats who were in office. Taking advantage of his ambition, they convinced him to run against an incumbent. Although he lost the primary, the incumbent was weakened and he lost the seat in the general election. Determined to be his own man, Dad realized he must create his own base, and he turned to the Alaska Education Association, for which he lobbied.

A key to Dad's lifelong success was the three-by-five-inch cards on which he recorded the names of everyone he met, their personal information, and their issues. He opted for public exposure and became a more professional, streamlined Nick Begich. In 1963, Dad became the superintendent of the Fort Richardson schools and the youngest-ever elected state senator, with a district of 1,200 square miles that included one-fourth of the state's population. By long distance during legislative sessions, he supervised the Fort Richardson schools and taught classes at the University of Alaska.

Already a father of three—Nichelle, Nick, and me—he announced his second candidacy for the Senate the year his fourth child, Mark, was born in 1962.

Part of growing up in a political family with a man who was a workaholic was that I didn't know my father. In those days, the legislative session was unlimited, and although the Democrats dominated, they were often not aligned,

265

and sessions could stretch into mid-June. My dad would drive to Juneau in January and not return for almost six months.

Before reapportionment made the previous geographic-based Senate districts invalid, Dad's district was enormous, stretching from Spenard to Adak. During the summer he campaigned, and Mom and we six kids drove, visiting relatives in the Lower Forty-eight. Sometimes Dad joined us.

At home, Dad had an inner sanctum that was off limits to us kids. Today it seems kind of funny: old photos show only a rundown teacher's office with jury-rigged shelves lined with books, most of which I now own. One of my first memories was when he invited me in and showed me the headlines of John Kennedy's assassination.

Throughout his years in the state Senate, Dad won twenty-three of twenty-four listed goals for teachers. By the time his Senate career finished, Alaska's teachers drew the nation's top salaries and benefits.

Alaska traditionally voted Democratic, but in 1966 we elected a Republican governor, Walter Hickel, and a Republican-dominated legislature. U.S. Senator Ernest Gruening, a Democrat, was seventy-nine years old. In 1968, Hickel appointed Republican Ted Stevens to replace Senator Bob Bartlett, a Democrat, who had just died.

In 1968, Nixon ran against Dad's mentor, Hubert Humphrey, and Dad ran for the Democratic nomination for the U.S. House against John Rader. Dad's teacher-based Democrats beat Rader.

Early on, Dad hadn't realized others played hardball, but he learned and built his own organization. He forged together the teachers and the Native Democrats and defeated Egan's establishment Democrats. In the general election, however, the nation went for Nixon and Dad lost to Republican, Howard Pollock.

The Begich family, Mark, Nick, Nichelle, Tom, Stephanie, Paul on Pegge's lap, Nick Begich, Anchorage, 1970.

Courtesy of Tom Begich.

Throughout 1960, '62, '66, and '68 (and later, 1970), Dad campaigned. When he ran for Congress, he campaigned statewide, not just in his Senate district. My Dad's obsession with work finally triggered my mother to file for divorce in 1969. Devastated, Dad offered to leave politics. Mom left us kids with him, spent the summer in Minnesota, and returned in the fall supporting a

Nick and daughter Stephanie Begich, Anchorage, 1972.
Courtesy of Tom Begich.

Nick Begich who had discovered there was more to life than political pursuits.

In 1970, Bill Egan was in the race of his life. Frankly, all the Democratic Party's resources were focused on Egan and his running mate, Wendell Kay. My dad was running against Frank Murkowski for the U.S. Congress, and many thought Murkowski would win, but Dad beat him soundly.

With the expected oil pipeline blocked by pending Alaska Native land claims, Dad had one goal: get a land claims bill passed. The previous Congress had gotten a bill through the Senate, but if a bill didn't make it through the House, the legislation could die. Dad asked Guy Martin, a lawyer who knew land claims well, to be his legislative aide.

The chairman of the Senate's Interior and Insular Affairs Committee, Henry "Scoop" Jackson, had a bill and was pushing hard for settlement. The chair for the House's Interior and Insular Affairs Committee was a crusty ol' guy from Colorado, Wayne Aspinall. In those days, a chair held that post for life and ruled with an iron hand. It was known that Aspinall didn't support Indians or favor settlement, and he didn't like being pushed around at all. He was a conservative Democrat, hard to handle, but he would favor a member who attended all his committee meetings.

Our family had moved by then to Washington, D.C. On the weekends, Dad would touch base back in Alaska, then return to D.C. twelve hours and five time zones later (this was before they changed the time zones in Alaska in 1983) and drive madly to the committee hearing room just as Aspinall convened the Monday-morning meeting.

From the day Dad first arrived in Washington in December 1970, he made sure he knew every person, Republican and Democrat, in the House of Representatives. He saw each one as a potential vote for the settlement act. Every morning he left his office for the House floor with a three-by-five-inch card with the names of ten congressmen, saying, "I am going to get to know these guys and find out the three most important issues to them."

When he met with the Alaska Federation of Natives, he said, "Tell me what you want." They said, "Half a billion dollars, ten million acres, and the corporate structure." He responded, "We can do better." So Dad carried the bill forward with forty million acres and a billion dollars.

He spent a huge amount of time on the bill, discussing with oil companies and talking with his aide, Guy. He supported issues relevant to the colleagues

House Majority Whip Democrat Tip O'Neil and U.S. Congressman Nick Begich, Washington, D.C., circa 1971.
Courtesy of Tom Begich.

he lobbied. He spent the entire first year positioning himself to get claims passed.

He didn't make the rousing speeches typical of his past but patiently worked his strategy, becoming a true statesman. When opposing members baited him, he nodded, made factual corrections, and didn't argue. He wanted a bill Natives could live with and one that worked.

Aspinall wanted to dictate the solution for the Natives. Dad and a supportive legislator from Washington, Lloyd Meeds, worked out a dynamic. Acting as a "no prisoners, no compromise" spokesman for the Natives, Meeds took the confrontational heat with the opposition, freeing Dad to be the connective tissue between Native and non-Native Alaskans and the politicians.

When Aspinall still wasn't delivering on Native terms, Dad called Aspinall's bluff, threatening to drop the bill. Aspinall replied, "Convince Bud Saylor of Pennsylvania, and we'll have a deal."

Before the final vote, Speaker of the House Carl Albert spoke: "I know of no one who has done more for his state in his first term of his first session than the hardworking, conscientious, never-say-die Nick Begich." On his chairman's advice, then, to combat possible amendments, Dad finally gave one of his fiery speeches, replying to all attacks with facts, dates, and numbers. In 1971 a billion dollars was a lot, and Congress was not so inclined, but the bill passed without amendment.

Later, I was told that if all the United States' indigenous land settlements were combined, they would not equal ANCSA's (Alaska Native Claims Settlement Act). While handling three committees, Dad, a first-session freshman, got a landmark bill that set the model for all subsequent Alaska land development. To this day, Dad is revered in rural Alaska.

From the outset, this quick-passage legislation was intended to be tweaked continually to meet the needs of the evolving Native community: addressing the rights of those born after passage, the descent of stocks, and the accountability issue of the new corporations. The great tragedy of ANCSA is that has not been done effectively. ANCSA is one of the most-amended acts ever, but only ten to twenty percent of those amendments have been to perfect the act. Rather, they have been to improve ANCSA's playing field, to get additional bites of the apple.

The morning of October 16, 1972, Dad, Louisiana congressman and majority leader of the House Hale Boggs, Dad's aide Russ Brown, and pilot Don

Tom Begich,
Anchorage, 2006.
Judy Ferguson
photo.

Jonz climbed into Jonz's Cessna 310 in Anchorage, bound for Juneau. The next morning, after the plane had not been heard from in twenty-four hours, our mother broke the news to us before we went to school.

As my brother Nick and I walked to classes, I looked up and saw a cloud formation. "See that cloud?" I said, "There's a plane and a mountain. You see, Dad must have made it through all right!"

When the votes were cast three weeks later, Dad won his congressional seat with 56.2 percent, even though he was suspected dead. Later, at the March special nominating convention, Mom,

U.S Senator
Mark Begich,
Nov. 19, 2008.
Courtesy of
Tom Begich.

though a candidate herself, threw her support to Emil Notti and put him over the top as Alaska's first Alaska Native candidate for Congress. That was an election Don Young won by about one percentage point.

At age thirty-four, Mom was a widow with six children.

When I was twenty-one, in an attempt to "find" the father I lost when I was eleven, I interviewed over eighty people and drafted a book about his life.

Unlike my grandfather's native Yugoslavia, our multi-ethnic issues in Alaska are addressed within the confines of the state and federal constitutions. One-fifth of the legislature in Alaska is Native, mirroring the population, which is unusual in a state with a "minority" population.

Before the pipeline, times weren't easy in Alaska. Sure, Republicans and Democrats fought—but when we were finished, we talked with respect. That legacy and the gift of our father's instinct for public service have helped keep five of his six children here in Alaska.

Timeline:

1957: Two years before statehood, Nick Begich family arrived in Alaska.

1960: Nick Begich Sr. ran for the Alaska senate.

1966: Republican Walter Hickel elected governor.

1968: Hickel filled U.S. Senator Bob Bartlett's (Democrat) vacated seat with Ted Stevens (Republican.)

1971: Alaska Native Claims Settlement Act.

1972: Nick Begich's plane missing.

2008: U.S. Senator-elect Mark Begich.

∞

Chapter Twenty-six

Nettie Suteen Peratrovich, Haida: Breaking Ground On Native Education

The Kaigani Haida migrated over two hundred years ago from British Columbia's Haida Gwaii (Queen Charlotte Islands). A matrilineal, warrior, seagoing culture, they are credited with the introduction of the totem pole and bentwood box. They also practiced slave trading. In their western red cedar canoes, they traveled to the northern

Frank and Nettie Peratrovich, Alaskans on the Potomac, Washington, D.C., 1969.
Courtesy of Frank and Nettie Peratrovich.

Bering Sea, and some traditions say they even went to Asia before the coming of the white man. In the 1700s, they moved into the southern part of the Tlingit Prince of Wales Island.

Their language is classified now as isolate. To my layman's ears when Nettie Peratrovich spoke Haida, it sounded melodic, like Polynesian.

Impacted early by European culture, the Haida and the Tlingit led the fight for citizenship for Alaska's indigenous people in forming the Alaska Native Brotherhood and Sisterhood in Sitka in 1912.

Nettie Peratrovich, half Haida, said, "Unlike the Alaska interior, for the most part, our land in Southeast was not infringed upon. Consequently, my lifelong focus has not been the land but education."

In 1998 while researching my first book, Parallel Destinies, *I met Nettie by telephone. From the beginning, clearly, she was a pioneer in Native education and a master teacher. A lightning personality, Nettie had my full attention as she guided me through the history of the Alaska Native Claims Settlement Act and the development of Native education. She began her story.*

A Haida-Scot, I was born at Steamboat Bay, Noyes Island, east of Prince of Wales Island, to Nettie Nix and Gilbert McLeod in 1936. I grew up when epidemics were raging and child mortality was that of a Third World nation.

HAIDA

x

x

x

Over two hundred years before, the Haida, famous for their large canoes, totems, and argillite carvings, migrated from Canada's Queen Charlotte Islands north to Prince of Wales Island. In 1911, three Haida villages (Sukkwan, Howkan, and Klinkwan) combined at the present site for their children to attend school; it was designated as the Hydaburg Indian Reservation. However the villagers were not comfortable with the arrangement and requested in 1926, that the land be restored to the Tongass National Forest. One-hundred-eighty-

Haida Warriors *painting by Nikola Kocic from* Alaska's First People.

Courtesy of Judy Ferguson.

nine acres were kept for the school and town site. My mother, Nettie Nix, was the first baby born at Hydaburg.

The Presbyterian missionaries (many of them from the Gould family) brought education early to Southeast. In 1877, the Sitka Industrial Training School (later known as Sheldon Jackson College) was established.

In the late 1800s, my paternal grandmother, Clara Martha Gould, came to Alaska as a seventeen-year-old Presbyterian missionary-teacher to teach the Haidas. She married William Donald McLeod, a miner and surveyor who named McLeod Bay and Gould and Peratrovich islands. My father, Gilbert McLeod, arrived in 1903, the first Caucasian baby born in Hydaburg.

In 1913, territorial schools were available only to Natives deemed "civilized." The Alaska Native Brotherhood and Sisterhood (ANB and ANS) were founded to secure citizenship and education for our people. My parents-in-law, Roy and Elizabeth Peratrovich and Senator Frank Peratrovich became heavily involved in ANB and ANS.

My maternal grandfather—my *"chenah"*—Frank Nix, was from Sukkwan, west of Hydaburg. My grandmother—my "NaNa"—Minnie George, was from Tongass village near Ketchikan. My mother had nine children, but we were half breeds so we could not go to school just anywhere.

I spent a lot of time with NaNa, who named me Suteen. A high-caste Haida, she had tattoos of frogs and eagles up her arms and neck. I loved to rub them with deer tallow. NaNa was so Presbyterian that she always wore long-sleeved, high-necked dresses to cover her tattoos. She used to comb my long, blond hair and say, "Suteen, you will save your Haida people. We are dying. Get an education to help or there will be no more Haidas left." Her words influenced me more than anyone else's.

We moved to Ketchikan at the beginning of World War II. The closest school was Caucasian, but my mother told them we would attend. When I was ten, my parents' marriage ended. My sister, brother, and I were put in an orphanage while my other six siblings went to Washington state.

I lived at the Craig Church of Christ children's home until it was closed for physical abuse. Then Dad sent us to the Presbyterian children's home, Haines House, which was as bad or worse. Until the Alaska Native Claims Settlement Act of 1971 (ANCSA), there was no enforcement of laws to protect Native children. Also, if Native adults were perceived as "loitering" on the street, they could be thrown in jail.

My generation was the first generation of Natives across the state to master modern skills on a large scale. In 1950, I began studying at Mt. Edgecumbe boarding school in Sitka. I met Iñupiaq, Yup'ik, Athabascans, and Aleuts from every corner of Alaska. Some of my classmates later became Native activists and the first presidents of the Native corporations: Cecil Barnes, John Schaeffer, Ralph Eluska, Morris Thompson, Joe Upicksoun, and Emil Notti, among others.

However, during the Eisenhower administration of 1954, Natives with white fathers could no longer attend Mt. Edgecumbe. I could not graduate, so I moved to Seattle, where I began working at a department store. Across the street one day I noticed an Army recruiting office. I signed up, and after getting my general equivalency diploma, I began my basic training in Alabama. One day when a Southern bus driver ordered, "All Negroes to the back of the bus," since I was a minority, I went to the back also.

Not until I began training at the Army Intelligence Center in Baltimore did I realize

Central Council Tlingit Haida Indian Tribes of Alaska, Juneau, 2003.

Judy Ferguson photo.

that the rest of the world didn't think of me as an Indian, even though I had a thick accent.

After I was discharged in 1957, I got a job in Juneau and saved money to attend the University of Alaska (UA Fairbanks.)

In Juneau, I met Frank Peratrovich, a former U.S. Marine and son of civil rights' activists, Roy and Elizabeth Peratrovich; we married in 1962. Four years later when Frank got a job with the state Department of Labor, we moved to Fairbanks. Frank's boss, Lottie Fleeks, ran the employment office and suggested he test for Equal Employment Opportunity. They wanted a rural interviewer to go out to the Bush, to test and to offer training. While Frank worked, I continued my education at UAF.

While a student, I got a job teaching urban survival skills to adult Natives during a five-week session for the Fairbanks Native Association (FNA.) With no handbook, I invented my own teaching methods. I wondered how I'd teach them the four basic math operations in that short session. One day when I walked in late, they were playing poker, slapping cards around with lightning speed.

Senator Ted Stevens, unknown, Nettie and Frank Peratrovich, Joe Briones Filipino-American veteran, unknown, unknown, Peggy Begich, unknown, American Veterans of Foreign Wars banquet, Washington, D.C., 1969.
Courtesy of Frank and Nettie Peratrovich.

"That's it!" I thought. I had them put petty change on the table, but instead of regular cards, we played with math flash cards. Not only did they learn fast, but they asked to up the ante. "No way!" I said.

At FNA, working with Poldine Carlo, Mary Jane Fate, Don Wright, and Tim Wallis, we had fundraisers to send elected representatives from the newly reorganized Tanana Chiefs Conference to the new Alaska Federation of Natives (AFN) meetings in Anchorage. Whenever Frank and I saw potential Native leaders, we invited them to FNA and appointed them to positions. Many remain big names today.

In 1968, the Tlingit-Haida received $7.5 million dollars minus expert costs for the extinguishment of indigenous land claims in the Tongass National Forest and Glacier Bay. As a result, my focus was not land concerns but the tools for our culture, education.

Fairbanks mayor H.A. "Red" Boucher created the Fairbanks Human Rights Commission and appointed Frank to the board. During the night, he rode

Frank and Nettie Peratrovich, 1987, Washington, D.C.
Courtesy of Frank and Nettie Peratrovich.

in police cars to ensure minorities and females were not harassed. He was promoted as the Department of Labor's minority groups specialist but he soon took a job with Bureau of Indian Affairs (BIA) as the employment assistance specialist. He helped Alaska Natives get training and find permanent jobs on the military bases. He got funding for house trailers, and in turn, they boarded rural students.

In 1969, Frank was chosen from a BIA national competition to train American Indians for upper management positions in Washington, D.C. While there, he researched the Indian preference laws, which ensured sustained policies for BIA that still stand today.

Since I was pregnant and unemployable, I sat in on Indian Affairs hearings. I discovered the Johnson O'Malley Act, which authorized BIA to negotiate federal funds to pay for the education of American Indians and Alaska Natives. I found out that the state of Alaska had been getting $7.5 million every year from BIA, who in turn had been signing the federal dollars over to the Department of Education. For years the state had used part of that money to ship Native children out of state to boarding schools while spending the majority of the federal dollars on urban schools.

At the same time, land claims were raging. Secretary of the Interior Walter Hickel threatened to lift Stewart Udall's super land freeze without Native approval. Frank called the Fairbanks Native Association and said, "If Hickel won't maintain the freeze, we won't support his confirmation as secretary of the interior and we'll get AFN to back us." We did and as a result, Frank got flak from every politician on the hill; even AFN wavered during the process.

There was a lot of traffic in those days from Alaska to Washington, D.C. as Natives testified for land claims. Frank and I organized "Alaskans on the Potomac;" we hosted many Alaskans in our apartment and showed them around D.C. Most Alaska Natives didn't have money to travel all the way to Washington, D.C. and to pay for their living expenses. Our organization helped them with their housing, eating, transportation, and directing them to the twelve congressional offices. Congressman Nick Begich's office helped us identify those people who were not listening to us and they pointed us to certain senators and congressmen.

Native groups also sent former beauty queens, some of the best looking Alaska Native representatives. I made a bunch of kuspuks for everyone so that after the hearings, we could recognize each other.

However the Tlingits and Haidas would not sit with the other Natives. I asked them why they wouldn't join us, but they wouldn't even answer. They thought that they were a little better than everybody else. It was really bizarre.

At the hearings, Don Wright did a fantastic job. He probably educated more senators and representatives than anyone regarding Alaska Natives' use of the land. You would have thought that he had read the Federal Field Committee report: *Alaska Natives and the Land* by the Department of Interior, a 565-page blueprint for settling land claims as well as paving the way for economic, social, and educational benefits. It was shocking to us that Tlingit and Haida didn't want to be involved with the statewide land claims however when ANSCA was nearly passed, Tlingit-Haida saw that they weren't going to get anything so they jumped on the bandwagon.

When Richard Nixon became president, the 1964 civil rights law began to get funded. Alaska's treatment of Natives ranked them on the same level as the deep South's abuse of the Afro-American. Before the poverty program would begin funneling money into the state of Alaska, the feds told the state to clean up its civil rights or there would be no grants.

To help implement that clean up—just before the passage of the Alaska Native Claims Settlement Act in 1971—Frank was made contract compliance officer with the Department of the Interior Office for Equal Opportunity in Anchorage, where he was soon promoted to assistant regional manager. As the pipeline era began, he conducted EEO reviews on federal contractors in Alaska. He found there were no females and very few minorities employed in construction. He also ensured that pregnancy leave was available and that tenure was open to all female employees at the

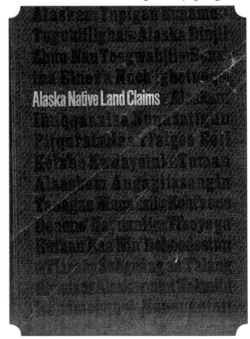

Alaska Native Land Claims *by Robert D. Arnold.*

Courtesy of Don Wright.

Frank Jr., John, Frank Sr and Nettie Peratrovich, circa 1989.

Courtesy of Frank and Nettie Peratrovich.

University of Alaska. The Department of the Interior Office for Civil Rights did more than anyone in getting Natives hired on the pipeline and in construction. However there were no Native organizations addressing the lack of minorities on TV, radio, or in journalism.

Even though he had begun working as deputy director for the Aleutian Pribilof Islands Association (APIA), he established and began volunteering his time to the Anchorage Native Caucus (ANC.) As the ANC, he confronted Alaska media moguls who ran the Anchorage television stations. Nose to nose with KTVA-TV founder, Augie Hebert, Frank protested the lack of good reporting of Alaska Natives and their industry's lack of minority and female hire. Frank told him that unless he hired minorities and females he'd file with Federal Communications Commission and suggest they delay the renewal of their license. Suddenly there were females and Afro-Americans in their news broadcasts, but very few Natives. However the reporting of quality Native stories increased.

As the APIA deputy director, Frank got the only national resolution through the National Congress of American Indians that year, pushing to clean up the World War II debris from the Aleutian Pribilof waters, a two-hundred-million dollar project.

While Frank was running APIA, I transferred to University of Alaska Anchorage to finish my schooling. Whenever Alaska Federation of Natives (AFN) had their meetings, we were frequently there. Since I'd had constitutional law, I helped them draft their constitution. Because RurAL Cap was getting some anti-poverty funds, that money helped support the fledgling AFN.

In those pre-pipeline days, the majority of the state's budget came from education monies; little of that went to rural Alaska. The main federal dollar built all the public schools with money that was meant for Alaska Natives; not a penny of it went to Natives. The state countered that they had had to build the schools for the military but no, the military had built their own schools. When I discovered that $7.5 million of federal Johnson O'Malley Act (JOM) monies intended for the education of Natives had been routinely signed over to the Department of Education, I protested. I went to AFN and said, "Alaska has been getting millions while sending our students Outside, where some of them are committing suicide. Don't let Morrie [Morris Thompson, the BIA director] sign the BIA JOM check over to the Department of Education. Let's create a statewide parent committee to see how the money should be spent." Even though the state was upset with him, Morrie stood with us.

At the same time, Judy Kleinfeld was writing a series in the newspaper citing data regarding the boarding student and suicide problem. With that leverage, we wrestled the legislature. I was made chairman of the new JOM Committee and served with Susan Murphy of Bethel and Mary Jane Fate of Fairbanks. Anyone accessing JOM monies had to apply through our committee. We were tagged the "Wicked Witches of Alaska," but that was before we learned to treat others not as we had been treated but as we wanted to be treated.

The summer of 1971, Senator Bill Ray met with our statewide JOM committee. He slammed his fist down: "Where were you when we were going through the education bills?" I asked, "How do those bills include us when you know where all the money goes?" I reminded him that we also had no bilingual program, even though we had five thousand non-English-speaking students in our schools.

When Frank was hired as the BIA superintendent for Southeast, he began a three-year stint in Juneau.

While I was finishing my degree in special education and in social studies, the Indian Education Law, Title IV, passed, providing grants for improving Indian education. Having heard about my previous innovative teaching at Fairbanks Native Association and knowing that I knew people from all over the state, Laura Bernhard of the State Operated School System came to see me in 1974.

"We have a program I'd like you to apply for," she said. I did, and I was accepted as the district director of Indian Education Act Programs in charge of Title IV for the State Operated School System. We developed bilingual and bicultural programs. With Dr. Michael Krauss, Elaine Abraham, and several others, I sat on the Native Language Board, where we studied the languages and our indigenous groups, made dictionaries, and developed the map *Native Peoples and Languages of Alaska*.

Because the main speakers of Haida were in Canada, I went to the governor's assistant and explained, "The Haida are a dying people. We have to have ALL of our Alaska languages developed or we'll know nothing about them."

I began traveling throughout the state, setting up parent advisory committees in 150 state-operated schools as well as forming regional and statewide boards. (Previously, the principal controlled everything in the village schools.)

281

We had to educate the people: "These books, these schools, these monies are yours, and only you can tell them how to use Indian education monies." I told them, "You have the right to fail as long as you try again."

We trained Native teacher-aides and bilingual/bicultural aides, and in the first year I hired fifteen Native teachers. I had a twelve-person board; we divided up the money depending on how many Natives were in each school. We queried the people and carefully set up regions along cultural and linguistic borders. There had never before been a Native education committee, ever. The regions became the model for today's Alaska Rural Education Attendance Areas. Some of those I trained still sit on those boards.

Indian education monies were used for many exciting programs including sending kids to Europe and to the Lower Forty-eight. One of the best projects was the *Alaska Native Land Claims* textbook published in 1976 by the Alaska Native Foundation and edited by Robert D. Arnold. Another important document was the Federal Field Committee report of 1968, which was the basis of land claims, "the bible." This report stated that five-eighths of Alaska, including rivers and ocean frontage, was used by Alaska Natives. It documented the lifestyle, ethnology, linguistics, numbers of Native language speakers, and acreage needed for subsistence foods. I tried to get both the ANCSA book and the Federal Field Committee report in every school.

In 1975, I was sent to Washington, D.C., to sit on the regulations board for Public Law 93-638, the new Indian Self-Determination Act, giving Indian tribes the authority to contract with the federal government to operate programs serving their tribal members. I made sure we were referred to as "Alaska Natives," not as "Alaska Indians," so all our indigenous cultures would be included. The Alaska Federation of Natives then contracted Johnson O'Malley monies from the Bureau of Indian Affairs. AFN funded the fledgling regional nonprofit corporations like the Aleut League and Tanana Chiefs Conference. This gave those in the Alaska Bush a viable organization, the means to be trained and, thereby, gain a voice.

AFN president Don Wright asked me to investigate the National Food and Nutrition Committee's new food stamp program in Washington, D.C. I tried to educate the committee on the widespread poverty, lack of food, and inadequate stores in rural Alaska. I suggested that food stamps might sufficiently boost the economy so that village stores might be able to install refrigeration but someone in Juneau said there was no accountability in the villages. I had to fight fourteen boards to get food stamps. Not only had the state of Alaska not referred the Bush as candidates for the food stamp program, but when I tried to get hot lunches for rural Alaska, lunches were improved only in the urban schools. There really were two Alaskas.

The Molly Hootch consent decree in the late 1970s was a godsend; the state committed to provide local high schools for Native communities as it had in predominantly white communities. Using oil tax dollars, rural schools began to be built.

During our time in Washington, D.C., Frank joined us to take a lateral job. Previously he had gotten 150 Alaska villages federally recognized; however villages like Haines and Kaltag had been overlooked, but D.C. lawyers were balking. In Juneau, he argued that BIA contract out to tribal corporations, but BIA wanted to simply go with individual hire. He also felt that Cook Inlet Region, Incorporated (CIRI) was not being fair with its stockholders so he felt it was time to retire.

By now I was employed by BIA in charge of subsistence issues, and I began funding the regional studies required by the 1980 Alaska National Interest Lands Conservation Act (ANILCA.) In 1983, I became BIA area rights protection officer in charge of all Native lands in Alaska. I funded the subsistence salmon, walrus, and waterfowl advisory boards and the new Eskimo Whaling Commission. I sat on the international salmon commission for subsistence.

Prior to ANCSA and ANILCA, Natives had nothing to say about their schools, resources, or the decisions the state or the BIA made relevant to them. Since receiving food stamps, welfare, and decent housing, the Native population has blossomed. I think we Natives have made a difference. My husband, Frank, and I have spent our lives trying to equalize things. (During those days, it seemed like that there wasn't anything we couldn't do. It was a wonderful ride while we were on it.) But I got to a point where I preferred that Native-looking people spoke out on the issues. As a non-Native looking person, I was a leader but as Native-looking leaders developed, the white world needed to hear a Native-looking speaker. I stepped aside; I'd given them the tools they needed but now, it was up to them.

I feel one of the state and the corporations' largest failures was in not educating non-Natives and Natives about Alaska Native Claims Settlement Act, nor were Natives properly prepared for the effects of ANCSA. A lot of Alaska Natives still feel today that they have no individual parcels of land, that they are landless. The corporations absorbed the acreage per head count, sold off vast areas, and many at-large shareholders have received neither land nor compensation from those sales.

At the time of land claims, non-Natives were stunned to find that our housing, water, and electricity were as bad as any developing nations. As a result. Alaska Natives began getting involved with various programs to meet those needs. That is the single biggest impact on village life: houses requiring payments and monthly bills for running water and electricity, which necessitated a monthly income. That changed rural Alaska; they became part of the rest of America and that was ANCSA's biggest impact.

ANCSA was meant to help Alaska Natives get into business. It has affected the villages as well as adding revenue statewide.

Today we need to train more Native teachers for urban and rural schools. In the village, we must compensate the Native teacher the same as the imported teachers who get housing and compensation for living in the village. In the city, if we can't get Native teachers, we should get Native counselors or trained individuals to bridge the gap between the school and the home. The dropout rate today is horrific. When we had BIA or the State Operated School System, there was no significant dropout rate and the standardized test scores were higher. At the college level today, Native students should be allowed to try until they succeed.

Frank Peratrovich, Anchorage, 2006.
Judy Ferguson photo.

Nettie Peratrovich, 2003, Anchorage.
Judy Ferguson photo.

Due to lack of finances, the parent advisory boards no longer exist. There needs to be a closer inspection today of how monies intended for Native education are used by the larger public schools. Getting involved is a requirement for change.

November 10, 2010, Nettie's husband, Frank Peratrovich, former U.S. Marine, CIRI board member, and superintendent of the Bureau of Indian Affairs, passed away in Anchorage. He was preceded in death by his sister, Loretta. He was survived by his brother, Roy; his wife, Nettie; his two sons, Frank and John; his five grandchildren; and seven nieces and nephews.

Timeline

1700s: Haidas moved from Canada to Alaska Tlingit territory.

1878: Sitka Industrial and Training School begun (renamed later for the Presbyterian missionary, Sheldon Jackson College.)

1911: Hydaburg Indian Reservation.

1912: Alaska Native Brotherhood begun.

1913: Territorial schools only for "civilized" Natives.

1924: Indian Citizenship Act included Alaska Natives as U.S. citizens.

1926: All but 189 acres of Hydaburg Reservation returned to Tongass National Forest.

1945: Alaska's Antidiscrimination law through Roy and Elizabeth Peratrovich.

1964: National Civil Right Act.

1968: Tlingit-Haida compensation for Tongass National Forest and Glacier Bay lands.

1971: BIA Johnson OMalley funds redirected to rural Alaska; ANCSA passed.

1972: Title IV of Public Law 92-318, Indian Education Act.

Mid-1970s: *Native Peoples and Languages of Alaska* map; parent advisory, regional, and statewide boards; bilingual programs.

1975: Indian Self-Determination Act, PL 93-638.

1976: Molly Hootch consent decree; schools built in rural Alaska. *Alaska Native Land Claims* published. Food stamps to rural Alaska.

1980: Alaska National Interest Lands Conservation Act (ANILCA.)

1985: Aleutian Pribilof waters World War II debris cleaned up.

∽

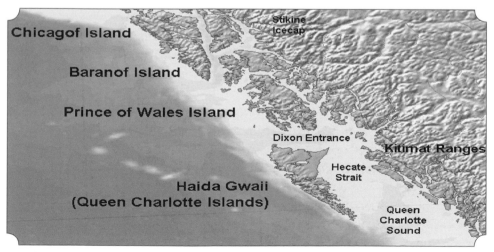

Haida land on Canada's Queen Charlotte and Alaska's Prince of Wales islands.

http://www.craigalaska.com/prince_of_wales_island_alaska.html

Chapter Twenty-seven

Child of the River Claude Demientieff Jr.

When my family and I canoed down the Yukon and up the Innoko River in 1975, we frequently saw the Demientieff barge and tugboat. At the end of our trip before flying home, we sold our nineteen-foot Grumman canoe to Luke Demientieff in Holy Cross.

In 2003 when I was writing the story of that life-changing trip, I contacted the widow of the owner of the Claude Demientieff family barge line, Martha Demientieff, to interview her. Martha was not feeling well, but twice she summoned her strength to talk with me in her Fairbanks apartment.

Claude Demientieff Sr. piloting the Ramona *tugboat, circa 1976.*
Courtesy of Martha Demientieff.

Like the Tanana and Yukon Rivers that Martha and Claude Dementieff navigated from 1960 to 1994, their lineage was also a flow of Alaska's varied cultures. Similarly, their family story reflected the braided channels of Alaska history.

Claude's great grandfather Nicholai Demientieff was a young man when Russia sold Alaska to the United States. On hearing of the change of countries, Nicholai's mother begged the Russian-American Trading Company, "Please send my boy back home." "Ma'am," the company's manager replied, "Nicholai is of age. If he chooses to stay in Alaska, now American territory, that is his decision." Thus the Russian-Deg Hit'an Athabascan family of Demientieff began.

Although Nicholai and his son Ivan were Russian Orthodox, Ivan helped the Roman Catholic priests at Holy Cross build their church and mission. Ivan married Mary, a Yup'ik; they had several children including Claude's father Stanley who married an Athabascan woman from Huslia.

A few months after my interviews with Martha Demientieff in 2003, I happened to see her and her daughter, Ramona, at Denney's restaurant. Nine days before she passed away, I was able to give Martha a copy of my new children's book,

DEG XINAG

Russians and the Creole Class in Russian America *from Claus-M. Naske's* **Alaska A History of the 49th State,** *pages 51 and 58:*

Far more impressive was the growth in numbers of the creoles, who became a significant factor in the life of the colonies, furnishing much of the needed labor supply, especially as skilled workers.... The company made an effort to aid those seeking to learn a trade or acquire the rudiments of science and navigation, and it even sent some to Russia for further education. Once he accepted such benefits, a person was required to remain in the company's service for ten to fifteen years. The creoles constituted a separate element in Russian America, never fully accepted by the Russians or the natives....Creole women almost never married natives, but creole men usually selected their mates from among native women....

In a ceremony at Sitka, General Lowell Rousseau, as the official representative of the president, formally took possession of Alaska for the United States. The treaty of purchase guaranteed Russians and creoles the privileges of citizenship in the United States and gave them the option of deciding within a three-year period whether they wished to become American citizens. A few remained in Alaska, many returned to Russia....For the natives, most of whom had never been under Russian rule, the change of regime seemed to be of little consequence.

❧

Nicholai Demientieff family: fourth is Tatiana Marie, fifth is Ivan Demientieff, Holy Cross, circa 1917.

Possibly Ira and Walter Wood Photograph Collection. ASL-PCA-191.
Courtesy of Claude Demientieff Jr.

Martha and Claude Demientieff, circa 1986.
Courtesy of Martha Demientieff.

a throttle back, it was time then to slowly pick up the RPMs again, one notch at a time—and then, go—go—go. We were always focused on getting to port and to offload before the wind might come up.

In the dark as we approached Grayling, I could see a dip in the ridgeline that I knew was the village. To stay in the deep channel going downstream, I began to plan my crossing. Because we had no sonar for determining the water depth and to be sure to miss the gravel shallows, I counted the fish camps, marked in my mind by notches in the ridgeline, until I passed the third one above the village. I was confident we were in at least forty feet of water. I shone a concentrated beam of red light that was mounted on a swivel on the wheelhouse roof. By using this narrow shaft of red light—adapted from twelve-volt aircraft technology—I could keep my night vision intact. (To also preserve our vision, we used no dashboard lights but relied only on a slender red beam to check our engine temperature, speed, and oil pressure.) Before crossing, I hit the searchlight and checked the windsock on the bow, then I located the cutbank across the river. It was a clear, calm night on the Yukon, one of my favorite times. I began to cross. Halfway across the river, I could see the lights of Grayling, five miles below. A pair of truck headlights appeared and began bouncing along the beach. He climbed up the bank to show me where the village slip was. I pointed the searchlight toward the town landing and toward the truck's receding taillights. The shine of the aluminum boats lined up along the gravel beach confirmed that we were in the right place.

The truck reappeared and flashed his headlights at us. Knowing that we had nothing to pickup or drop off, I took it as a "Hello" from an unknown Grayling friend. I acknowledged with my searchlight and flashed the running lights to say, "Goodbye." His parking lights flashed back.

Always on the river, there was the danger of high wind. If the wind got too bad, we would take a break and camp on the bank until the wind dropped again. When I was small, taking a break from the wind was fun. My little sister, Ramona, and I loved to get out on the gravel beach to explore and gather driftwood for a beach fire. As I got bigger, I always made a big fire for wind camp. I'd use a whole stump so it would burn all evening. Dad would look out at the blowing willow leaves and say, "It won't be a long blow" or looking up at the shape of the clouds, he'd say, "It's going to last three days." Mom could not handle the wind. It made her very nervous from seeing what weight and momentum could do to a barge going at even the slowest of speeds. Twenty-five miles above Grayling, at Fox Point, the waves could grow into big whitecaps. The point jutted out into the gravelly shallows and forced vessels to go around it. The only hiding spot, a slough two miles down, could have bigger waves at its mouth than even at Fox Point. But when the rolling and rippling barge was caught in the river's swells, we had no choice. We had to steer against the wind and run for it. In a really rough situation, a pilot might have to cut loose from the barge and hope to catch it later, hung up downriver on tree sweepers. Landing in the wind was also a problem. There were too many big waves to ne-gotiate a turn. We put the engine in full reverse, came in close to the gravel beach, swung the bow toward the main river, and then tied off to the largest possible tree stump. Using a small skiff, we pushed the tug stern back in toward the bank. We hoped the wind would keep the tall, vul-nerable tug from swinging back out. Once the barge and tug were protected in the slough, we

Martha Demientieff en route by boat to Reindeer Lake to install the headstone for Claude Demientieff Sr., 2003.
Courtesy of Martha Demientieff.

got our coffee, sat back, and watched the Yukon rock and roll.

One of my fondest childhood memories was of lying in my bunk in the pitch dark, warm and comfortable. I felt a deep sense of absolute secu-rity with my dad at the wheel. The hum of the engine and a gentle rock of the tug were the only reminders that we were still moving on the river.

Sometimes to deliver freight we had to go up a very narrow tributary. As the pilot, I kept my eye on our bow wave, always watching for telltale willows or timber stands, indicators of shallow water. If the barge began to push the wave ahead, I knew that the water was getting shallow; I had to immediately adjust or throw the engine into full reverse. About these times, Dad said, "A good pilot is always right, seldom wrong, and never undecided."

Come out and be heard.
Be heard in school where our children are.
Aunties are there smiling, making kids happy, training the tongue.
Tell your Native name,
say the parts of your body,
talk about your relatives,
sing about the world,
voice it in your language.

In 1960, Dad quit a secure DEW Line job and with a third grade education, he believed he could support his family and still keep us all together.

As a pilot, one of my navigational markers on the Tanana River below Manley Hot Springs used to be a crooked aspen that had curled from growing out of the hillside. When I last saw it, the tree no longer had two curls but three.

When I look at the river, my concerns melt away. I smile and feel free. I know I am where I am supposed to be, come hell or high water. If I trust my instinct and my life markers, my boat will stay on course. Such is the silt-washed soul of a lifelong river rat.

Claude Demientieff Jr. is a graduate of Harvard University and the former assistant vice president of National Bank of Alaska in Fairbanks.

In 1995, Claude Demientieff Jr. suffered a stroke, leaving him with partial paralysis of his left side. Today he and his service dog, Missy, enjoy life at the head of Yukon River barge navigation system in Nenana, Alaska.

Timeline

Early 1840s: Lt. Zagoskin met 170 people at "Anilukhtakpak."

October 18, 1867: the United States took possession of Alaska.

1880: The village had thirty "Askhomute."

1880s: A Catholic mission and school were built in Holy Cross by Father Aloysius Robaut. Deg Hit'an migrated to the mission and school.

1899: A post office was opened under the name "Koserefsky."

1912: Koserefsky was changed to "Holy Cross" after the mission.

1954 to 1957: DEW Line built.

1956: Holy Cross Mission boarding school closed.

1970s: Johnson O'Malley funds directed to build schools in rural Alaska.

1976: "Molly Hootch" case settled.

1983: Our Lady of Sorrows mission school closed in Nulato.

∞

Chapter Twenty-eight

Opening Doors to Native Education: Dr. Angayuqaq Oscar Kawagley

Angayuqaq O. Kawagley with his mother, Amelia, in Akiak in 1935. Both of his parents died when he was two years old.

Courtesy of Oscar Kawagley.

The Yup'ik/Yupiaq are in-digenous people who live in western Alaska, including the Yukon-Kuskokwim Delta, the Kuskokwim River, and St. Lawrence Island (the Siberian Yupik). In southern Alaska the Alutiiq are closely related. Across the Bering Strait, there are Yupik people in the Russian Far East. As western Eskimo, they are distinct from the Inuit. Many of the Yup'ik still speak their own language.

In 2006 as I was preparing my children's book, Alaska's First People, *Dr. Angayuqaq Oscar Kawagley of the Center for Cross-Cultural Studies and the Alaska Native Knowledge Network agreed to review my text and its drawings to ensure all was correct. Also, he was the cousin of my long-time friend, Harvey Anderson, of both Bethel and Delta Junction. Dr. Kawagley was very receptive and gentle, a man of practical wisdom. Together with Dr. Ray Barnhardt, he has de-veloped a much-needed hub for indigenous research and information. To exemplify their approach, Ray Barnhardt, co-director with Oscar Kawagley of the Alaska Rural Systemic Initiative, once offered advice to non-Native teachers hired to teach in an unfamiliar indigenous cultural setting:*

> *Whatever piece of the curriculum you are responsible for, embed it first in the world with which the students are familiar and work out-ward from there. Adapt the content to the local scene. Then help the students connect it to the region, the nation, and the world. Keep in mind the adage, "Think globally, act locally," as you pre-pare your lessons. If students are to have any influence over their lives as adults, they need to understand who they are, where they fit into the world, and how 'the system' works. It is your responsibil-*

ity as a teacher to help them achieve that understanding.

For more, please see http://www. ankn.uaf.edu/.

Dr. Kawagley died on Easter Sunday, 2011, but in 2006 at the Center for Cross Cultural-Studies, he shared his story with me:

Dr. Angayuqaq Oscar Kawagley, Fairbanks, 2006.

Judy Ferguson photo.

My Yupiaq name, Angayuqaq, "parent, leader, or chief," was given to me by my grandmother, Kinaven Matilda Oscar. From her, I lived the life of my ancestors.

Barry Lopez stated in his book *Arctic Dreams*, "the landscape forms the mindscape, and the mindscape forms the landscape." In the same way, our Native children must interpret modern reality with perceptions from our Yupiaq world.

I was born Oscar Kawagley on November 8, 1934, in Mamterilleq, today called Bethel. My parents were David Kawagley, a reindeer herder from Akiak, and Amelia Oscar of Bethel. When I was only two, my mother died of a ruptured appendix; my father died shortly after from an accident, complicated by tuberculosis.

As she was dying, my mother insisted that my grandmother (who spoke only Yupiaq) raise me. Because she did, I skipped a generation, and I am fluent in my own language.

The first part of my life was my best education. Completely free, I learned as I played. In my waterproof sealskin boots, I walked with my grandmother through the marshy muskeg, hunting for eggs. She taught me where to find a ptarmigan nest and mallard and goose eggs. I loved going with her in the springtime to set out muskrat traps. Paddling among the lakes and streams, sleeping on reindeer hides in a tent, I absorbed who I was and how to look at life. I learned about the personal relationships of humans, weather, plants, and animals. When I asked her about plants that I didn't know, she'd say, "Oh, that's just part of the plant world." I realized then that we only gave names to the plants that were medicinal or edible; all the rest were lumped together as part of the ecology. I loved fish camp: watching the rhythmic wheel and especially jumping into the river. The first two feet were fairly warm but when your legs let down, that lower water was cold. I never learned to swim, but none of us did, even though we were born and raised by the river. When I was seven, my uncle gave me one of his handmade canoes and a pump BB gun. I wasn't strong enough to pump it, but I learned to shoot… boy, did I learn.

Oscar's grandmother, Kinaven Angngnaq with him and his cousin Carrie Avigyaq, Bethel, 1943.
Courtesy of Oscar Kawagley.

When I was nine, I got my first .22. My poor grandmother—I don't know how she managed to keep me in all that ammunition. I shot anything that moved except the two-legged ones. I got pretty good. When I was thirteen, my grandmother got me a shotgun, and that sure enlarged my world, getting lots of ducks and geese. She got me a small canvas-covered, wood-frame canoe and ordered us a little 2.5-horsepower motor from Sears and Roebuck. It ran for years. In the summer, I was one of the most popular guys because I had a boat and outboard.

My uncle traveled greater distances than I, going everywhere in his open canvas canoe. Most people at home made their own boats. By then, we had waterproof paint; my favorite was battleship gray.

Thank goodness we didn't have radio or TV, so in the evenings my grandmother shared magical, mythological stories with me, producing pictures in my mind and getting my internal camera going. She told how the crane got blue eyes; I became a part of that story and it became a part of me.

During the winter, I went down to the Kuskokwim River to fill our water can, chop trees for firewood, and haul it all back on my little sled.

When I was almost eight, my family was told they had to obey the compulsory schooling law; that was the end of my beautiful education. For the last time, I went to spring muskrat camp. Suddenly life became strenuous work, going every day to a four-walled classroom in Bethel. I was introduced to a segregated school system. The Bureau of Indian Affairs had a two-room elementary school, grades one through eight. About 150 yards away, there was a school for whites and halfbreeds whose families had "a civilized life." There was always rivalry between the two schools. During my first three grades, I went to the BIA school. At the beginning of my fourth grade, seventeen of us Native boys were integrated into the territorial school. I found out later that the antidiscrimination act presented by Roy, Elizabeth, and Frank Peratrovich and signed by Gov. Gruening in 1945 ended the dual school system in Alaska. At the territorial school, the older Native boys got into trouble, but to survive and succeed, I became a conformist to the extent I could. We seventeen boys graduated from eighth grade. Although there was a high school in Bethel, every Native student had the opportunity to go to a boarding school. Most chose to go to Mt. Edgecumbe High School in Sitka or Chemawa Indian School in Oregon, but my grandmother wouldn't allow it. All my friends were going, but my grandmother needed me to get firewood, pack water, and trap. So three of

us Native boys stayed, but by tenth grade, I was the only one left at Bethel Regional High School. All the teachers, particularly the superintendent, treated me very well, probably because of my trying to blend in. When I was seventeen, I joined the local National Guard.

Boy Scout troop in Bethel, 1948. Front row, fourth boy from right: Oscar in plaid shirt.
Courtesy of Oscar Kawagley.

To help give me some spending money, the superintendent gave me a job as a janitor. Every so often, he would call me into his office and ask me about what I wanted to do. He said, "Have you ever thought about college?" "No," I answered. How could I, with only my grandmother for help? He asked, "If you did go to college, what would you want to study? Have you ever thought of teaching?" The following semester, he suggested, "If you want to go to college, you can take the balance of your high school classes here in the mornings, and in the afternoons, you can be free to work at the National Guard, to save up your money."

In 1954, with twenty-seven other Natives, I began studying at the University of Alaska Fairbanks. I discovered that my education at Bethel High School wasn't that good. I had to do remedial work, particularly in English, to catch up. I refused BIA grants and instead I washed dishes and translated for the Fourth Judicial District. In my senior year, I lacked forty credits. I decided to take twenty each semester and work at the same time.

After four years, only four of us Natives finished. I graduated from ROTC as a second lieutenant in the Medical Service Corps and with a degree in biology and a minor in military science and tactics. I became the seventh Native teacher in the territory, and later the first Eskimo in the officer corps.

I applied for a teaching job at the Department of Education in Juneau. They wouldn't allow me to return home to teach, so I took a one-semester job in

Oscar Kawagley promoted in ROTC class at University of Alaska Fairbanks, late 1950s.
Courtesy of
Oscar Kawagley.

Tok during the fall of 1958. It was really strange to enter an Athabascan culture, but they respected me okay. That spring I had another immersion experience. I was sent to Fort Sam Houston, Texas, for active-duty training. I was such an oddity that the officers asked, "Do you live in an igloo?" The staff didn't know how to racially classify me; they had four choices, including Oriental. I said, "Well, anthropologists say we're from Oriental stock." When the officer returned my papers, for the first and last time in my life I was called a Caucasian. I have a copy on my table at home. Nice as they were there, they had no experience at all with an Eskimo in Texas, none at all.

In the early 1960s I got a job teaching school in Glennallen, where I heard about early Native land claims; Robert Marshall of Tazlina represented some Ahtna holdings.

I decided to quit teaching, and I moved to Anchorage to try the corporation world, running my own consulting service. But it's tough being a Native. I didn't have many clients. I attended some early Alaska Federation of Native meetings at Alaska Methodist University. I got a job as president, writing grants for ESCA-Tech Corp., a subsidiary for the Calista Corporation. At that time, Calista was building the Sheraton Anchorage Hotel; one of my grants was for teaching Natives how to become hotel management. But the corporation was having problems with the building. It was an incomplete steel skeleton, the biggest fish rack in the state. I hired an East Indian who knew the financial world. By the time we finished the Sheraton, I was so proud that the elders couldn't tell me anything— but boy, they clipped my wings. Ever since I've been a different person, humbled and more human.

After the Sheraton, I worked in Bethel as the director of Native education for the Lower Kuskokwim School District, and then I returned to UAF to get my education

Dr. Alfonso Ortiz (1939 to 1998) was a renowned Native American anthropologist from the Pueblo of San Juan, New Mexico. A professor, he also served as president of the Association on American Indian Affairs.
http://www.unm.
edu/news/photos/
Alfonso%20
Ortiz.jpg

303

Timeline:

1000 AD: Yupik related to Aleut and Inuit languages. With Thule Eskimo migrations to the east, the languages diverged.

1728: St. Lawrence Yupik related to the Siberian Yupik. St. Lawrence was the first place visited by Russian explorer Vitus Bering.

1867: Russia sold Alaska to the United States.

June 14, 1988: Siberian Yupiks rejoined with Siberian relatives in Friendship Flight to Siberia Apr 6, 2007: The four Yupik languages, Alutiiq (Sugpiaq), Central Alaskan Yup'ik, Naukan (spoken by about seventy people on the Chukotka peninsula), and Siberian Yupik (who live along the coast of the Chukchi Peninsula in the Russian far northeast and on St. Lawrence Island), are distinct languages with limited mutual intelligibility.

∽

Excerpts from: **Native Alaska scholar Oscar Kawagley ...** *by Reba Lean, Apr 27, 2011,* **Fairbanks Daily News-Miner***:*

...Kawagley was an Alaska Native elder with big ideas that profoundly affected many of his students and colleagues. Ray Barnhardt, with the cross-cultural studies department at the university, worked with Kawagley for more than 40 years. Barnhardt was his faculty supervisor and first met Kawagley in 1969.

"He was an original thinker...." He is a Yup'ik Eskimo, but referred to his heritage as Yupiaq in all his writings and references. "It was his effort to reconnect with the older pronunciation," Barnhardt said, explaining that Yup'ik is now the more common spelling and pronunciation.

He was the first Yupiaq to graduate high school in Bethel, encouraged by his grandmother to learn both a Western education and a traditional one....His focus was on developing and implementing Native ways of knowing. He claimed that phrase." Barnhardt said when Kawagley first developed the idea in the late 1980s, it was not something one heard or saw often. Now the university offers courses with that title... The idea implemented indigenous story-telling methods and ecological knowledge. "From my perspective, that was kind of his signature contribution," Barnhardt said.

"He had...a different way of looking at cross-cultural studies. Fortunately for many of us, Oscar Kawagley paved the way ... to do research in many of our communities. His book is a foundational piece." Throughout his life, he received many prestigious awards, including the National Indian Education Association Lifetime Achievement Award."

∽

Chapter Twenty-nine

Bob "Moose" Henrichs of Eyak and Cordova

In Delta, our neighbors to the south are Valdez and Cordova on Prince William Sound. In 2003, when Bob "Moose" Henrichs was running for state senate seat E, he campaigned at the Delta fair. Bigger than life and very friendly, Moose made an impression.

Two years later I took the illustrator of my new children's book, Alaska's First People, *to Prince William Sound so he might better illustrate the Eyak people in the book. Moose not only kindly*

Robert "Moose" Henrichs, president of the Native Village of Eyak, 2012, Cordova.
Courtesy of Bob Henrichs.

hosted us but as president of the Native Village of Eyak (NVE), he gave me an interview, and explained NVE's history and their vision. That night in his living room, Moose began to share.

Originally the people of Prince William Sound called themselves Sugpiaq, "the real people," but the Russians began calling them Aleut, which became accepted. My mother was the daughter of a half Eyak, Russian Orthodox priest and an Alutiiq mother. She was born on Nuchek, one of the first places the Russians headquartered during the early Russian period of 1788.

The Sugpiaq term for Aleut is Alutiiq. Today, all three names—Alutiiq, Aleut, and Sugpiaq—are used. I prefer Sugpiaq because that pertains to Cordova, while I feel that Alutiiq refers more to Kodiak. The Alutiiq language is similar to Yup'ik, so anthropologists have also called us Pacific Eskimo.

My mother, Rose Mitvitnikoff Henrichs, was born in 1913. When my father, Hollis Henrichs, arrived in Alaska with the Coast Guard, they met and married. I was born in 1942.

During my childhood, we Natives were not treated well. Even though my father was a non-Native postmaster, it made no difference. In the hospitals, we got secondary treatment. My mother died of appendicitis. My father always felt that she didn't get the treatment a White woman would have. Today, non-Natives claim there was never discrimination in Cordova. But during the fight for Alaska Native land claims,

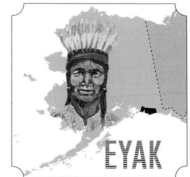

many of the residents got so upset that they had meetings of their own, called "White Rights." They only needed their white sheets and hoods.

Three years after I graduated from high school in Cordova, the 1964 earthquake destroyed Cordova's clam industry. They used to catch a million pounds of Dungeness crabs and razor clams here, right within sight of town. We were the clam capital. But after the earthquake, the sea otter population moved in and destroyed the rest of the clams.

I had been in college two years when fishing began to really take off. During the 1970s and 1980s, we made a fortune fishing until 1989 when Joseph Hazelwood hit the reef and yes, that [Exxon *Valdez*] oil spill made a big difference. It wrecked the herring industry.

I used to run two boats, a 135-footer and an 86-footer. I had twenty-five to thirty people working for me. I tendered (hauled what others caught) salmon and herring. I fished crab here, as well as in the Bering Sea, in Kodiak, and during the Lower Forty-eight season, I crabbed out of Westport, Washingon. Here in Cordova, I also gillnetted salmon and longlined halibut and I seined herring in Togiak. But the boats cost a lot to operate. At the end of the year, I found that I didn't have any more money than when I fished alone. So now I am down to three smaller boats.

I was perfectly happy going broke as a commercial fisherman when, in 1993, I was asked to run for the Chugach Alaska Corporation board. I had no idea why anyone wanted me to help. However, that same year, I was also asked to take over as president of the Native Village of Eyak [NVE], a federally rec-ognized, nonprofit tribe, which also had for-profit subsidiaries.

Our tribe was recognized late, in 1981. Because there are only a few living Eyak, NVE is an umbrella term that incorporates other indigenous regional tribal members: some Tlingit and a lot of Aleut, known now as Alutiiq. There are over five hundred in the Native Village of Eyak tribe. During the winter, the Cordova Native and non-Native population amounts to about 2,200.

Prince William Sound near Cordova.
Nikola Kocic photo.

During the summer, it may be as much as 4,000.

The new cultural labels have created confusion. There's a big difference between the Chugach Eskimo, the Sugpiaq, and the Alutiiq. The Russians enslaved the Alutiiq in Kodiak but the people in the Cordova area of Prince William Sound [Chugach Eskimo] were not easily managed. We had a reputation of being difficult, and today it is still true. I must say that the Yup'ik were not thrilled to find out that we Sugpiaq were related to them. On the other hand, we don't really want to be affiliated with Kodiak's Alutiiq culture, but apparently, it's all considered one.

I am related to Makari Chimaviskey, who anthropologist Dr. Frederica de Laguna interviewed in the 1930s. Makari was not Eyak but was what we called an Aleut but today is called Alutiiq. De Laguna paid people to talk with her, but not everyone would. It's nice that she wrote a book but people here don't regard her as gospel on our culture.

As "Aleuts," we didn't have clans like the Eyak, Tlingit, and Haida. Our people lived in small villages; we traveled seasonally wherever the food source was.

Before the era of White Rights meetings, many Natives could not escape looking obviously Native while others could slide by the racial divide. I don't hold grudges against those who had it easy. People did what they had to do to get by. However, after it became both popular and profitable to be Native, those who had borne the stigma would note how many "new Natives" there suddenly were.

The Alaska Native Claims Settlement Act [ANCSA] allotted land to the corporations, not to the tribes, aka the villages, which caused a lot of angst, along with lack of control over our land and risk that through incurred debt the corporations could also lose our land.

At the time of the ANCSA legislation, the United States formally claimed only out to three miles on the outer continental shelf (OCS.) In 1983, President Ronald Reagan issued a proclamation extending the U.S. Exclusive Economic Zone to two hundred nautical miles from the shore. ANCSA extinguished indigenous land claims in Alaska but not on the continental shelf. This has tremendous implications regarding both fisheries and oil resources.

After the Restricted Access Management Program of the Alaska Region of NOAA Fisheries began issuing individuals a fishing quota, as president of the NVE I asked the former director, "Where's the tribal share for NVE?" He replied, "There is none." In 1995 I filed a lawsuit for aboriginal rights to our continental shelf: *Native Villages of Eyak, Tatitlek, Chenega, Nanwalek, and Port Graham v. Evans.* It stated,

> *According to the Native Villages of Eyak, Tatitlek, Chenega, Nanwalek and Port Graham, regulations promulgated by the Department of Commerce for the management of halibut and sablefish fisheries violate their rights to the exclusive use and occupancy of the OCS. The Native Villages are located in the Prince William Sound, the Gulf of Alaska, and the lower Cook Inlet regions of Alaska. They claim that, for more*

> *than 7,000 years, their members have hunted sea mammals and har-*
> *vested the fishery resources of the OCS. The Native Villages maintain*
> *that a majority of their members still maintain a subsistence lifestyle*
> *heavily reliant on the fish and wildlife of the OCS, and that their con-*
> *tinued social, cultural, and economic wellbeing depends on their con-*
> *tinued ability to hunt and to fish in their traditional territories on the*
> *OCS. The Native Villages argue that they are entitled to exclusive use*
> *and occupancy of their respective areas of the OCS, including exclusive*
> *hunting and fishing rights, based upon unextinguished aboriginal title.*

We were countered with the Magnuson-Stevens Act that extended federal control to 200 miles offshore. Judge Russel Holland, a federal judge for the United States District Court for the District of Alaska, ruled against us for exclusive aboriginal rights, which I never thought we were going to get anyway. So we sued for nonexclusive aboriginal rights, saying

> *The Native Villages challenge the Secretary's fishing regulations on*
> *the ground that they improperly authorize non-tribal members to fish*
> *within the Native Villages' exclusive aboriginal territories while prohib-*
> *iting Native Village members without Individual Fishing Quotas (IFQ)*
> *from doing the same. The Native Villages have requested an injunction*
> *against the Secretary's fishing regulations and a declaration that they*
> *hold aboriginal title and exclusive aboriginal rights to use, occupy, pos-*
> *sess, hunt, fish, and exploit the waters, and to the mineral resources*
> *within their traditional use areas of the OCS.*

The Supreme Court would not hear our case. An eleven-judge hearing was set up under the Ninth Circuit Court of Appeals. Three of the judges ruled that this was not about fish but about oil. Twenty days later they vacated Holland's decision and sent it back to him to determine what our nonexclusive aboriginal rights were, saying,

> *The Native Villages maintain that, although a few of their members*
> *possess IFQ permits, the vast majority do not. The district court decided*
> *only the aboriginal title issues, . . . [and left] for another day the ques-*
> *tion of what nonexclusive fisheries rights, if any, plaintiffs might have in*
> *the OCS which are not dependent upon aboriginal title.*

Finally in August 2009, the federal court held that although the five Chugach Tribes had established that they had a "territory" and had proven they had used the waters in question, the court ruled that the Tribes could not hold aboriginal rights as a matter of law. The Chugach appealed to the Ninth Circuit en banc panel. Oral argument was held in San Francisco but after losing the case the summer of 2012, the Chugach appealed the case to the Supreme Court.

In 1993, when I became president of the NVE, the budget was $24,000 a year but today it is seven million dollars a year. When an intertribal organization I was involved in began to fail, I told NVE, "The best we can do is to lead by example," and we have become not only one of the best tribes in the state but also in the nation.

For years, we operated the only community health center, based at the hospital. The two local doctors and several physician's assistants all worked for us.

In January 2013 with one of the local doctors, we will now be operating out of the old hospital. We not only cater to all of the outpatients in Cordova but we offer the only sliding fee schedule, dependent on a person's ability to pay.

As the representative for NVE, I have served on the Alaska Native Tribal Health Consortium board that runs the Alaska Native Medical Center in Anchorage. Because I have served a long time on the Chugachmiut board, I was also asked in 2004 to serve as chairman of Chugach Alaska Corporation. We got into government contracting, both on our own and in joint ventures. At its high point, Chugach Alaska was worth billion dollars a year. Today I am no longer chairman and the corporation is valued now at only seven hundred million.

After the Exxon *Valdez* settlement, Alyeska, the federal government, and state government all put money into building a road and a dock five miles outside of Cordova, called the oil spill response facility at Shepard Point. The Native Village of Eyak took on the project but the environmentalists stalled it until I got involved in 1995. It's a thirty million dollar project.

Through contracts with the Fish and Wildlife Service, we operate research projects on the Copper River, totaling about $600,000 to $700,000 a year. We operate a couple of camps and fishwheels up the river for researching various types of salmon. Our results validated us as a credible source of fisheries data.

At NVE, we have fifty people working for us year-round. We have one of the largest Bureau of Indian Affairs roads inventories of any tribe in Alaska and also larger than in some places in the Lower Forty-eight. For that, we get annual funding. We don't own any land but this *is our* traditional homeland. Anything that happens in our area, we get a seat at the table with government agencies. Anything that we oppose, we start chewing up. We are in the middle of sovereignty and local control issues right now.

We have a pretty good working relationship with the city, but it was not always so. Since I've been involved, we've probably brought eighty million dollars into this town. They don't have to love us, but only respect us. From the beginning, we have agreed to pay property tax on our land. We probably could have avoided it, but we pay our own way.

Before we started running the health center in the late 1980s, a lot of Natives would not go there because of the treatment they had gotten there previously. They said they'd rather die than go through those hospital doors.

When I took over, the government funding for physician and hospital care for Natives only lasted ten days into each month. Then the hospital would put up a sign, "No more Indian Health Care Services this month." So if a Native needed care, he had to pay out of his own pocket or go without. Even worse, at the drug store, Native prescription coverage lasted only two to three days into each month. Those with chronic prescriptions had to go there during the first few days of every month or they went without.

When I took over, I knew the money game. I told the administration, "With what we as a tribe are paying you, we could hire our own darned doctor and open our own clinic!" The new director came running to me and agreed, "You're right! With what you're paying us, we could supply you all month, not just for the first ten days." It was same old story of the Indian agent stealing from the government and pocketing the money.

When we started to open our own clinic, the hospital and the community raised heck because they had three doctors already that the town could not support. We really had to swim upstream against all the garbage coming at us. Ultimately by an act of Congress, we became one of only twenty-six cosigners for the Indian Health Service (I.H.S.) Alaska Tribal Health Compact, allowing us, rather than I.H.S., to provide services. We were declared a regional health entity by Congress.

Racism still lingers today. Sometimes people say to me, "What's the matter today, didn't you get your dividend?" But I don't care. We keep servicing the community's needs. If we had not been providing this medical service, the Coast Guard would have pulled out. Their admirals made it clear to me that they had to have health care available to their people.

For twenty-five years, development at Hartney Bay Subdivision, which includes 420 lots of two and half-acres each, did not move forward. We built an access road to open the first hundred lots. The beauty of that area is that it's outside the city limits so there is no planning commission and no city taxes. We got funding to run power out there.

The fallacy of the corporations is that they were designed to serve only those born before 1972. But with the NVE tribe, any indigenous Alaskans living in our area are tribal members. Ted Stevens said that the corporations have made a lot of money but they only exist for their own shareholders. As a tribe, we have never given out dividends but we offer consistent health care and social services as well as giving thousands of dollars of scholarships to our young people.

It has been said that in ANCSA Alaska Natives chose the vehicle of the corporation over the tribe but today, the tribes are stronger than ever.

In 2004, for the first time, I ran for office in the Democratic primary for seat E in the state senate. Seat E is the largest senate district in America, 250,000 square miles, from Southeast up. I had only a week to campaign. I got 1,000 votes but Al Kookesh beat me with 2,300 votes. As chairman of both Chugach Alaska Corporation and NVE, I had no time to campaign. Besides that, I was concerned that the senate summer session would cut into my fishing job, which pays a lot better than public office. (Since I have an individual fishing quota, gill and seine net operating permits, and the boats to do it, I can fish whenever I want.)

About fourteen years ago, a local substance abuse counselor asked, "Why don't we have a sobriety celebration?" I asked, "What the heck is that?" He said that it was something he studied in college. I said, "What the heck, why not?" So we and our tribal council organized some speakers and dance groups from Seward, Copper Center, Tatitlik, Kake, Yakutat, and Juneau. We promoted wellness and presented our rich tradition of social and spiritual order, which goes back thousands of years. Over two decades, it has become a tradition, evolving into a two-day event. In 2012, we had 175 dancers making the grand entrance along with speakers who focused on sobriety. In 2013, we'll host our twentieth celebration. Last year, they really got cranking; it sounded like they

Native Village of Eyak (NVE) dancers at the Annual Sobriety Celebration and Memorial Potlatch, Cordova, 2012.

Courtesy of Bob Henrichs and the NVE Tribal Council.

were going to blow off the roof with the drums and singing. Those Southeast groups don't give any warning but they start ratcheting up their performance, competing with and challenging each other. Afterward, we always have a big dinner.

Before he passed away, the traditional chief for the Ahtna, Harry Johns of the Native Village of Kluti-Kaah [Copper Center on the Copper River] asked if I were a leader of the Eyak. He said, "You gotta come up and talk to our tribes." Not only are we Chugach but we are at the mouth of the Copper River; we and the Ahtna have a lot in common. I went and he met me like I was his long-lost son. He sat me with the elders who were testifying. When he passed away, 1,500 people came to his three-day funeral potlatch. They asked me to speak and to be a pallbearer. Six moose—two from Canada—were harvested for his potlatch, which solidified bonds between the Alaska and Canadian tribes. They gave away 285 rifles, a stack of six hundred blankets that you couldn't see over, and thousands in groceries. Those Athabascan potlatches really get to cranking. They put bandanas on a clothesline. So as not to overcrowd the floor, when someone wants to dance, he grabs a bandana and dances with it. When finished, each dancer puts his bandana back on the line. In the grand entry, those closest to the deceased come in first, circling around to form the innermost circle. Only the drummers and singers know when a dance will end; they love to catch the other dancers off guard, like a game of indigenous musical chairs. They roar with laughter when they trick those remaining, still dancing.

Dancer, Annual sobriety celebration and memorial potlatch, 2012.
Courtesy of NVE Tribal Council.

The Cordova area is tied culturally with Nanwalek and Port Graham on the southern tip of the Kenai Peninsula on Kachemak Bay, more than we are with Kodiak, which has its own traditions. The culture in Cordova was trashed very early by the presence of the Copper River and Northwestern Railway. Since their establishment of the town in 1906, we have been surrounded by non-Natives. At our first sobriety celebration, I saw the damage our cultural tradition had suffered. When the kids started singing the old Russian Orthodox Christmas carols in the liturgical Slavonic language, the elders began to cry.

At the beginning of our sobriety celebrations, we had no idea what we were doing. At that time, we had no youth dance group but now we have a strong one. Today we rent the Masonic Hall where we have a bidarka [a one- or two-hole kayak with a bifurcated prow] on display. We also have the Ilanka cultural center, which has a twenty-eight-foot killer whale skeleton hanging from the ceiling. The center has had a huge impact on this town.

During the spring of 2006, we made a traditional pre-Russian-period, very large *umiaq*, the first one built here in over three hundred years. Historically, the Russians would not allow the Aleuts to build the thirty-two-foot-long boats because they could've put the whole village in an *umiaq* and taken off. We put over a ton of ballast in our new boat to test it. The hide covering was pretty thin. I think our ancestors must have been only five feet tall and weighed a hundred pounds! [Moose is six feet one.]

In recent years, I've been involved in repatriation, the return of ancestral bones to graves on nearby Hawkins Island. After the initial seven feet of dirt, archeological digs in old settlements reveal layers and layers of clamshells. Also in the caves they used, there is a forty-foot pile of more clamshells. Their clothing was made of sea otter pelts. Funny, we make baseball caps of otter now. I have heard that at one time, during the Ice Age, there was ice all the way to Middleton Island, southeast of us. As it melted, the land began to show.

Spotted seal on ice floe near Cordova.
Nikola Kocic photo.

In 2010, property on Prince William Sound's Mummy Island was donated and repatriated to NVE by Ecotrust, a nonprofit group based in Portland, Oregon. Mummy Island was of ancient significance to us, the Chugach people. It was home first to the Shallow Water people and later to an early clam cannery. As we walked the land with its weathered trees on a beach strewn with barnacle-covered rocks and clam shells, we knew this land was a beginning of our restored culture.

A well-known Bethel fisheries and subsistence activist, Harold Sparck, set the precedent for subsistence preference for marine fisheries. He plotted a strategy that helped push the Japanese driftnet fleets out of the North Pacific and usher in an era of record Alaska salmon harvests. He was one of the early proponents of a federal program that now endows western Alaska villages with shares of the billion-dollar North Pacific bottom-fish harvests. In all his efforts, he tried first to safeguard subsistence values and then helped develop new sources of income for the Yup'ik people. He helped design a strategy that won the support of the trawl fleet and ushered in a new era of partnerships that has put village people to work on the Bering Sea factory ships. The plan also funded small-boat fleets that villages use in coastal harvests. The village Individual Fishing Quota communities are now doing so well that they are buying out the Seattle trawlers. Initially they were only given ten percent but now they have eight to nine hundred million dollars in assets. The big boy trawlers from Washington state are really crying.

It is Sparck's spearheading efforts that encourage us to pursue our own lawsuit for the continental shelf. After all, Cordova was once the clam capital, and despite early exploitation from the Copper River and Northwestern Railway-Guggenheim-J.P Morgan mining, followed by the 1964 earthquake, the 1989 oil spill, and today's labels for our cultures, we have survived. We "Aleut," Alutiiq, and Sugpiaq welcome visitors to our traditional homeland and we provide services to the community as a whole.

In January 2012, Bob was elected president of the NVE again by a landslide. In November 2012, he ran for the newly reapportioned Alaska Senate District R, which represents Yakutat through Kodiak, Dillingham, and out to Nelson Island west of Bethel but lost the general election. Bob said, "If everyone likes you, you haven't pushed the envelope enough for social change."

Chapter Thirty

Clarence Alexander, Former Grand Chief of the Gwich'in of Alaska and Co-founder of the Council of Athabascan Tribal Governments

Before the arrival of the Hudson's Bay Company (HBC) in about 1795, Ditsii was the patriarch of the great Gwich'in chiefs.

In the eighteenth century, the Hudson's Bay Company explored the Mackenzie River. A principal Hudson Bay explorer, Alexander Murray, discovered around 1837 that the center of the Gwich'in population was west of the Rocky Mountains. With the

Clarence Alexander, Grand Chief of the Gwich'in, circa 2004.
Courtesy of Ecotrust.

help of the Gwich'in, he traveled across the Continental Divide and down the Eagle and Porcupine rivers to Old Crow. Along the way he established trading posts. Ten years later, in 1847, at the confluence of the Porcupine and Yukon rivers, he came to the center of the Gwich'in population at Gwichyaa Zhee. Making it his headquarters, he called it Fort Yukon.

Over the adjoining rich, wide river tributaries, there were more than sixty large Gwich'in villages. The population may have been eighty thousand, or even twice that.

In 1851, a smallpox epidemic devastated Gwichyaa Zhee. When Alexander Murray returned to Fort Yukon from a three-week resupply trip, he found dead bodies everywhere—a thousand people had died. Within the next few months, the epidemic swept through other villages; more than half of the Gwich'in population perished. The fortunate survivors were those who lived in the outlying fishing and hunting camps.

Belle Herbert (ca. 1855 or 1880-1982, Chalkyitsik) and her mother were the lone sur-vivors of their band. Belle lived to be well over a hundred years old. She died in 1982 and in her book, Shandaa, *many of her memories were recorded.*

In 1898 during the heyday of the gold rush, a post office was established at Fort Yukon along with an opera house, saloons, and professional ser-

GWICH' IN

Chief Esias Loola, Titus, Gabriel, Elijah, Jimmie, and Chief Christian of Christian Village, St. Stephens Hospital, Fort Yukon, circa 1920s.
Dr. Ernest A. Cook
Photograph Coll UAF-2003-109-68

vices. With the influx of newcomers, there were more epidemics, including the Spanish Flu, followed by tuberculosis.

At the turn of the twentieth century, Episcopalian Archdeacon Hudson Stuck (1863-1920) began ministering in Fort Yukon. Called "Big Preacher" by the Gwich'in, he traveled by dog sled and by boat to share the gospel with Alaska's indigenous people. He headquartered at Fort Yukon. During the time of Chief David Wallis and Second Chief Jonas, Hudson Stuck built a hospital and a school for Fort Yukon. He brought in the medical doctor, Dr. Grafton Burke.

However, Hudson Stuck died of pneumonia in 1920; not long after, Second Chief Jonas also passed away. He was succeeded by Chief Esias Loola, the son of William Loola and the foster father of Gwich'in linguist Katherine Peter and Athabascan fiddle player Bill Stevens.

As transportation evolved with motor launches and later, air travel, Bush living improved.

In 1949, Fort Yukon suffered a cataclysmic flood. In the 1950s the United States Air Force built a base and radar station called the Distant Early Warning system, or DEW Line.

During the 1960s, President Lyndon Johnson's "War On Poverty" impacted the Alaska Bush both with needed help but also with an increase of government dependency.

In the fall of 2005, I flew with Janet Curtiss and Chief David Salmon to Fort Yukon for the installation of the newly elected chief, Bruce Thomas. David's niece, Nancy James, introduced me to Jonathon Solomon, founder of Gwichyaa Gwich'in Ginkhii, and Clarence Alexander, former Gwich'in grand chief and cofounder of the Council of Athabascan Tribal Governments (CATG). After driving to what remained of the old village on the Yukon River, we knocked on Clarence's door. A six-foot-eight Draan'jik

Jonathon Solomon, 2005, Fort Yukon, founder of Gwichyaa Gwich'in Ginkhii, organized to fight construction of Rampart Dam in the late 1960s.

Judy Ferguson photo.

Gwich'in Athabascan man opened the door. After agreeing to an interview, Clarence, a bridge from the original Gwich'in, began to share his story and that of Fort Yukon.

Nadehtee Solomon David, Jonathon Solomon's great grandfather, circa 1900, probably Fort Yukon.

Courtesy of Jonathon Solomon.

Gwich'in means *one who dwells here.* Our grandfather said that once there were so many of us that our campfires resembled "a mountain with porcupine quills on it." After Fort Yukon was established, our grandfathers came in their canoes to trade. As they approached the fort, they shot three times, then waited for the welcoming three shots.

Our people did not *subsist,* a borrowed term in regard to government subsidies for Lower Forty-eight farmers. We as a people recycled and sustained our natural resources. We had no jails. If people broke our strict laws, they were exiled permanently from the community, becoming brush people, *naa'in.* (Only one exiled person ever reentered our society.) We worked for everything; there was no other choice. However, many of our people died in epidemics. Very few descendants of those original thousands of people exist today. There may be only fifty, of which I am one. The vast majority came here from other villages.

I am very fluent in my language. Today, many leave the village for the city but this homeland is the most precious place.

Today, there are about nine thousand Gwich'in, most of whom live above the Arctic Circle. We are the northernmost Alaska Indians, living in Venetie, Chalkyitsik, Arctic Village, Birch Creek, Beaver, Stevens Village, Fort Yukon, Circle, Canyon Village, and Rampart. We are made up of different groups but we all share the same culture and language. We were nomadic and still, traveling is in our blood. In one form or the other, we like to keep on the move.

Fort Yukon was a place for seasonal trading. From its founding, it became a community of many Gwich'in dialects: Vuntut, Teetl'it Zheh, Edhiitat, Danzhit Hanlaih, Neets'aii, Dendu, Draan'jik, Gwichyaa, Dihaii, and Tsiigehtchic, along with people from other areas: Yup'ik as well as Irish, German, Finnish, and Danish immigrants. If newcomers asked, we taught them survival. In turn, they brought their skills: a bakery, theater/dance hall, and restaurants. From first contact the people here learned to do business in a very formal way. Growing up, we became part of that system, accepting the values of others. A motor launch pushed a big barge upstream and supplied the villages. In the spring the Gwich'in came into town for the summer where they camped on the banks, enjoying the lucrative life. Salt, fifty cents for pie crust, seventy-five cents for a pound of sugar, twenty-five cents for a pack of cigarettes. At three dollars a cord, our people cut firewood for the steamboats.

Clarence's mother, Mary Jane Steven, and her mother, Charlotte Williams Steven, circa 1922, Fort Yukon.

Dr. Ernest A. Cook
Photo Collection, 2003-109-73

In 1910, my father, Alexander, was born to Samuel Alexander Jr. and his wife. My mother, Mary Jane Steven, was born in 1919 to Steven John and Charlotte Williams Steven, but the following year during the Spanish flu epidemic, everyone in her family died but her. Her father, Steven John, an education advocate, was close friends with the primary founder of the Venetie Indian Reserve and the first Alaska Native college graduate, John Fredson. Mother went on to become a health provider at Hudson Stuck Memorial Hospital in Fort Yukon for twenty-five years until its closing in 1957.

Top right: David Wallis, chief during Archdeacon Hudson Stuck's era. Bottom center: Clarence Alexander's "grandpa" John Herbert, circa 1900, Fort Yukon.
Shandaa: In My Lifetime
by Belle Herbert and Jane McGary, Ed.

I was born March 12, 1939, in Hudson Stuck Hospital, the oldest of ten children. When I was young, territorial wars were still real. We were taught to sleep so lightly that we'd know if someone were in the room. Everyone practiced genealogy, careful not to marry within the same clan. (I came from the *cha'sa*, worker, clan.)

My family's home is Alexander's Village (*Shoo Taii*, the happy hill), by a lake on the Christian River, about twenty miles north of Fort Yukon. Until I was ten in 1949, most people lived in their traditional locations. In Fort Yukon, a community of six sections grew up, each with its own values and mentors. Beyond a line of trees, there were mixed Gwich'in-Europeans

319

in downtown Fort Yukon. [Alaska had a dual school system. The Nelson Act of 1905 allowed for only non-Native and mixed blood children to attend the territorial schools. The Bureau of Indian Affairs taught the mostly full-blood children.] I didn't even know those other kids. I lived downstream on the banks of the Yukon, where our first language was Gwich'in. (After the passage of Alaska Native Claims Settlement Act, December 18, 1971, it was amazing who suddenly became "Native.")

In 1954, only the head clan members could afford a motor launch boat. The social scale was partly based on how you traveled. My grandfather, Steven John, had a motor launch but very few did.

The first ten years of my life, from 1939 to 1949, were peaceful, sliding down hills dressed in a fur parka and caribou pants, mittens, and thick moosehide booties. I was surrounded by elders born in 1850 who prophesied that hardship was coming. I assumed they meant famine, not social and economic upheaval. The message from our elders was "Go to that western school, learn their information better, and do it nicely."

In fourth grade, I was at the BIA's Alaska Native Services school, a one-room, log classroom. In 1947-1948, we were kind of blessed with a devoted teacher, Alice Wilson, who was honored later for her service. I spoke only my language but I learned a lot by listening to the kids in the upper grades as they discussed in Gwich'in. By listening, I can pretty much record everything.

About 1950, all children under sixteen were required to attend school. We could no longer be out with the clans helping trap, which increased the family's burden of support. School met only three months of the year, so it took three years for me to get past the fourth grade.

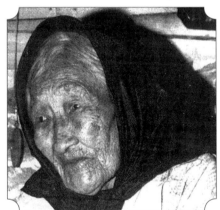

Belle Herbert.
Shandaa: In My Lifetime by Belle Herbert and Jane McGary, Ed. Photographer Rob Stapleton.

As the steamboats arrived in the summer, we could smell the fresh, pungent odor of apples and oranges filling the air. We were not allowed to eat much sugar, salt, or tea; that could lead to addiction. My family didn't like king salmon, so one entire summer, they sent me downriver to Jacob Flitt's fishcamp to learn to work.

As children worked alongside their elders, a transferral of mindset and skills was always naturally taking place. When I was four, my blind "grandfather," John Herbert, (who was married to Belle Herbert, memorialized in her autobiography, *Shandaa*) called to me, "Come, I want to see the leader," and he felt my face.

One day in the spring of 1949, I was sent uptown to James A. Carroll's store with a muskrat skin to trade for groceries on the list under my arm. The Carrolls were eating lunch, so I waited outside the store. All of a sudden, water began pouring over the bank; everyone began running. I didn't know what was happening. I ran all the way to the airport, out of reach of the water. There I sat while all around me life was changing. An older friend came by in a car and gave me a ride to my house. The water and ice had come so fast that cabins were bulldozed, dogs were swept out, and long-saved possessions, regalia, all disappeared.

Suddenly we were cut off from our heritage, homes, and our belongings. The Assembly of God mission had 160 acres on top of the hill which they turned over to the community. Contrary to our tradition, the Red Cross deeded surveyed house lots to us. Outsiders decided we were impoverished, and they put our mothers with dependent children on welfare.

Also, with no concept of tribal law, government agencies began issuing rules dictating when, where, and how much we could hunt and fish. With these regulations along with mandatory school attendance and welfare from the Bureau of Indian Affairs, the family unit began to fragment and government dependence began to become a way of life.

During the 1950s, our hundred-year-old elders began disappearing. Suffering some illness, our Chief Loola was taken to Seattle, but they never brought him back.

About 1950, the Johnson O'Malley Act began the transfer of schools in Alaska to the administrative control of the territory. It was decided that there were too many of us Indian kids in the log cabin school. To minimize construction, the territory unified the two-school system into one building serving all three groups: non-Native, part-Native, and full-bloods. I didn't even know those other kids; I only knew that they were part Gwich'in.

When I was fifteen, thirty of us were shipped off to Mt. Edgecumbe boarding school in Sitka. We took tests before entering the classroom. They said, "You're supposed to be in seventh grade." "Okay," I said, "whatever you say."

I could read the Gettysburg Address, but when I was on the playground and if I started speaking Gwich'in with someone from my village—WHAMMO!—I got beat on the head. It hurt really badly because I didn't understand what the heck I was getting beat up for. My forefathers gave me our traditional life, but somehow I didn't feel included in the other forefathers' "certain inalienable rights." But our elders told us not to make rebuttal and to listen, no matter how we were treated. I listened, but it seemed like no one else was listening. It made me distrust the system for a long time.

There were also language syntax conflicts. For example when I say "*nikah gwahdah*," it means literally, "tomorrow, next day." But in English, it should be translated, "day after tomorrow." Language, social patterns, and protocol were being remapped in my head, all scrambled up. When I entered the classroom, without understanding what the problem was, I had to reverse word order, and I had one hell of a time grasping what was expected.

When I was seventeen, the Air Force's Distant Early Warning system [DEW Line] suddenly brought in 130 new people into Fort Yukon. It created quite an impact. The women thought the new guys were a more lucrative choice so they married them. Some were abused and then returned to the village. But with children, they found it difficult to remarry. Child neglect resulted, and those children became an additional burden to the state and federal subsidies. These generations have continued to propagate and to become government-dependent.

My family experienced a disaster. In 1959 when I was twenty, my father drowned. A few years later, a new construction project determined that our family home was in its way. Based on the right of eminent domain, the State of Alaska gave my mother the assessed value and took our house. She was now not only alone but she had no place to go.

My political interests began. I wanted to know out how to work with the state, but at that time, we were not considered equal partners in any way, shape, or form. I left for Fairbanks but I was not welcomed with open arms. Okay, no one is, but my education had told me that we were equal. However, when I left Ft. Yukon, I found a completely reversed standard, and I didn't know how to deal with it. If I wanted to become a carpenter, there were no funds for me to attend an apprenticeship school in Fairbanks. Since I had only a tenth-grade education, I could not enter the university. As a Native, I was the last possible choice for hiring. Finally I got a job for three months, reporting every morning at 8 a.m., but every moment, I had to watch my step.

I returned home, believing that the answer was in our own self-development. I pushed aggressively for a local economy but I almost got kicked out of town. In 1960, my views were not yet acceptable. I heard that the girls in California were good-looking so I decided to go see what the Lower Forty-eight had to offer. I said to myself, "Okay, Clarence, keep on going."

Nineteen-year-old Clarence Alexander, just after two family disasters, en route to California, Yukon Territory, circa 1960.

Courtesy of Clarence Alexander.

The next year just after statehood, Senator Ernest Gruening was pushing for the world's largest hydroelectric project, the Rampart Dam, which would inundate nine Athabascan villages on the Yukon, Porcupine, and Black rivers and irrevocably damage the Yukon Flats waterfowl habitat. Also, the state was filing on Native lands throughout the state. These intrusions led to area-wide meetings at Nucha'la'woy'ya/Tanana in 1962-1963, which led to the reorganization of the Tanana Chiefs Conference [TCC]. After our chief asked Jonathon Solomon to protect our land from Rampart, he organized and chaired "Gwichyaa Gwich'in Ginkhii (GGG)/A Person of Fort Yukon Speaks" in 1964. Two years later, Alaska Federation of Natives [AFN] began, ultimately resulting in Alaska Native Claims Settlement Act [ANCSA].

Ten years after I left Fort Yukon and shortly before the passage of ANCSA, I returned home. Although the Gwich'in are all connected by language and cultural activities, ANCSA drew a line arbitrarily, saying this village is where you belong, whether you're related to that dialect or not.

There were many shortcomings in ANCSA, including the lack of local control as well as there being no subsurface rights at the tribal (village) level. Also, neither ANCSA nor the Alaska National Interest Lands Conservation Act [ANILCA] recognized the right of indigenous peoples to manage wildlife on their lands, a right exercised by many tribes in the Lower Forty-eight. Regional nonprofit organizations like Tanana Chiefs Conference were set up to support the villages, but never forget that the nonprofits like TCC are mini-operatives of the Bureau of Indian Affairs and of the state.

TCC employs people in the city, but at the village level we needed direct control of our own education, realty, tribal government, and justice as well as the means to create business. My vision for local development was finally timely, but there was a lot to learn. I could see that the basics of running a business were the same whether it was trapping or running a

Jonathon Solomon (1932 to 2006) was a member of the U.S. delegation to the International Porcupine Caribou Agreement between Canada and U.S. He served as the Traditional Chief of the Gwichyaa Zhee Gwich'in, a lifetime designation, from 2002 until his death in 2006. He was a founding member of the Gwich'in Steering Committee formed by the Gwich'in at Arctic Village (Vashraii K'oo) in 1988, and dedicated to the preservation of the Porcupine Caribou Herd. He was awarded the Goldman Environmental Prize in 2002, together with Norma Kassi and Sarah James. They received the prize for their struggles for protection of the Arctic National Wildlife Refuge from plans of oil exploration and drilling. Oil and gas exploration would disturb the life cycle of the Porcupine caribou, which has been a foundation for the Gwich'in culture for 20,000 years.

Edward Alexander, Wikipedia.

323

store. I paid Larry Dworkin at the All American Tobacco Shop in Fairbanks to teach me modern transactions. I paid him $800 for eight hours of teaching. I also read a book on corporate structures. When I returned home, we created a fur cooperative, owned by trappers. (In the 1980s, the animal rights movement in Europe put a kibosh on the fur industry, and a ten million dollar industry nosedived.)

In 1973, we set aside land for a clinic, then we waited patiently to fulfill that dream. By the late 1970s, frustration and anger had replaced our expectations. There was little local economy. Our historic independence, generosity, and pride had been replaced by diabetes, cancer, and alcoholism, and, we were no longer mentoring our children.

In 1980 while I was away, the tribal council began thinking about my 1960 ideas for self-development. They asked if I might consider becoming chief. I accepted and began by asking, "What has been done here since 1953?" "Nothing," they answered, "but accepting checks." I said, "Well, things are different now. We are going to do whatever is necessary to become responsible, accountable Gwich'in, in control of our own lives." But part of the "hardship" that our elders had prophesied was that the government-dependent generation were the very ones who kept propagating. A leader is only as strong as the support he gets. I discussed the problems with Jonathon Solomon, who was my mentor.

When I traveled, I personally paid for over half of what I was doing. Every year, I took off six weeks to do the necessary politicking. I was involved up to the brim; I didn't even see my kids grow up.

I got on the executive board of Tanana Chiefs Conference with a very determined agenda: to take over the business of the health program for the Yukon Flats and to co-sign on all our BIA programs. I figured if TCC has a $100,000 program to administer for us, why should we give them $30,000 of it when I can train someone in Fort Yukon—who knows the land—to do the commu-

Clarence Alexander, circa 1990s.

http://www.catg.org/

nity allotments? I reopened the Native village of Fort Yukon (Gwich'yaa Zhee Gwich'in), hired a consultant, and began creating. We had to build a functioning tribal government that existed on its own to receive the programs. There were six levels of society in Fort Yukon, each with its own values and mentors. I went to the leaders' homes and asked, "Come sit on this new council; you have ideas we need." We started pulling in programs, hiring from our own community, and teaching them new skills. With that training, some have gotten jobs at the regional corporation, state, or federal level.

Chief Esias Loola, Fort Yukon, circa 1920s.
Dr. Ernest A. Cook Photograph Coll UAF-2003-109-68

With the local council launched, one day I stopped in at Beaver to see my friend Paul Williams. He waved me in, saying, "I have a muskrat baking" [a Gwich'in traditional delicacy]. As we ate, we talked of Chief Esias Loola, our revered father figure, who died in a Seattle hospital in 1957 and was buried there. Paul said, "The time is now. Let us pay our last respects to him at an area-wide gathering. We'll visit the villages and suggest an organization that would base in the flats and create economic opportunity for the Yukon Flats people." He decided to go to Stevens Village, Rampart, and Birch Creek while I would go to Fort Yukon, Circle, Venetie, Arctic Village, Chalkyitsik, and Canyon Village.

The Loola family agreed to the memorialization. In 1985, we invited all the Alaska-Canadian Gwich'in.

Fifteen villages gathered, speaking Gwichin only. In the evenings, Chief Loola was honored with song, speech, dance, and ceremony. During the days, we discussed the problems and brainstormed possible solutions. I said, "I find that we are lazy; we have been holding our hands out for too long. We've been deteriorating ever since the flood and its reorganization. We were put into a little box of house lots and city streets. We used to run our own traplines and hold summer jobs. Let's put our heads together and come up with an economic development plan." John Titus of Venetie said, "We don't unite as a Native people. When one of us advances, we get jealous, and then we turn our hatred against him—because that person is doing better than us. Our number one enemy is the jealousy among us. Let's go back and be Indian, and start over again." Simon Francis of Chalkyitsik, one of the last indigenous snowshoe craftsmen, added, "Long time ago, 1940, there were lots of smart people. We didn't get any help, no pension, no check. It was a tough life, but people were smart, that

Paul Williams, chief of Beaver, 2004, Chalkyitsik.
Judy Ferguson photo.

time. We'd go out in the woods and get anything we wanted: meat, trapping, fishing, and then, work all summer. Nowadays, it's not like that. Nowadays, we just check the post office for checks. I never gone school, but I always got carpentry job. I make snowshoe when I was kid. Today, I still make snowshoe... But we say we got no jobs. Lots of things in this world: lots of wood, lots of fish, lots of game. We got to work for it." The meeting had planted a good seed, but we knew if we did not take action soon, nothing would grow.

To better connect us, we decided to get a radio station. Over the next seven to eight years, I campaigned and contracted one of the best grant writers at the Federal Communications Commission in Washington, D.C. Finally we obtained KZPA 900 AM Gwandak Radio. We made a Yukon Flats board and came under the tribal umbrella, the Council of Athabascan Tribal Governments [CATG.]

Clarence Alexander continued:

I decided to try to return to school. Interestingly enough, the university had changed its requirements from demanding a high school diploma for those wishing to start a program. The policy now was, "Anyone who feels they can handle the courses can take them," so I put in for the University of Alaska's Alaska Native Knowledge Network Alaska Arctic Rural Teacher Training Corps program. In 1973 under a thirty-day, very intensive course taught by Dick Mueller and Lincoln Tritt, I learned to read and write my language. As an intern in the program, I was asked if I'd like to develop a bilingual program, training teachers to teach young children. I went to the villages, watched, and then talked to them. I saw weaknesses and strengths. After a few years of work-

Council of Athabascan Tribal Governments (CATG:)
Back: Clarence Alexander, Fort Yukon; third: Steve McGinnis.
Second row: Nancy James, Fort Yukon; far right, Patty Salmon, Chalkyitsik.
Front: Adlai Stevenson, Fort Yukon; third, Jonathon Solomon, Fort Yukon;
James Nathaniel, circa 1985.

http://www.catg.org/

ing with my fourteen teachers, I went to our district office to inquire if there were any federal programs with courses that could shore up my teachers' weak spots. I conferred with the director of the Alaska Native Language Center, Dr. Michael Krauss. To encourage my teachers to take courses, I took a class in Cross Cultural Communication. I went out to the villages and urged them to also take a course, saying, "This will make it better for you." I talked to a man

The history of CATG: http://www.catg.org/ourstory.html

Assisted by an Administration for Native Americans grant, villagers gathered in Beaver the following July. Many ideas were presented - sawmill development, marketing fur, creating a tourist industry. People spoke of their frustration with all the different government systems that had been created elsewhere and which were staffed by people from other places but which sought to extend their powers into the Yukon Flats and to control everything, from the management of fish and game to education and health care. The people of the Flats had little input into these systems, and felt no sense of ownership over them.

The following September in 1985, the fledgling organization began a series of meetings to determine where they wanted to go and how they could best get there. Rejecting the idea of a non-profit corporation, they chose to create an organization under the authority of the tribal governments. Its board would be the elected chiefs from 10 villages, reaching from Circle down to Rampart on the Yukon River, and out into the drainage areas to include the communities of Canyon Village, Chalkytsik, Birch Creek, Venetie and Arctic Village. Pat Stanley was hired as Executive Director, a job she would hold for 17 years. So began the Council of Athabascan Tribal Governments.

According to its constitution, CATG is "to conserve and protect tribal land and other resources; to encourage and support the exercise of tribal powers of self-government; to aid and support economic development; to promote the general welfare of each member tribe and its respective individual members; to preserve and maintain justice for all..." The power would be in the tribes, which would decide for themselves where to pool their efforts, and where to act individually. They agreed to operate on a consensus basis, with each village, from tiny Birch Creek (population 30) to Fort Yukon (700) having one vote. If one village strenuously objected to any course of action, even though the others all voted in favor, that action would be dropped or tabled.

∽

ANCSA was the government's opportunity to handle indigenous land claims in a fair and liberal manner, and it was hailed as a positive step toward the government's policy of self-determination without termination. ANCSA failed to address Indian country, however, and the Supreme Court's decision did not quell the disagreement. In the aftermath, where tribal governments in Alaska are not afforded the same rights as tribal governments in the contiguous states and the Supreme Court has denied them the basic designation of Indian country, some have questioned whether they really have achieved self-determination. ... Some argue that justice was served. In 1997, Joseph Matal wrote, "ANCSA employs language which, from the beginning of the Supreme Court's Indian jurisprudence, has been understood to extinguish tribal sovereignty and invite state jurisdiction." He goes on to say that the definition and application of sovereignty has been conflicted in the last 50 years, that proper application of the definition shows Indian country does not exist in Alaska outside of Metlakatla Reservation and that the Venetie case was "merely a symptom of a current confusion in which the Indian sovereignty doctrine is degenerating into one based solely on ancestry."

It seems that the State of Alaska won the battle, but perhaps lost the war. This case alienated the state from tribal governments and further divided the people of Alaska.

May 7, 2010, Karol Dixon is an Athabascan Indian from Shageluk, Alaska. the granddaughter of Adolph and Margaret Hamilton. Dixon graduated with a bachelor's degree in economics from the University of Alaska-Anchorage. She started attending law school at the University of Oregon in fall 2003, and is a graduate of the American Indian Law Center's Pre-Law Summer Institute. http://www.alaskool.org/projects/ancsa/ARTICLES/afn_newsletters/AFN_Newsletter.htm *states:*

The Alaska Native Claims Settlement Act of 1971 granted fee simple title to Alaska Natives of some 44 million acres of land. It also directed the state and federal governments to disburse almost $1 billion over a period of 12 years for the capitalization of 12 regional and over 200 village corporations. Native people each received stock in the regional corporation of their choice, and one of several village corporations within that region.

Under the terms of ANCSA, the stock could not be sold or lost for a period of 20 years. Land received by the corporations was similarly protected for 20 years after it was conveyed.

But the protections on the stock would be lifted automatically on Dec. 18, 1991. Many Native people feared that sale or loss of the stock would result in loss of the Native land base, which was made an asset of the respective corporations.

The U.S. House of Representatives passed AFN's 1991 amendment package to the Alaska Native Claims Settlement Act on March 31. 1991. The bill, H.R. 278, was introduced by Alaska Congressman Don Young, and passed without amendment by unanimous consent.

Congressman Don Young, in his address to House colleagues urging passage of the bill, stressed that H.R. 278 had nothing to do with tribal sovereignty.

Of the so-called 1991 issue, Congressman Morris Udall of Arizona, Chairman of the House Interior and Insular Affairs Committee, said, "Unfortunately, the controversial question of the continued existence of tribal entities in Alaska has become a focal point of this legislation. . . I want to reiterate my position that neither ANCSA as passed nor these proposed amendments affect in any way the question of whether there continue to be tribal entities in Alaska."

Native concerns with the bill was its inclusion of a strong anti-tribal disclaimer in the section which would make it easier for corporate share-holders to transfer land and other assets to non-profit, tribal or other entities.

For more, see: http://www.alaskool.org/projects/ancsa/ARTICLES/ afn_newsletters/AFN_Newsletter.htm

∽

we have a complete consensus of the 747 shareholders to do it, but we did, and we are the only ones who have.)

From 1980 to 1994, I served as the chief of Fort Yukon. During the 1990s, I founded and served as chairman of KZPA 900 AM Gwandak Radio. Even though I am not a businessman, I served as the chairman of the Gwichyaa Zhee Corporation.

In the early twenty-first century, I translated Gwich'in to English. My wife, Virginia Alexander, and I wrote the *Gwich'in-English Dictionary*. With Fort Yukon's Dinjii Zhuu Enjit Museum, my wife sponsored the funding of the initial fieldwork for the Belle Herbert autobiography, *Shandaa*, for the Alaska

June 2012, Tyler won the Yukon 800 and became the first person to win both the Iron Dog and the Yukon 800, each considered the most difficult race of its type in the world. The twenty-six-year-old captain of Miss Riverboat Discovery *and his crew of navigator Patrick Captain and engineer Richard Sommer guided their vessel to the title. The crew finished the two-day total time of twelve hours, fourteen minutes and twenty-four seconds in the the world's toughest riverboat race. After stepping off the* Miss Riverboat Discovery, *Tyler immediately greeted his sons, Trevan, five, and Hayden, three. He later gave a hug to his ninty-seven-year-old grandfather, Sidney Huntington, who had just arrived from Galena. Tyler beamed about being the only person to win the Yukon 800 and the Iron Dog. "It hasn't sunk in yet. I can't believe it," he said. "It's something I've been wanting my whole life and I finally got it. It feels good."*

However in February 2013 while training for the Iron Dog, Tyler Huntington was seriously injured. He is recovering as Windows to the Land *went to press.*

Tyler Huntington with his oldest son, Trevon, gazing from his father's arms during the 2010 Iron Dog, Pike's Landing, Fairbanks.

Courtesy of Tyler Huntington

Index

B

F

G

S

T

U

Windows to the Land: the story of great-grandfathers, grandfathers, and fathers for the next generation to remember the sound that came before ... to mark the trail.

Jerry Isaac's grandchildren with Kenny Thomas drumming, 2009, Tanacross.
John Rusyniak photo.

We welcome reader response to
Windows to the Land, An Alaska Native Story, Volume One:
Alaska Native Land Claims Trailblazers

2013 to 2014, look for **Windows to the Land, An Alaska Native Story,**
Volume Two: the Iditarod and Alaska River Trails

Books and Materials by Judy Ferguson

Bridges to Statehood: The Alaska-Yugoslav Connection
Blue Hills: Alaska's Promised Land
Parallel Destinies: An Alaskan Odyssey

Children's Books
Alaska's Secret Door
Alaska's Little Chief
Alaska's First People
Lesson plans based on state performance standards on CD

Online store: http://alaska-highway.org/delta/outpost/:
1-907-895-4101; outpost99737@gmail.com; Box 130, Delta Junction, Alaska,
99737, U.S.A.